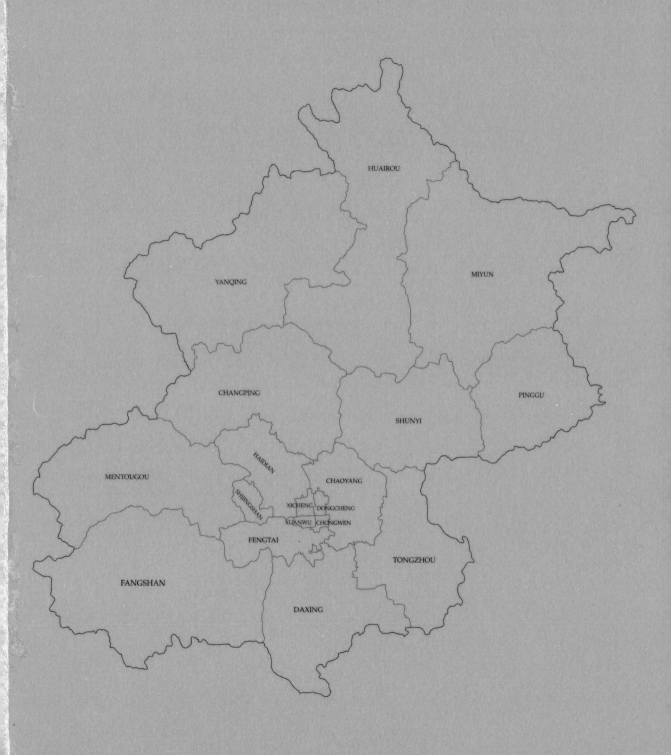

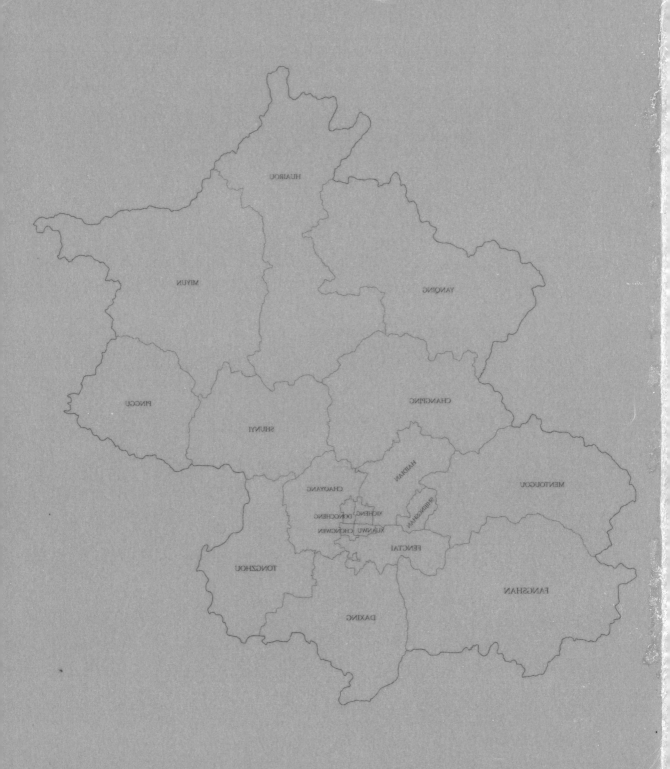

*Virginia Stibbs Anami*

# ENCOUNTERS WITH ANCIENT BEIJING

## Its Legacy in Trees, Stone and Water

CHINA
INTERCONTINENTAL
PRESS

## 图书在版编目（CIP）数据

寻访北京的古迹：古树，雄石，宝水 = Encounters with Ancient Beijing: Its Legacy of Trees, Stone and Water/ (日) 阿南史代（Anami, V.S.）著. —北京：五洲传播出版社，2003.12
ISBN 7-5085-0381-3

Ⅰ.寻... Ⅱ.阿... Ⅲ.寺庙－简介－北京市－英文 Ⅳ. K928.75

中国版本图书馆 CIP 数据核字（2003）第 116633 号

**寻访北京的古迹：古树，雄石，宝水**

著　　者：（日）阿南史代
摄 影 者：（日）阿南史代
策　　划：李德安　宋坚之
责任编辑：邓锦辉
装帧设计：田　林
制　　作：北京原色印象文化艺术中心
出版发行：五洲传播出版社（北京北三环中路 31 号 邮编：100088）
承 印 者：深圳利丰雅高印刷有限公司
开　　本：889 × 1194mm 1/20
印　　张：16.6
字　　数：250 千
版　　次：2004 年 2 月第 1 版第 1 次印刷
书　　号：ISBN 7-5085-0381-3/K·491
定　　价：120.00 元

# Contents

*I find a rock with sun on it, and a stream where the water runs gentle, and the trees, which one by one give me company, so I must stay for a long time...* (N. Wood)

# *Preface*

## Admiring Beijing's Legacy of Trees, Stone and Water

Looking at Beijing within the framework of trees, stone and water is a way of appreciating the city's heritage, based on a special relationship of man and nature. In the process of exploring Beijing's ancient ruins, what I often found as markers of the past were a well or spring, a couple of gnarled pines, and sometimes a stele or an abandoned stone cave. They took on the mantle of the sites' history.

It was these three aspects of nature that held Beijing's past. They helped me define and respond to the sites I was searching for. Often they maintained the atmosphere of these places, long after rituals there ceased. Moreover, they led me to the people of Beijing, who readily shared their knowledge and stories.

It became my passion to study and explore the city for historical sites during my three extended periods of residence in Beijing since 1983. Although I was looking for the physical space of the old relics, what I experienced spanning these 20 years was the exposure to the dynamics of neighborhoods, to the changes of village life and to the destinies of their peoples. It also afforded a very personal peek into individual values. The rekindling of interest in traditional customs gave a sense of continuity with history amid all the changes around those ancient places. Many of the old sites like temples and shrines had been converted for other uses, so I learned to talk my way into factories, schools, residences and other units.

The following stories and episodes are only a fraction of my adventures. I chose those that were the most exceptional or that pointed to a variety of the experiences and places in this capital. This is not intended to be either a guide or a comprehensive presentation of historical facts. I have instead emphasized encounters with people from all walks of life. Some of these are put under the heading

of "Unforgettable People", as these short essays went beyond the focus of a particular tree, stone or body of water. They are part of the city's collective history.

In searching the streets and hills for old temple remnants I got to admire the hospitality and resiliency of local people. That was the satisfying part of these adventures. Sometimes residents would leave what they were doing and spend the whole day walking around with me. This kind of "walking and talking" method of studying the past made each place come alive.

In these ramblings I also became more and more aware of the importance of environmental concerns. When you go around rural Beijing these days, the talk is often of water, the desertification and the period of "dry." No wonder there is a growing popularity of visiting the old springs and bringing home a load of filled plastic bottles.

Trees caught my eye particularly when they were sometimes the only vestige of history left at an abandoned temple or gravesite. How many times they helped me to identify former historical sites! I love learning the background of their unique nicknames and respect these ancient sentinels for their living history. Fortunately, there is an increasing appreciation for the city's old trees and understanding how to maintain them.

Walking in the mountains, I developed a new way of looking at stones. The natural boulders have always impressed me, but I particularly focused on their environmental importance when they started to be destroyed. I also keep an eye out for inscribed stone slabs (steles) that give evidence of past constructions of temples, imperial patronage, grave commemorations and the like. These steles have had lots of upheaval with urban development, but many have remained at their original locations.

For me, the timing was right because a lot of old Beijing still remained in the 1980s and 90s, not yet transformed by modernization. It also was right because of the opening up of the system

and society, which allowed me to mix easily with citizens. Moreover, it was timely in that people were still around to remember earlier settings of various sites and could relate what they had lived through in the more than fifty years since Liberation.

During my stay in Beijing, I was able to meet specialists who helped me greatly with their knowledge of the city's history. I am indebted to their assistance. Most importantly was the encouragement and support of family and friends, often companions to these excursions, and the warm welcome always extended by people both in urban and rural areas.

It is my sincere hope that these short essays will bring attention to the wonderful variety of legacies of this great capital city. The ancient trees bring you back in time. The taste of spring water continues to nourish. The engineering feats of canals to meet the challenges of mastering the water supply for the capital are still worthy of respect. Or just walk up to an older person seated on a stone left along that *hutong*, and there will sure to be a long tale. Follow along the deep cart ruts cut in bridges or the pilgrim path stones and you will feel the moss of history. I am always exhilarated setting out on a new exploration, ready to walk through time, curious about the next encounter.

V. Anami

I. Aged Trees as

# I. Aged Trees as Living History

"If the trees could speak, they would tell such stories..."

# Introduction

## Trees from Ancient Times

One of the greatest rewards from the search for old sites in the Beijing area was the acquaintance with so many imposing ancient trees. Most of these trees are left in what were Buddhist temple compounds or former imperial villas. In these places they were protected and revered over the centuries. Often it is only the trees that are left to mark the spot of the former site. In my investigation of temples around the outskirts of town, it was the trees that always stood up to greet me. A cluster of dignified tall pines can sometimes be spotted from a distance deep in a valley, so that even if there is nothing else left, one knows that they protect the memory of a special place.

In Greater Beijing, there are more than 6,000 living trees of 29 species with a heritage over 300 years old. Those with longest longevity are ever-greens like the cypress and pine varieties. Deciduous ginkgo, sal and scholar trees also can span more than one thousand years. These venerable trees were treated with respect and acknowledged to have spiritual qualities. They were the trees of choice to surround temples, imperial buildings and tombs. In contrast, domestic trees were more likely to be flowering acacia and fruit trees like jujube or persimmons.

These majestic trees scattered around the city and environs, make a map of Beijing's past. When visiting these places, I often feel that if these trees could only speak they would tell ex-

citing stories of the city's long history. Sharing the encounters I have had with some of these trees is a way of giving them voice and recognition.

The robust cypresses at Zhongshan Park, for example, stand in two rows leading up to the place where the 10<sup>th</sup> century Liao Dynasty

Xingguosi (Temple of National Restoration) once stood. The site was later incorporated into the Altar to Land and Grain. Trees of such enormous girth are rare inside the city. Even though this is now a busy park, it is possible from the trees to recognize the old sacred way. Their powerful endurance is awesome.

Likewise, Ditan, the Altar to the Earth, is full of sturdy cypresses. As part of morning exercises people often circle these trees as a way of gleaning energy from their extended life force. Many of them have wonderful polished knobs on their trunks coming from years of interaction with man. These knobs have been rubbed by backs and stiff necks until they gleam a golden brown. The trees, too, must have felt the massage and appear all the more healthy.

Aged trees of Beijing are felt to have strong personalities. Both in the city and in the countryside, the greatest ones were often

venerated and given nicknames by emperors or locals, such as "the Emperor Tree", "King of Cypresses", or "the Tree to Which a Horse Was Tied." It is a wonderful way to honor these living symbols of history.

Often the name describes the tree's shape, like "Lying Dragon Pine" with branches spreading laterally or "Incense Burner Cypress" that indicates two branches that look like handles at-

tached to a round trunk. The Worker's Cultural Palace has one ancient cypress that bends in such a way as to suggest: "The Deer Which Turns its Head."

Because Beijing was the capital over many centuries, it boasts a wide variety of unusual trees. Gardeners of imperial gardens and great monasteries purposely pruned or splayed branches to give beautiful and unique shapes. Other species were planted to admire amazing bark patterns or root systems that grew above the ground.

Unfortunately, the vast forests that had once covered the Beijing area were severely decimated by the falling of a great deal of the former tree cover to make the grand cities of each succes-

sive empire. This gradually changed the environment. Today's expansion of the urban area has also threatened many of the survivors.

When I first visited China in 1976, I had my first encounter with Beijing's ancient trees. Great gnarled cypresses and pines lined the original road from the city to the Ming Tombs. It was a sacred colonnade. Upon returning in 1983 I drove again on this road. To my shock, the giant trees were being uprooted to widen the road. Scattered all along the way were the torn-up root stumps of these 500-year-old trees.

There is now a concerted effort in Beijing to preserve all aged trees. A fence is usually built around them and they are identified with an official number on a color-coded metal plaque nailed onto the bark of the tree. Those trees over 100 years are given second rank; those over 300 years are first rank. The Forestry Bureau keeps track of them that way, so even if the old temple compound that had once been the protectors of the trees has gone, they are acknowledged as treasures. As neighborhoods are being demolished, trees from the traditional *siheyuan* courtyard houses have sometimes been kept, and hopefully they will landscape the new setting.

The many kinds, ages and shapes of Beijing trees not only give us a connection with the past but they make us aware of the need to keep them and the sacred sites for future generations to appreciate and enjoy. Maybe we should give them all unique nicknames.

## "The Trees Would Know!"

Trees are magnificent testimony to the importance of Beijing's sacred sites. One of the finest spots to enjoy a number of millennium trees is Jietaisi (Temple of the Ordination Altar). The Liao Dynasty scholar tree, its trunk raw with age, proudly guards the main gate. It probably was planted when the temple was rebuilt by chief cleric Fajun in 1069. His stupa pagoda is embraced by the outstretched limbs of an equally ancient pine. Nearby, vigorously spreading its nine massive branches upward, is Beijing's oldest lacebark pine, known as the "Nine Dragon Pine." Just below the temple is the Pagoda Forest, graveyard for the temple's monks. Many stones of the stupas lie strewn about, but numerous magnificent "Chrysanthemum"-shaped pine trees continue to give dignity to the hallowed ground. This monastery's trees have stood as witnesses to history and outshine any other cultural relic.

In the foothills of northwest Haidian District, two grand ginkgos at Longquansi (Dragon Spring Temple) are conspicuous. One tree towers 30 meters over an ancient stone bridge. The other tree stands just before the foundation relics of a vanished hall. It is pleasant to sit on the ancient stone steps under this tree with its deep fissures and watch the water from the spring meander through the lonely courtyard. The living trees of these sites still breathe the history

from 1,000 years ago.

Like old wise men confident of their knowledge over the years, these trees reticently watch the unfolding of time. What is the number of prayers offered to the memory of the great 12th century abbot Tongli at his nine-storied pagoda at Tanzhesi (Temple of the Pool and Wild Mulberry)? The city's oldest sal trees that give shade to the pagoda have stood there all the time. They would know!

How many visitors have trudged up the hill in search of the famed spring water of

are preserved the typical one-storied quadrangle houses built around central courtyards. These neighborhoods are like mazes of gray walls broken only by the dark entranceways to each house. Old maps reveal small temples nestled in remote corners of the labyrinth.

The Small Black Tiger *Hutong* is a long, winding and narrow alley. On one morning in early December, 1996, walking along that alley in search of places noted on my historical map, I noticed that the land level of one courtyard

Jinshanquan (Gold Mountain Spring)? The "Sister Pines" that have watched over the pathway there for over 800 years would know!

And how can we measure the solace given to those who sat under the pair of "Listening to the Sermons" Pines of temple ruins in the Fragrant Hills? We do know that emperors and their retinues came here for relaxation. We also know that these two strong and upright pines were there when the temple was totally destroyed one hundred years ago during the Eight Allied Powers' bombardment of the place.

The trees would know! Only they survived.

# Old Trees Hide an Imperial Cook

I n the area west of the Drum Tower in central Beijing, the narrow alleys haven't changed for several centuries. Here, too,

compound was quite low. That usually means that the place dates back at least several hundred years. Beyond the entrance a scholar tree with a massive trunk and thick branches stood clinging to life among brick and metal edifices built right around it. This had once been a garden but it was taken over by many families making shelters where they could during the massive migrations into the city for the past 50 years.

Here and there potted plants put some beauty into the chaotic setting. A small bonsai pomegranate tree cheered up the communal water spigot. Two aged jujube (Chinese date) trees

reached high for life, their branches being used to hang laundry and connect electric and telephone wires. One tree was living in symbiosis with an entangling *gualou* gourd vine, its light orange fruit hanging on the tree like tennis ball-sized Christmas ornaments. An elderly man came out of a room and declared that this place had once been a nunnery and pointed to the broken tiles on the roof. Sure enough, my mid-18th century map showed it to be Wanfu'an (Convent of Ten Thousand Good Lucks). He didn't remember the nuns, but he did recall that there used to be many giant trees there. During the

Cultural Revolution, unfortunately, they were cut down for housing. Only the three survived. And their determination to keep living among the clutter makes them admirable heroes.

In the convent's front room bright with the winter sunshine, a large pot was steaming on a charcoal brazier. The rich stew-like aroma made it hard not to ask what was cooking. Mr. Liu Jingquan said proudly, "You can't buy anything good like this anywhere." His wife beamed and announced, "My husband was the cook for the last emperor Puyi."

Liu, 82, proceeded to tell the story of how his family had been cooks for the Imperial Family for four generations. They specialized in pastry and made the famous mini cornbreads, bean paste cakes and the pan-roasted sesame rolls. When he was a boy, he traveled with his father who accompanied the last emperor into exile to Tianjin and former Manchuria. His father even went to Japan. With that, Mr. Liu threw in a few phrases of Japanese. After the war they came back to Beijing and his father started a restaurant for Imperial Cuisine at the north shore of the Beihai Park.

Mr. Liu worked most of his career in Xi'an, and regrettably none of his children wanted to learn the imperial cooking. I am afraid that the secret recipe for that delicious stew will be lost! These tree heroes will also likely be lost in the rapid urban development. But for now, Beijing's narrow *hutong*s probably hide a legend behind every door.

## Survivors of Tumultuous Times: Monk, Eunuch and Catalpa Tree

Guanghuasi (Temple of Great Transformation) is the headquarters of the Beijing Buddhist Association. On one quiet spring evening in 1996, when I visited the temple, only a handful of clerics and lay believers walked in the compound. Passing through one courtyard after another, I heard the strains of ancient Buddhist music. A catalpa tree over 500 years old stood high against the backdrop of the two-storied library hall in the final courtyard.

In one corner, a secluded patio was filled with peony plants. This was the residence of the temple's senior abbot, now deceased, the Venerable Xiu Ming. When we met him, the abbot was 91, still spry and able to greet visitors in French, English and Japanese to meet almost any occasion.

As a young man from a wealthy Beijing family, he had traveled to France, studying in Lyons, with a group of Chinese students. Premier Zhou Enlai was part of that group, as was Marshal Chen Yi, a foreign minister in the 1960s. He remarked that of the twelve students that roomed together, he was the only one that didn't go into politics and, he added with a mischievous twinkle in his eye, was the only one who was still alive. "They were all concerned with how to save and reform the country," he added. But Xiu Ming turned to a reflective life and Buddhism.

He had always been affiliated with the Guanghuasi, but not always been able to live on the premises. There were times in the 1950s when he was forced to work as a laborer. During the Cultural Revolution he had to leave. The books and manuscripts of the temple burned for seven days in the front courtyard. Buddhist statues were destroyed beyond recognition, and steles were smashed. Two pairs of lions were not ferocious enough to hold back the Red Guards. Finally, the army came to protect what was left.

Xiu Ming was back as abbot in 1983, when the temple began its revival.

The upright posture and kind but sure glance was of a man of great depth, self-discipline and peace. His character pervaded the atmosphere of the temple.

Nearby is another secluded enclosure. One small hall faces a garden with a single tree. There, on the same day, we met China's last imperial palace eunuch, the late Sun Yaoting, sitting dignified in the corner of the room wearing a brown leather jacket and black-padded pants. He lived there until his death the following year, aged 98.

Sun had a smooth but swarthy face and hair cut to a short stubble. His eyes glistened as he acknowledged our presence. "Gong gong," we had to yell to get his attention with these words of respect. You can't call a eunuch "eunuch", rather the term "gong gong" (honorable father-in-law) is the polite form of address. In these circumstances one had to ask simple and direct questions, like "where are you from?" He said that his "Old Home" was Jinghai County in Hebei Province, "a great source of eunuchs for the Qing Dynasty." "Gong gong, when did you come to the palace?" He recalled that he came to serve the emperor in his early teens.

The Qing Dynasty crumbled soon after, but he continued to live within the walls of the Forbidden City. His rank was "four dishes and one soup", meaning what he was entitled to at meal time, and denoting a rather high position. "Then I went with Puyi to Tianjin and later to Changchun when it became the capital of so-called Manchukuo." The move to the northeast was in 1932, when he was 33 years old. After Liberation he returned and became a Taoist priest. However, he also had to do a bit of "reform through labor."

Sun and six other eunuchs came to live at the Guanghuasi in 1983 and were given total care. He was served by an elderly helper from the temple. Often he slept during the day and stayed awake in the evenings. He said he ate simply now. No more "four dishes and one soup"!

After the ten-minute meeting, his delicate yet gnarled hands reached out to bid farewell. From the outside we could see his face by the window, peering out at the small courtyard from the darkened room. This image seemed to reflect his life, behind the walls far from the real world outside.

Walking back to the gate, I admired the resilience, too, of the great catalpa tree. It was just about to bloom, in time for the Buddha's birthday.

# Pairs of Trees Welcome Visitors

## Tall Pines Perpetuate Temple's Memory

In the countryside ancient trees dominate the landscape and are easily spotted in winter. They usually mark where an old temple or grave once was located. Deep in a remote valley, tall pines stand before the gate of Ruiyunsi (Temple of Auspicious Clouds) and tower high above the temple halls. These buildings have been rebuilt and restored many times during the trees' long thousand-year lifetimes.

Searching out the history of this temple one springtime, I found a stone stele almost incognito in the surrounding blossoming orchard. It described the temple's history during the 12th and 13th centuries, its monks and the temple spring.

Such temple trees were always revered by the community. Planting of trees in temple compounds has been a Buddhist custom going back to the importance of the great *bodhi* tree (pipal) at Bodhgaya under which Buddha Sakyamuni in the 6th century B.C. reached enlightenment after meditating for forty-nine days. A pair of sal trees served as a canopy for Buddha's deathbed and his entrance into *nirvana*. But in China and Japan, the subtropical bodhi tree did not take well in the northern regions and the ginkgo, pine and others were given sacred treatment instead.

Temple compounds were, thus, to become the preservers of trees, their wood not used for kindling or cut for lumber. So these pines of the Ruiyunsi stake out their territory and fearlessly continue to grow.

## Cypresses Lead Way to Eminent Trees

Two old trees, one gnarled, the other straight, will often stand at the entrance of many temples as a balance

of the *yin* and *yang*. One finds this same symmetry of trees in front of the Japanese Kyoto Imperial Palace, too. I can think of no better example in Beijing than the 800-year-old cypress trees leading into the Dajuesi (Temple of Great Enlightenment). They were planted at the time that the 12th century Jin emperor Zhangzong adopted this earlier Liao Dynasty Qingshuiyuan (Clear Water Temple) for one of his imperial retreats.

With its halls facing east toward the rising sun, following the Liao shamanistic tradition, it has been restored over successive regimes. An ancient stele of 1068 stands a bit lonely at the back, but is still legible and declares the site to be the "best known pool in the Ji area, located at the foot of Yangtai Hill." If that stele were written today, though, I would write in praise of the fine trees.

It is hard to say which is the best season here as there are good memories from all times of year. In early April I was awarded with a dazzling view of the valley below the temple all covered with apricot blossoms. In a small courtyard the famed *yulan* magnolia was in bloom. It was planted more than 200 years ago by Emperor Qianlong when he lived here doing a stint as a monk. Locals are still furious at the Red Guard who chopped down the other tree that had been paired with it. "How could one go against the trees?" they asked. One of the greatest luxuries of Beijing is to sit beneath its white blossoms in

spring or later in the fall under the grape-like fuchsia-colored fruit bursting with orange seeds. Next to it stands a straight cypress with a buckthorn growing around its waist as a parasite.

In the middle of the summer heat, Dajuesi is much cooler than the city and one can sit out comfortably in the evening under the celebrated 1,000-year "King of Ginkgos" tree undisturbed by insects. Its girth of eight meters keeps growing as shoots of following generations grow alongside the weathered trunk. Talking late into the night with friends under this great masterpiece of nature, we were accompanied by the

trickling of the spring water as it passed lightly in the mossy stone aqueducts.

In autumn, golden leaves of the 30-meter-high ginkgo stand out against the deep blue sky. While photographing upwards into the mass of yellow, I heard a man tell his young son that he'd seen me interviewed on television about visiting the temples and trees, and then said to me, "You look so excited to be with the old tree!"

In the solitude of winter, the "King's" many branches rub together with the wind and its deep patterns of broken bark show strength rooted in time as regal commander. Steam rises from the famed spring pool causing a light mist in the last courtyard, where a pair of venerable trees powdered with snow, seem to protectively hug the bulbous relics pagoda to keep it warm. Shivering, I found warmth in the temple's fine tea.

# Emperor Knights Ginkgo Couple

Temple trees were often planted in balance like the most celebrated couple, the two ginkgo trees, male and female, planted in front of the main temple halls of Tanzhesi. Fittingly they are called the "Emperor's Tree" and the "Tree Which Matches the Emperor Tree." The titles were bestowed by Emperor Qianlong himself in recognition of their grand stature. They are indeed wondrous specimens and the energy from the two is increased by yet another pair standing parallel before them, two sal trees with more than 500 years existence.

Trying to photograph them at the height of

their fall colors, I found it difficult to make a picture of one whole tree and impossible to get the pair of them in one frame, since the ginkgos are so enormous. The dark trunks show up as silhouettes in the midst of the glittering yellow leaves. It was like the shadow of a body beneath a diaphanous dress. There used to be an old Buddhist hall from the Ming Dynasty situated between the two trees, but it was removed to give an open area and the trees have been given more space to expand in the next thousand years. Someday, the couple will be holding hands.

## Dual Lacebark Pines

Two shining "White Tiger Skin" pines, also known as lacebark pines, grow in the courtyard of the Chang'ansi (Temple of Eternal Peace), the first temple of the Eight Grand Sites (Badachu). More than 600 years old, they are relics of the Yuan Dynasty. Their mottled skin gives a unique chalky brightness and, because of this exceptional appearance, these trees were planted at only special sites. Radiating a life force from their long existence, this hardy duo must be a help healing patients in the sanatorium now located there.

One is reminded, too, of similar lacebark pines from the Ming Dynasty planted at Fahaisi (Temple of the Sea of the Law) nestled in the Cuiwei Mountains. The small main hall is practically

dwarfed by their mighty presence. In fact, the pair, one tree on either side of the walk to the main hall, are so exceptional that they at first take the limelight away from the prize within the hall.

I still remember when the temple was first opened to foreigners on May 1, 1985. I rushed there with my children for a picnic under those great branches. It was only after we ate that we went into the darkened room with our flashlights to gaze at the well-preserved Ming Dynasty Buddhist murals, amazed at the brightness of color after 600 years.

The frescos of the front part of the main hall had been half hidden and thus protected by sculptures of the three Buddhas in front and the 18 arhats along the two side walls. However, the figures were destroyed during the Cultural Revolution exposing the vibrant colors on the walls behind them.

Along the back wall is the great fresco of Indra and the Twenty Companions, rich in representation of the Buddhist pantheon. The two sides are balanced with male and female, sun and moon, etc., that would satisfy the symmetry, just like the pair of trees in the courtyard. Those trees seem to serve as beacons to draw attention to this magnificent art treasure.

## Crouching Tiger, Twisting Dragon

On the west side of the Yongding River is a village with a long history, Longquanwu. Here was the ancient kiln for the Liao Dynasty Tricolor Pottery of one thousand years ago. Equally ancient are the ruins of a temple in the hills south of the village. The site is cut off by railroad tracks, but even when I found a way to the other side, I got lost running around unmarked dirt roads. One led to a canine center, another to a military compound. At last I followed a track running along a narrow creek bed. Just standing without any fanfare among thorny bushes in a nondescript ravine are two pairs of incredible trees, the only temple heirlooms left.

Two cypresses have grown there for a millennium flanking the eastern oriented entrance. One is growing straight and tall, its trunk with a fine spiral pattern winding up to the branches at the top. It is as if a dragon is twisting in flight up toward the sky. The Tiger cypress is also true to its name. The thick trunk is firmly planted as a fat sumo wrestler ready to pounce. Bulging growths from its bark epitomize the giant head of a crouching tiger.

A legend goes that the trees are really the spirits of the elderly caretakers who wept wildly when their valuable incense burner was stolen. After three days the neighbors heard the loud wailing suddenly go quiet. The couple had vanished, but instead two old trees stood before the temple gate.

The other pair of trees, two strange-shaped ginkgos, are also viewed like an odd couple. One is upright and aloof while the other seems to be bowing in obedience. Villagers call them the "Husband and Wife" ginkgos.

Only a few yellow and green pottery shards from the former kilns lay scattered about. But it didn't seem so lonely. After all, there stands a crouching tiger, a twisting dragon and an odd couple.

# Familiar Trees in the Neighborhood of the Bannermen

One April day in 1997, the air of Beijing was full of the flying white cotton-like willow catkin, *liuxu*, which was drifting on the breeze like snow, a sign that spring had arrived in north China. On this comfortable day, my friend Professor Deng Ruiling was eager to share his childhood memories of growing up in the neighborhood just west of the Zhongnanhai, which today is the site for the headquarters of the Chinese Communist Party.

Professor Deng, now over 70, is an old Beijinger. His family members for several centuries were among the elite. They served as Pure Yellow Banner officials for the Qing Dynasty

emperors, even though they were Han Chinese, not Manchu. "Grandpa was sent as an official to Jiangxi Province in the south. As all the orders came in Manchu, only he could read and translate them. My father also spoke Manchu," he recounted.

"We lived in the western part of the old Imperial City of Beijing on Fuyou Street. The name means 'to the right of the prince's residence', because the father of Emperor Xuantong used to live to the west of here. That place is now part of the State Council complex."

The family compound consisted of seven garden courtyards extending from south to north. There was also a western axis. "The rooms facing smaller gardens at the back were for the family and the halls around the larger ones at the front were the formal areas for the guests," he recalled as we drove there. His house actually covered almost an entire block. But all the courtyards are now occupied by families and different work units.

It was the trees that helped mark the former layout. A pair of scholar trees still defined the southern border. They stood upright and distinguished as before, and although the way is now blocked, one could imagine the old formal entrance gate between the two trees.

Professor Deng continued to talk nostalgically about his memories. "There weren't too many people around in this neighborhood in those days. People we met were always courteous and still used the Manchu greetings." He continued, "The Ying family lived next door. They were Mongolian bannermen and Catholic. We rented some of our front rooms to them in the 1930s."

He also recalled that the army had living quarters just south of his Guangmingdian Primary School. "We could hear the trumpet blowing in the early morning and at night. To a little boy, it seemed so far away, but it really is only a ten-minute walk."

Three entrances still open up on the east to Fuyou Street. The first one is a police station. The next one led into a maze of small living quarters. A resident was quite friendly when Professor Deng recognized two other trees. The last entrance led to the central government nursery school.

"That elm tree, that toon tree, those juniper trees, they were ours!" Deng was clearly at home. "There's a well at that corner. One day when a Japanese soldier came through our house, we all hid behind the well. He just walked around slowly and left from that gate," he rambled on as he relived the moment.

Professor Deng showed me a painting of what this courtyard used to look like. "This back garden was really pleasant. In the summer evenings there were fireflies and bats."

In 1951, Deng's family moved out of their family home of many generations. But all those fine trees continue to stake out the family compound, harking back to the days of the bannermen.

# Lone Sentinels of the Past

## Basking in the Winter Sun

In the little village of Tiankai, two aged trees, a cypress and a scholar tree, shade the daily market and give a communal gathering spot. They are all that remain of their

village central shrine. On a bright winter day, I walked past this place where people were chatting and playing chess. One elderly man had his back against one of the trees, his green cotton padded coat slightly open and comfortable as a cat basking in the sun. Carts with brightly colored materials, dried foods, piles of cabbage, a large platter of fresh bean curd and sacks of flour were all set up for the late morning market.

The remnants of another temple, the "Big Temple", are now used for the Tiankai Junior High School. A teacher in a shiny pink coat told me that they have 200 students. She pointed out some of the stones used in the foundation and I could detect Sanskrit writing on them. Joining our group conversation was a wizened 74-year-old man named Zhang. He remembered studying in the school when it was still part temple. Adjusting his fur cap, he looked around and pointed to the main classroom on the elevated earthen platform and recalled that there had been a big statue in that hall.

"Do you want to know why is our village called Tiankai?" he asked. "Well, there is no other place in China with this name. The story goes like this," he puffed on his small pipe and continued, "This area used to be very dark and foggy all the time and the sun never shone. But one day a magic animal came and opened the skies to let in the sunshine, and that became the name of our village, *tiankai*, 'the sky opens'."

Zhang rambled on about the village history. "We're only about 600 families now, the young leave to find work." And that explained why there were mostly older people sitting outside that day. The village center and its two trees seemed like a place lost in time and very far from the rapid development of Beijing. On that January morning, the "magic animal" had indeed opened the skies to let in the sunshine.

## Hollow Tree Guards Convent

A haggard 1,000-year scholar tree in Xihuang Village has seen its share of drama. It was set on what was once a coal transport road leading into the capital. As an old soul of several hundred years, it must have witnessed a nun of the temple behind it come out and warn the Ming emperor Yingzong, leading his troops out to battle, of an impending defeat and temporary imprisonment. This was something for which she was strongly chastised. When her forecast turned out to be true, the emperor honored her daring outspokenness with a title for her convent, Huanggusi, as its name indicates, the "Temple of the Emperor's Sister." Some legends say that she even visited him in prison and brought him food and water. Some other tales go that he actually had her killed when she had tried to block his way to battle and that he later built the monastery in her honor.

In following years, only this nunnery stayed open when all convents in or by the city were shut, as the nuns were supposedly raising money by other means. Its unique title gave it protection. The temple's bell is now preserved at the Big Bell Temple in town. On its surface cast in bronze are inscriptions confirming continued imperial support.

Today there are only a few rooms of the abandoned convent. Many migrant workers were occupying the premises when I last visited inside in the late 1990s. Their laundry and sheets hung along lines drawn between the pillars of the former temple halls. The still sturdy stone-enclosing wall gave an impression of what the area must have looked like. At least it has kept a bit of its history.

The scholar tree, though, is pretty worn out with its hollow trunk. Nonetheless, it still holds fast in its prominent position of honor before the entrance gate.

## Catalpa Tree Left on a Playground

Even in the city, such lone trees can also be found. One large catalpa tree grows on the playground of the Baizhifang Primary School. It is a remnant of Chongxiaosi (Temple of Supreme Service), which claims origins from the 7th century. When I visited in search of the temple in 1995, I was also looking

for the tree, as well as for the famous *mudanhua,* tree peonies, that used to bloom there. It is said that they were over 200 years old and included rare green and dark purple varieties.

The tree peonies are all gone, their roots transplanted in Zhongshan Park, but the catalpa tree still stands firm, now surrounded by a protective fence. A gate hall and the two-storied sutra library, both from the Ming Dynasty, have been incorporated as part of the school compound. The library once held a fine collection of the *Diamond Sutra*, but no more.

Nobody was on the playground, so I sauntered forth for a better view of its one living heritage specimen. Just as I had taken photos of the tree, the gatekeeper had a change of heart and asked me to leave rather brusquely. Perhaps she wasn't quite sure whether or not old trees could be photographed.

# Only the Tree Remains

**L**ooking for the ruins of Heishansi (Black Mountain Temple) in an overgrown valley in northeast Beijing, my eyes caught the Great Wall snaking along the ridge of the mountains behind it. No other edifice was around. Finally by searching among the tall autumn grasses, I found a few carved marble stones. Nothing else. Yet a lone straight standing ginkgo juxtaposed against the deep blue sky maintained its watch over the once sacred site.

Its leaves were just changing as they have for hundreds of years, but very few visitors come to enjoy its beauty.

Farmers winnowing their grain nearby told me that this once was a thriving Buddhist center from the Tang Dynasty times, however, it met its demise 200 years ago at the hands of angry locals who accused the monks of stealing their daughters. Only the ginkgo was spared destruction.

This reminded me of another location where the only clue to its former glory was a set of trees. Three giant white poplar trees almost 30 meters high stand in a tight circle hidden within a forgotten corner of the famous imperial Yuanmingyuan (Garden of Eternal Brightness). There is literally nothing nearby that in any way relates to the former surroundings in which they had once stood. But you know just by looking at these imposing trees why they were spared the destruction wrought on the rest of the garden by foreign troops in 1860. Nobody dared touch them! It is an amazing experience to stand among the three trunks and look upward to their towering intertwined branches.

## Mammoth Ginkgos Hidden from View

The village of Taitou has practically forgotten the old Fushengsi (Temple of Abundant Success). If you ask in the neighborhood, don't try the young people. They will only give you a blank stare. An elderly gentleman seated by the side of the road finally acknowledged that there had been such a place. He pointed to a side street and a high wall, motioning that one can get behind it.

Climbing up a slippery dirt path behind a brick building and a garbage heap, I found the way. There stood two massive ginkgo trees that had been hidden from view. After clawing carefully to the trees through a thick growth of prickly weeds, I realized that one tree has eight large branches extending from a trunk, over seven meters in girth. Except for a single stone column base, they were the only indication of an earlier monastery having been there.

Local historian Hao Zhongquan later told me that the temple's ginkgos were already famous at the beginning of the 19th century. A stele once found near the trees dating from that time described their size and splendor. Hao claims, "They have to go back to the temple's founding in the Liao period, almost one thousand years ago." According to him, the temple covered a large area and that there were numerous other trees as well. The trunk of one scholar tree was over fifteen meters high. It was so large that when the cadres cut it down after Liberation, they made 67 school desks from it for the primary students studying in what had been the temple compound.

Fortunately, the ginkgos remain and these

mammoths just keep expanding in their neglected seclusion.

# Pine Marks Cave Temple

In late March when all mountains of Beijing are covered in flowering fruit trees, it is a good time to climb up the hilly path to the Tianhua Cave. Above the cave, the Great Wall meanders with no attempts at restoration and without tourists. The cave has few visitors as well, for it is at least an hour's hike.

When I asked directions of the local shepherds, they just replied, "It's by the green tree." I looked up to the high ridge in front of me. And there it was. I could easily spot the lone pine, perhaps over 700 years old, which marks the site looking very much like a tall solitary sentinel. On that day its evergreen needles stood in contrast to the light pink shades dominating the mountainside.

Sure enough, the slightly curving tree was standing just in front of the cave entrance. It was almost like a bending arrow pointing the direction saying, "Here it is!" Peering into the deep cavern I saw that several natural rooms had been made into a multiple Buddhist sanctuary. Supposedly an underwater river once made this a livable place for monks. Buddhist figures there are all new, but the use of the cave as a place of worship has had a very long tradition, at least as old as the tree.

# Persimmons Offered to a Forgotten Japanese Monk

Only one persimmon tree graces the graveyard for the monks of Tanzhesi, Beijing's foremost sanctuary for over 1,000 years. The tree's towering branches, thick with dangling bright orange persimmons, appear to hug the top of one pagoda.

The graveyard, called the "forest of pagodas", lies below the temple on a flattened section of hillside. But most visitors miss the spot as they take the curving road up to the main temple halls.

The place is usually empty. But there are a number of large stones to sit on. I often went there in the 1980s with my family for picnics. And in the 1990s it was a special spot to let our dog have a bit of freedom to roam. But as often as I had gone there to relax, I had failed to notice that one particular pagoda, until the colorful persimmons drew my attention to it in the fall of 2000.

Birds were picking at the ripe persimmons and half-eaten fruit splattered on the grey bricks of the five-storied pagoda. The inscription on the pagoda face reads: "Stupa of monk Wuchu Deshi, 33rd abbot." A weathered sign in front makes for interesting reading. I was startled by the identification of the interred abbot with the persimmon tree. He was in fact a Japanese. Arriving in China at the beginning of the Ming Dynasty (1368-1644), it goes on to say that the abbot's Japanese name was Musho Tokushi and that he went by the novice name of Shukyu. He was from a region of Japan then known as Shinshu, present-day Nagano Prefecture, where he joined a monastery at an early age.

Musho was an abbot at several well-known temples in Nanjing, Chengdu and Beijing. Yet it was his acquaintance with Yao Guangxiao, tutor to Emperor Yongle, that led to his appointment as abbot of Tanzhesi in 1412. The only other snippet of information about the man said, "During his tenure he worked unceasingly on the repair and construction of the temple. He passed away in 1429 and this pagoda was built for him."

His being in China was a result of diplomatic connections between the Ashikaga Shogunate and the Ming court. Clerics who returned to Japan after studying abroad were often exalted

and became leading monks in their respective monasteries. Many never returned and were forgotten. Still, it seems strange no mention is made in Japanese history books of this man who obviously won great respect in China and was an outstanding Buddhist leader.

This Japanese monk also distinguished himself as a calligrapher. The stele inscribed with his writing can still be viewed at Shaolin temple in Henan province. The stele is dated the fifth lunar month of 1392 and is signed "Monk Tokushi from *Fusang*", the ancient name for Japan in Chinese meaning "from the east where the sun rises."

Musho Tokushi's accomplishments offer a good example of scholarship exchange of earlier days of Japan-China relations. He was here as a member of the Buddhist community, a cosmo-

politan group which had no borders. He was accepted in China as an individual by virtue of his scholarship and leadership capabilities. He not only made the perilous journey to China, but he overcame language, culture and other obstacles to rise to the top of the Chinese Buddhist hierarchy.

Unquestionably, the persimmon tree was planted as a form of tribute, a tree well known in his native Nagano. The birds seemingly complied by dropping bits of the sweet fruit, offering the long dead cleric a nostalgic taste.

I felt it was fitting to offer Japanese tea to this roving Rinzai monk. Joining me on May 17, 2001 were monks from several Beijing temples, along with officials from the Buddhist Association. We were having a tea friendship excursion with teachers and students of the Urasenke Japanese Tea Ceremony School of Beijing. As we stood by quietly, a monk reverently put the *tenmoku* tea bowl in front of his pagoda, prayed and then poured the tea around the base. Five hundred and seventy years since his death, I was sure his spirit must have enjoyed the taste of Japanese tea. The following year the persimmons were probably even sweeter!

# Beijing's Oldest Trees

## The Monk's Tale of Ancient Roots

Pink and white *furong* hibiscuses were in bloom on the day in early August when I met the Honorable Hai Feng, the 81-year-old monk of the Hongluosi (Temple of the Red Spiral Conch). Hai Feng, now the temple historian and calligrapher, claimed this monastery dates back to the 4<sup>th</sup> century, thus often declared the oldest temple in Beijing. It was an important center of the Pure Land Sect of Buddhism and has the stupa pagodas of its famous abbots in one of the courtyards.

Hai Feng slowly told his story. When he was just eleven he joined a nearby temple and was ordained at nineteen. Then he was allowed to come to study at the prestigious Hongluosi for a year. Unfortunately, his own temple was destroyed in the 1950s in the land reform movement, and he was forced to return to lay life. During the sixties, he witnessed the smashing of the Hongluosi. As the Red Guards trampled around destroying the buildings, they forgot, or in ignorance didn't notice, that the grand trees kept the spirit of the temple, that they in fact were shrines, that they were the treasures.

According to Hai Feng, this was the most important center for *qigong* (breath exercise) practice in the Beijing region. "The temple and the surrounding valley have strong *qi* (energy)," he said, declaring that the energy came from the ancient trees assembled there.

A pair of famous 1,100-year-old ginkgos stand over 30 meters high dwarfing the main hall. They are champions in motion! The myriads of deep green fan-shaped leaves waved in the wind like the fan dancers practicing at dawn in Beijing's parks.

Another one of the treasures is an energetic gnarled pine that is said to have been planted in the Ming Dynasty 500 years ago. It appeared to be performing a swirling tango with the entangled embrace of a wisteria vine. The pine has to be energetic because this dance has been going on for several hundred years!

Hai Feng pointed to the Lohan valley at the side of the temple and proclaimed that *qigong* was born there. I felt the extraordinary energy of the trees and knew they kept the spirit of the original temple. I didn't have to be convinced any more.

## School Protects Its Tree

It took a long time weaving the back roads east of the capital to find Tangzi Village. There stands a beautiful 1,500-year-old ginkgo tree. Its unrestrained branches hover high above the back play yard of the Tangzi Elementary School. One teacher said there was once a temple there, fittingly nicknamed after the tree, Baiguosi (Temple of the Ginkgo).

Another ginkgo used to stand as its pair, but no more. Mountains and hills surrounding the village have probably helped the tree survive harsh winds. When Japanese troops fought here the tree was burned and one can still see charred bark as evidence of this tragedy.

Today school children play around its nine-meter round base, lightly jumping over the roots

Neighbors of Xinchengzi Village told how a Guandimiao (Shrine to the War God) from the Tang Dynasty used to stand behind it, so the tree is at least that old. Where the temple used to be is now a martyrs' cemetery for those locals who died fighting against the Japanese invasion. When a road was cut beside the tree, a fence was put around it for protection.

Fortunately the fence has a big hole in it so people can crawl in and touch the tree. Humans are dwarfed easily by those eighteen branches, each one of them thick enough to be a great tree in itself. From its appearance, it may have had a life of at least 2,500 years. I liked the tree best by looking at its silhouette against the sun and reflecting on what it means to be alive for

and playing hide and seek. It was lovely to see them on that early autumn day, crowding around the robust tree as if they were caressing it. I am sure the weathered bark was rejuvenated by their touch and laughter. And the children in turn grow with the powerful life force of the aged tree.

## Nine Hands Round and Eighteen Branches

The "Nine Hands Round and Eighteen Branches" name describes the great girth of a cypress around which nine people could join hands and has the forking of eighteen branches. Its bark is deeply creased, the craggy wrinkles of time.

that long. How did this living fossil manage to survive more than anything else in the Beijing basin? Was it the water, protection from wind, remoteness from man or just good luck? Perhaps all of the above.

## "We Three Kings of Orient Are…"

There are one thousand steps leading up to the formerly great monastic community of Shangfangshan (Mountain of the Upper Place). Today it is a national park and the once flourishing 72 monasteries are left as scattered ruins taken over by nature. I had the pleasure to tramp up those steps on several oc-

casions and enter this seemingly enchanted woods. In the dense forest, it is almost dark under the heavy canopy of trees of late summer, the trees ever reaching upward for sunshine.

I followed a map done by a Belgian engineer over 90 years ago. His markings were quite exact and I could easily identify old stupas and temple relics as I went along. The soft light was beautiful. I felt overwhelmed by the lushness of many mossy stupas and towering pines above them. I wondered which one of them was the tallest, making it a "king."

Further up the mountain in a rare clearing of the green cover stands a partially restored temple, Doushuaisi (Temple of Responsible Command), from the Ming period. The keeper of the temple, Mr. Wang, has been protecting Shangfangshan for over 20 years. Looking out to the forest, he

said there were quite a few ancient trees in the woods. Certain trees had been singled out for attention and dubbed as the "Three Kings": the "King of Cypresses", the "Pine King" and the "King of Scholar Trees." Wang noted that the handsome cypress in the temple clearing there

was over 30 meters high.

I showed him the old map and how a foreigner noticed his temple in the 1910s. He looked, too, at the sketch of the graveyard and the pagodas. Then he undid a wire lock at the back gate and let me in to an overgrown grassy courtyard. A number of stones were scattered about and he said that they were all from the graveyard. And right there standing in the grass was the Liao Dynasty octagonal stone pillar I had been looking for. Carved on the front was the small seated image of a monk, one of the early abbots.

Wang talked on about the other temples and convents further along. Not much left, he added, but the magnificent trees. A rare sal tree had one branch stretching protectively over the remaining gate of some temple ruins. Further on, in the middle of the path, stood the "King of Scholar Trees." It stretched high to pierce the forest dome; its leaves were almost out of sight. It was over 3 meters round. These slower grow-

and 1.54 meters in diameter, or 4.9 meters in circumference! On its bulky trunk there was a large lumpy growth. Sitting in front of the giant tree, I thought of all the life it had seen; the people and ever-present mosquitoes that had lived with it in the compound over the centuries.

These thriving majestic trees make Shangfangshan such an exhilarating place to visit. They have stood as silent witnesses for over one thousand years. Now back down the thousand steps to the busy world below!

## Godmother of 2,000 Years

She looks like some giant wild hag out of the pages of Celtic mythology attempting a backbend or from a distance a gargantuan black widow spider raised to strike. Yet this scholar tree is really a gentle creature who has been severely injured over the years. Villagers from surrounding areas bring their children to bow and pray before the great *Gan Ma* (Godmother) in hopes of ensuring them long life. And that for sure is what this tree has accomplished. A small altar stands before the open hollow of the trunk.

Growing by the Yanqi River in Huairou district, this tree once had a girth of 7.5 and a height of 20 meters. Tragically Red Guards lopped off arms and a large part of its body to use as their firewood. This sad story was related to me by the tree's watchman, Sun Zhengming,

ing trees can extend to a longer life, but they have to compete for the light with the faster growing younger trees around them.

Crossing a stone bridge spanning a small ravine, the path led into an old convent with a couple of lonely gutted halls. The buildings didn't matter. This was the space of the "King of Cypresses": 1,500 years old, 28 meters high

72. He remembered how seven kids used to be able to get within the old hollow trunk, or four adults could have a game of poker inside. And then there is the serious drought. In 2002, its leaves began to fall in July. County officials were alerted and Mr. Sun pumped river water night and day for a week all around its base. Despite all his efforts a couple massive branches died and broke off.

I peered into the old trunk and found the remnants of charcoaled wounds where old fires had left their tattoos. "When I was in my early teens, I used to come here with my friends," commented Sun dressed in a common blue jacket and a cap as he looked out on this flat site by the river. This had once been the village center. A few years ago, the place was turned into a weekend resort lodge by a developer, but was since abandoned. "Right here is where our Baiyachang Village stage was. Performances were held for all the holidays." Five other old trees were cut down. But this tree was special, as it was from the Han Dynasty, more than 2,000 years old, and no one had dared cut even a limb until the turbulent 1960s. Sun added that behind the tree there used to be a shrine to the local god, "but that also disappeared."

Another mystery of the tree is that insects avoid it. It is cool under the tree in summer and if you rest, no ants or flies will bother you. Sun said that first there was the tree, then the old shrine and only later did the village build up here. It was a logging village that cut the forests of cypress trees on the tusk-shaped mountain behind. Thus the village name "Baiyachang" means "Cypress Tusk Factory".

Each angle of the tree gave a different face. And as I walked around on that winter day seeing the hag, the spider, or even a giant *bonsai*, I preferred the view of its gutted hollow topped by a large curling branch. This was the godmother face, the grizzled yet caring fantastical spirit, the longest living tree of its kind in the Greater Beijing area.

## Courtyard of the Old Tree

Huafangzhai Studio in Beihai Park boasts the oldest tree in the city proper, a Tang Dynasty scholar tree. Going there in the summer of 2002 for the re-opening of the studio to the public, the greatest reward was to be able to view this most venerable tree in the back courtyard, named for the tree, *Guke* (Old Tree) Court. As part of a detached palace garden for at least 700 years, the tree was respected by Emperor Qianlong who wrote couplets to praise it. This court was also used by the later Emperor Guangxu as his study. The tree's bright green canopy rises high above its stocky frame and bears itself with dignity. After all, it has associated with nobles its entire life.

*Unforgettable People*

# Team Spirit the Hallmark of *Qigong* Master

Barrel-chested *Qigong* Master Wan Sujian, 52, is unquestionably gifted. Just a moment with him in his Taoist Medical *Qigong* Headquarters, Wan can detect a person's strengths and weaknesses. Master Wan looks at someone for 10 seconds and then draws on paper what he sees. "Balance is the key, for too much of any emotion can effect the organs of the body," is a typical diagnosis. With his penetrating gaze, he perceives areas in the body that give off little heat or don't radiate health. He then tells the patient about their weak areas, anything from nagging back pain to potential coolness or overheating of the liver or kidneys, which might be susceptible to disease in the future. "It is there that the imbalance lies," he may caution.

Based on the ancient precepts of Taoist healing and the power of *qi* (energy) spirit, doctors like Wan have been traditional healers in China over the centuries. Wan himself is an army man and is associated with several military hospitals where he has practiced Chinese-style healing. Like so many in his profession, he sees the need for traditional treatments to work hand-in-hand with modern healing methods. Master Wan himself learned the techniques from his mentor, Luo Youming, a famous female bone setter who still practices medicine even though she is well over 100. As he learned from her, "the purpose of *qigong* (breathing exercise) and Taoist meditation," instructed Wan, "is to control one's breathing and push energy through the meridians of the body for good health."

Energy coming from the doctor and his young assistants, working in groups of four or five, is directed at the weak zones of the patient. The patient can feel the heat radiating from their palms which are held some distance from the body. Trained to harness their own *qi* through meditation and *Taiji* exercises, they then emit their energy to the patient and that, Wan says, helps cure or ward off disease. Wan's innovation to Taoist medicine is using the team approach. He calls this the *Bagua Qigong*, or *qi* of the Eight Trigrams.

Wan has 64 assistants, all personally trained by him. Ranging in age from 10 to 25, they each specialize in one of the many schools of martial arts. They give spectacular demonstrations of their skills in which they accumulate *qi* energy. Their education doesn't stop there. They all have mastered a musical instrument which are used in Taoist music health treatment. Wan trains them, too, to "collect" *qi* from mountains, aged trees and even water.

The ancient trees have the energy of their longevity. The many old trees of Beijing provide good opportunities for tapping some of this life force. That energy is perceptible not only from the trunk but from the branches above and the roots below. With knees slightly bent, one stands about a meter before the trunk of an aged but vigorous tree. Hands sway up and down as if to pull the force of the tree in through the top of one's head and release the energy back to the tree through one's legs. Thus one becomes part of

the tree's energy cycle between its branches, trunk and roots. Another way is to position one's palms towards the tree and move one's arms forcefully up and down taking in the energy through the center of the palms. Some people even embrace trees directly.

Dr. Wan Sujian's therapy, though, is not limited to these personalized treatments. He provides community service at a number of clinics in Northern China in affiliation with the International Red Cross, reflecting his group's commitment to helping those in distress. Under Wan's dynamic leadership, Taoist medicine still has an important place in today's modern society.

# Along the Old Pilgrim Paths

## Shade for the Faithful

Trees were also planted along the pilgrim routes to mountain temples and one can easily spot them winding up an old path or clumped where there had once been tea-rest houses, *chapeng*, that gave the pilgrims shade. Looking out over the northwestern hills, a number of these dilapidated rest houses and trees follow the past routes that go over the mountain ridge leading to Miaofeng Mountain.

One can spot a large pine here and there and know that a teahouse would probably have been nearby. For over 1,000 years pilgrims have walked past one such ancient imposing pine shading a dilapidated shrine. The tree is aptly named "Welcoming Guests Pine." From there the faithful made their way to Ruiyun'an (Convent of Auspicious Clouds) where a curious site of a small pagoda perched on the tip of a giant boulder awaited

the travelers. Further on, the old stone walk also forks to the west, and more pines along the way confirm that this was one of the four well-trodden routes of the Miaofeng mountain monastery pilgrimage circuit.

## The Twisting Trees of Eagle Peak

A similar pilgrim route goes over Jiufeng (Eagle Peak) also in the west. It leads first to the Ming temple of Xiufengsi, meaning "beautiful peak." Old trees dominate its several courtyards terraced up the hill. Pines, cypresses, and scholar trees in clusters or standing alone, give a distinguished elegance to the almost deserted premises. Only the shrill screeches from squirrels pierced the quiet as they leapt between the temple roofs. Below the largest group of these trees, broken stone tomb doors from the grave of some forgotten eunuch have been realigned as picnic tables, looking lonely in the middle of winter.

It had snowed the day before and my crunching footsteps resounded on the stone trail of this once crowded passage. En route to the peak were impressive rocks with nicknames, like "lizard boulder." I wondered how long had they borne these identifications.

Eagle Peak has stone bases and steps left from 1,000 years ago. The stones have telling furrows, about the width of a finger, indicating their

antiquity. Each leveled terrace up the peak has its sacred space, some as cave temples, but most are in ruins.

Higher up this rugged land affords dizzy views of the Beijing basin below. It also has some magnificent trees at the top. One named the Eagle Peak Old Pine is an outstanding natural treasure standing beside a great stone. Close by, an oak tree stands in front of another giant rock, right at a wind passage, so all its limbs bend in one direction, its leaves curled from constant blowing. The stone path continues on. One can see evergreen trees here and there that follow the route as it goes over the ridge. Even Hansel and Gretle could find their way!

53

## Bitter Dates of Yaji Mountain

Crumbled shells of old temples scatter down the hillside of this strangely shaped Yajishan, Mountain of the Double Knob, to the east of Beijing. The summit looks as if hit by a meat cleaver giving it the shape of the letter "Y." Its shape obviously marked it for a special mountain.

Trudging up the mountain we were joined by keeper of the keys and ticket seller, 72-year-old Mr. Zhang. Here, too, the trees give the sanctified space a special aura. Some "Guest Welcoming" pines and a "Cypress Embraced by a Pine" were the most notable on the route. "We exploded lots of crackers for the new year the other night," Zhang remarked as he plodded on.

In the village is the lodge where the emperor stayed on pilgrimages here. "During WW II, over 100 Japanese troops lived there." Zhang noted, "Yajishan's 51 Taoist priests were all sent away in 1947. For the yearly festivals these days the priests come from Beijing's White Cloud Temple and Mount Wudang in Hubei."

At the summit, the eastern part is the Hall of the Jade Emperor; the west knob has the temple for the popular deity Bixiayuanjun, Lady Sovereign of the Azure Clouds. The shrine itself has been rebuilt and inside are the three main statues, "but not as fine as in the old days," commented Zhang. Piles of tiny shoes are given as thankful offerings, when prayers for childbirth have been answered.

Growing out from the crannies of the stone boulder embankments for the shrine were many clumps of prickly bitter date trees. Only they thrive in this rugged terrain. This is a poor area, and villagers, too, barely eek out an existence. Even so, the old custom, noted Wang, the knob's current gatekeeper, was not to eat the bitter dates.

A local legend tells of a hungry shepherd who

one day, while tending his flock on the hillside, tried out the bitter dates and found them a good meal. He ate and ate until he was full and even greedily picked more to stuff into his pockets. When he looked around, he couldn't find his sheep. He met a long-bearded Taoist priest to whom the shepherd explained what had happened and the priest quickly scolded him for eating the bitter dates. Whereupon the priest said that the only way to get his sheep back was to pray to the four goddesses of the mountain. When the shepherd prostrated himself before their images, the priest came out and told him, "Your sheep are by the old oak tree." And there was his flock waiting for him. The moral of the story is: Yajishan bitter dates, don't cut them, don't pick them, and don't eat them. Maybe that is why they have so many thorns.

# Pines Line the Route to Holy Site

"Do you want to go on a pilgrimage?" asked Feng Jianhua, proprietor of a small teahouse in one of the back alleys off Liulichang, the famous antique section of Beijing. I first met Feng when I unexpectedly came across his teahouse the day it opened in April 1996. His shop is a simple place with only a casual wood sign, with the word *cha* (tea), hanging at the nondescript entrance. Inside there are only eight square tables and wood benches. But Feng electrifies the place with his personality.

All of a sudden, there is Feng in make-up doing stand-up comedy, slapstick and Beijing's well known "cross-talk" humor. Then before you notice, he is back to his rounds pouring tea and chatting with customers.

Feng, 29, returned to my bench and embellished on his earlier question. "I'm leading a *shenghui* (sacred association) to pray and provide tea to other pilgrims next month at Miaofeng Mountain." His voice was low and serious. "It's the feast day of the popular deity Bixiayuanjun, Lady Sovereign of the Azure Clouds — you know she's the real protector of Beijing."

It was the tradition in Beijing to join a pilgrim club. That would ensure traveling arrangements and accommodations along the way. Often one person in the family was chosen to make the pilgrimage, for many a once in a lifetime excursion. Support groups made it a religious vow to help the pilgrims by providing free tea and places to rest, especially when climbing the mountain. That was the origin of the Tea Societies, the "sacred associations."

"All of this stopped after the war. But recently we got the 'Tianping Shenghui' (Heavenly Peaceful Sacred Society) going again," continued Feng. "Our organization is special. Only those whose troops have performed for the Imperial court can use the term 'shenghui'. The other tea societies are just known as 'laohui', or old club. We got the honor because our troop performed for the birthday of the Empress Dowager Cixi in the early 20<sup>th</sup> century."

The 18<sup>th</sup> of the fourth moon is the goddess's birthday and

several weeks before that, the temple fair begins its annual tribute to this patroness of women, giver of children and saintly protector of the common man. She is one of the most loved divinities in all of the Taoist pantheons.

It took about two hours to get to the remote Miaofeng (Mystic Peak) Mountain monastery, also known as Jinding, or the Golden Peak, about 70 kilometers west from central Beijing. Although the temple is more than 1,300 meters high, one can go part of the way by car. The last ascent, however, is a steep footpath lined with regularly spaced ancient pines. It gives a fabulous panorama of rocky mountains and valleys filled with wild roses below.

Feng suggested we go on the first day of the festival. There was a steady stream of pilgrims winding their way upward along the path. Dressed in good clothes, most pilgrims festooned themselves with long rosaries, colorful scarves, and charms. Everyone was in a holiday mood. Friendships developed quickly with the common bond of the spiritual quest. "Here, have a rose for your hair," called out one seller of pine walking sticks.

Going up the final leg of the path, there are more grand trees. These are treated as holy trees. Red ribbons, prayer banners and cut papers were tied to the trunks. Feng led us first to the main shrine sitting on an outcropping of the peak.

A heavy cloud of smoke covered the inner courtyard. Crowds jostled in front of the huge incense burner to present their offerings. The altar was covered by dolls in all shapes and sizes. Prayers accomplished, the pious turned their attention to the fun of the fair. The elaborately decorated tent of Feng's "Tianping Shenghui" was the largest and his troop geared right into action.

Heavily made-up men and women, mostly over 70 years old, gathered in a semi-circle. To the rhythm of clackers and drums, with fans and sticks as props, an ancient folk story was acted out, like a passion play of Medieval Europe, it entertained and moralized.

People loaded up on souvenirs. I got Feng a bumper sticker. It read: "Good people will have peace all their lives! The Fourth Temple Festival of Miaofeng Mountain." We also bought good luck talismans, especially the red braided bat corsage, and pinned them to our clothes. As we descended, we slowly followed the route of pines to the road below.

# Time Capsules

## Where Have All the Flowers Gone?

Fengtai District in the southwest corner of the modern capital is in a construction boom with urban sprawl encroaching on farmlands. Yet this area was known as "A Land of Flowers" for more than 600 years and almost all flowering trees and plants for the city came from here. Even now Fengtai boasts over 200 hectares of land for flower cultivation.

Not far from the southern ring road in Fanjia Village is the site of a former small temple, Huashenmiao (Temple to the Flower Gods). While consulting an old map in the late spring of 1997, it was good luck to meet Mr. Guo, age 70, a local of long residence. He was seated outside of an elementary school gate waiting for his granddaughter. Asked where the Temple to the Flower Gods was, he swept his hand from the far road all the way to the school gate behind him, "It was right here." He then reminisced about the place as his granddaughter looked on.

"This was a popular gathering place. The flower farmers prayed for rich blossoms and scholars came to write poetry." They came at sunrise, the hour of perfume, when the blossoms begin the day with their fresh fragrance. "At festivals a stage was put up here for Peking Opera performances. Lots of people came to watch the free shows." Guo continued, "The market was great for flowers, seeds and gardening equipment. I remember a lot of people from south China came to the fair to sell plants, we could tell by their accents."

The most important festival was the 19th of the fourth moon. That was known as the festival of "The Washing of Flowers." Garden parties used to be held on that day and people proudly displayed their most beautiful peonies, the King of the Flower Gods.

Guo recounted an old legend. "The beautiful goddess Tree Peony (*mudan*) and eleven other gods in Heaven committed crimes and were condemned by the Jade Emperor (the Taoist Lord of Heaven) to go to earth where they became flowers of different colors, each one presiding over one month of the year." Guo couldn't remember which flowers were there, but a source on folklore said that the the flower-fairies had a certain order beginning in the first moon of the lunar New Year which was *ying chun* (yellow winter jasmine), then *yulan* (tree magnolia), lilac, tree peony, jasmine, the lotus blossom, begonia, sweet-scented osmanthus, chrysanthemum, camellia, narcissus, and plum. The peony (*shaoyao*) was a kind of secondary flower god. In addition, the rose, apricot, peach, climbing rose, pomegranate, balsam and marigold also served as flower-fairies for the monthly fetes.

As popular belief, the cult of the flower gods was perpetuated by the farmers. Guo went on, "No monks ever lived here. The village acted as caretaker. It was the headquarters for the Flower Association." Guo's granddaughter stood transfixed as he recounted the past. "I remember there were three halls, but the main hall had the statues of the flower gods made of clay and grass. The Jade Emperor was represented, too. All were more than one meter high and dressed up in many colored cloths. If the door was open we could see them all seated on an altar facing south."

"They tore down the last remnants of one hall just last year," he lamented. "I saw them bury three steles under the ground where the cement is there." Today that cemented space is a lot for selling cars. The parked yellow and red taxis have replaced the clay statues and colorful flapping flags denote daily sales instead

of the monthly fairs.

Guo left, but a little girl who had been listening motioned to follow her. She and her friends giggled as they walked along the dirt road. Finally they pointed to a carved dragon, its four claws and extended nose still discernible on a broken slab forgotten behind their school. It was the last monument to the flower deities.

Fengtai's history is gradually being eclipsed by urban development. The Temple to the Flower Gods is gone, but many parks in the city still provide places for the avid followers of the flower calendar. Old-timers still remember the flower that is "in charge" each month.

## A Patriot's Tree Bends toward the South

The trees, too, are like time capsules. Take one tree in a small courtyard on Fuxue *Hutong* for example. This part of Beijing's Eastern District still preserves quite a few large residences. But one place is set very low below street level. This is one of the clues that a site has maintained its older history and not been built up with the surrounding neighborhood.

A shrine was dedicated here to the famous 13th century Southern Song general Wen Tianxiang. He was taken prisoner and held captive for seven years by the Mongols. They later beheaded him due to his continued defiance of their takeover of China. In the subsequent Ming Dynasty this shrine was built to commemorate his loyalty. And the proud jujube tree that grows in the second courtyard was rumored to have been planted by General Wen himself.

When I first visited Wen Tianxiang Shrine, I felt that stepping down to the sunken courtyard was like stepping down through the ages. As in some kind of time warp, I could actually stand in Ming Beijing. A curator told the story of the jujube tree and I saw the many branches all bending in one direction: south. It was like another famous general whose statue stands prominently in my hometown of New Orleans. But there, General Robert E. Lee always faces north in defiance, whereas the patriot Wen, and the tree that embodies his spirit, always faces south in support of his beloved homeland, ever loyal to the emperor of Southern Song.

## Monks Tend History among the Lilacs

Certain places in Beijing are known for their glorious flowering trees and it is a must to see them in their season. The most famous lilac trees in the city are at Fayuansi (Source of the Law Temple). During the April blooming season, it has often been referred to as the "Fragrant Sea of Snow." I like being

well near the back of the temple. Emperor Qianlong also frequented the temple, sometimes in the guise of a monk. Today it is the center for the research of Buddhist studies. The temple is filled with artifacts, ancient steles and even a 700-year-old lacebark pine dating from the Mongol period.

But the most pleasant experiences at Fayuansi have been associated with the Japanese tea ceremony. The long history of tea in its relationship with Buddhism is also the history of Buddhism's transfer to Japan and the introduction there of tea drinking by Japanese monks who had studied in China. Now in a reverse course, Japanese tea ceremony masters are reintroducing the tea etiquette into China. There in a hall by the blooming lilacs, young Chinese monks whip powdered green tea in glazed pottery bowls.

It was amusing to see the young monks scurrying about doing a formal tea ceremony. They were very proud of their accomplishments. One young acolyte, who had just finished tea ceremony practice, asked me if I wanted to see his room. There inside were all the things that any young person would have on their desks. In addition to study books, there was a tape recorder and piles of tapes ("language study," he winked), a tennis racket, barbells, some candy and gum, several popular magazines, and a picture of his family. He seemed just like any other student, and his room like any dorm room. And we took photos together by the lilac blooms.

inundated with the sweet lilac aroma and listening to chanting monks. As one of the oldest temples in Beijing, Fayuansi was founded in the Tang Dynasty to pray for the soldiers who died in the campaign against the Bohai State in the north. It was here in 1127 that the Song emperor Qinzong was kept under house arrest by an old

# Wisteria and Crabapple Withstand the Noise

One evening in 1985, I was having dinner with a group of American friends at the famous Shanxi Restaurant, Jinyang Fanzhuang. Always crowded, the restaurant was full of energy, good spirits and good food. The magnificent wisteria vine of over 200 years gracefully curled up a trellis and made a grand canopy with its lush foliage covering the entrance.

We got a table in the crowded main hall. Soon we were munching on toasted onion rolls. The room was so packed and noisy that we had to shout to make ourselves heard. We dug into the Shanxi pressed chicken. My eardrums and vocal chords were stretched to maximum load. The "cats' ears" curled noodles were served. And we gave a toast with Fenjiu, the white distilled liquor made with the waters of the Fen River that

ambles down the center of Shanxi province. We screamed, "To Ji Xiaolan and his beautiful home!" For in fact the restaurant was operating in the old home of that great 18th century scholar. Under the sponsorship of Emperor Qianlong, he edited the imposing work, "The Complete Collection of the Four Libraries."

And more yelling back and forth about his life. "They say the crabapple tree in the courtyard was planted to remember his childhood sweetheart." She died of a broken heart. "A toast to the crabapple tree!" Then the great staple of Shanxi Province, *daoxiaomian*, knife-scraped noodles, was put at each place. "In the old days, the chef would put the flattened dough on his head and whip his knife around in a swirling motion to cut the noodles." "How awful," blasted one American, "his hair must have gotten cut, too." All of a sudden, we realized that most of the customers were gone. And the one remaining table of guests was staring in shock at the boisterous foreigners bellowing at the top of their lungs.

Ji Xiaolan's spirit must have been taken aback as well. And his spirit does survive for it dwells in the wisteria and crabapple he planted there. In verse he wrote about wisteria flowers draping down as drooping clouds of purple hue and their aroma sending out shock waves of perfume. He visualized that their beauty would continue long after he was gone. Another poem was for the crabapple as a symbol of his lover whom he compared with the beauty of the tree's blossoms. But it is a sad composition of the tree in late autumn, reflecting the passing of time.

The restaurant is no longer on the premises as the home has been restored as a historic site in honor of Ji Xiaolan. Both trees are now thriving in peace, having survived all that noise. "Cheers!"

# Beijing's Butterfly Tree

O n the day of the first snow of 1995, February 27th, I made another attempt to get into Bailinsi (Cypress Grove Temple). The challenge was always to find a way into what used to be one of the Great Eight Temples of Beijing. This temple of the Yuan Dynasty was where so many of the ancient records and their printing blocks were once stored. Since it has not been open to the general public, it keeps a kind of timelessness in its courtyards with historic cypress trees.

Having checked the names of the units using the halls as offices listed outside, it seemed natural to me to pick up the name of the International Friendship Museum. Being both international and friendly, it was easy to convincingly

fool the guard and proceed to the first courtyard. A "man in charge" approached and warned against photos of the two large stele. When the museum was mentioned, he instructed to go all the way to the back, adding that all of the buildings have been recently repaired. He pointed out one horizontal plaque with the writing, "Cypress Grove of Ten Thousand Ages", by Emperor Qianlong hanging on the main hall.

At the back, the courtyard of the two-storied Sutra Hall was littered with metal display cases, perhaps with a plan to show off international friendship. I quickly had a look around, but in my hurry, forgot to recognize the temple's unique "butterfly" scholar tree for which the temple was also well known. A friendly gateman said that the museum people were all in a meeting

and he yelled up to them that there is a visitor. They yelled back to come in the afternoon. Relieved, I said I'd return, maybe tomorrow, and hurriedly departed.

Back around the north side outside the temple

wall is a splendid view of the Sutra Hall. Two old men came up and told me, "The temple was so big, and its garden went far to the north. One needed to ride a horse to get from one end to the other. During the Ming Dynasty, the city wall cut through the great grounds of Bailinsi. Oh yes, before Beijing, there was Bailinsi." Seems there are similar sayings for several temples in town.

I knew I had to go back to this temple, having missed its great tree, but it wasn't until September 2002, that I ventured back along the familiar *hutong* by the entrance gate. I went with the sole purpose of getting a glimpse of the "butterfly." Planted in the mid-Qing Dynasty, it is supposed to have unusual leaf formations. The leaves grow in clusters of seven leaves and thus earned its nickname.

A group of foreign young women working there spotted me lurking around the entrance. They let me in with them. Back in the courtyard of the Sutra Hall, I mentioned the butterfly scholar tree, but an officious looking lady abruptly declared that she didn't think there were any butterflies here. Unexpectedly, a young watchman all of a sudden piped in and pointed out that there was in fact a butterfly scholar tree in the compound. The lady, caught off balance, just quietly looked on as I photographed the tree's branches spreading over one of the temple halls with its rich green butterfly-like leaf clusters. It was well worth it to have wormed my way in there again!

# A Thousand-Year Village Lost in Time

One of Beijing's earliest inhabited areas can be found along the upper reaches of the Yongding River. This was an important route cutting through the mountains from the west and even today some villages have been continuously lived in for over 1,000 years. Lingshui Village in 1996 was like a place lost in time. Going along a dirt track, we came upon a setting of stone homes, relics of crumbling temples and a number of extraordinarily grand trees.

Following stone steps to the higher back part of the hamlet of 700 persons, I went searching for their temples and shrines. The overall feeling from the trees is that the village is from the 10th century Liao period. There is even an inscribed reference to the village on a 992 A.D. stone pillar. Locals say that the shape of today's village is basically the same since the Mongol times and that many houses stand as they are from the 16th century.

I found the village community center when I came upon a remnant of a former opera stage. Probably most of the population used to gather here to watch traveling troupes perform at festival times. They would have crowded into this space between the stage at the south and the Shrine of the South-Seas Fire Dragon forming a backdrop on the northern edge. A decrepit gate

leads into the shrine compound which is dominated by unusual trees. The hollowed out center of an aged cypress is host to a younger, but already 300-year-old and ten-meter-high elm. The locals call it "Cypress Holding an Elm."

Nearby, another strange combination called, "Embracing Mulberry and Cypress" stand as happy lovers wrapped in each other's arms. The locals say that they are the most beautiful when the white mulberries hang together with the green of the cypress.

I walked inside one of the courtyards. Residents were using the same utensils as their ancestors. Several water cisterns and earthen jugs for storing food stood in the shadow of a squash vine breaching the wall and the slate roof. They

showed me a mallet for hitting their clothes on a special laundry stone and a large beater for winnowing grain. Out on the stoop neighbors sat in the warm autumn sun. One 95-year-old lady with tiny deformed feet boasted that she still did her own cooking.

Higher up only a gateway stands in memory of a temple dedicated to the local spring. Two giggling girls poked their heads out from behind its wooden doors. Although the temple is only imaginary now, its dignified patriarchal trees give it some character. Where the halls once stood, a makeshift building served as the village school. A retired teacher took us around. "This tree was supposedly planted when the temple was built. But it's hard to tell. Lingshui at one time had more than fifteen shrines and temples crammed in and around the village." He continued sharing village history and pointed out a rare ginkgo that only has fruit on one strange branch which is longitudinally attached to the host tree.

In the distance, another ancient tree, a sturdy robust cypress, stood in silhouette against the fields of millet and corn. Known as the "Sacred Mushroom Cypress (Lingzhibai)", its location marks the spot of another lost temple. Returning through the maze of medieval stone alleyways, I came upon a pair of statuesque old scholar trees near the village entrance. Underneath their extending branches, a donkey plodded repetitively in a circle pulling the primitive grinding stone across the newly harvested grain. It was a timeless image of Lingshui's past.

*Unforgettable People*

## A Jujube Tree with History

Crossing in front of what had been the old Huguosi (Temple to Protect the Country) is the *hutong* by the same name. The temple no longer exists, but a couple of buildings still stand as storerooms. They are the only traces left of the important history of this neighborhood. At the great monthly temple fairs in the past, people from all over the city flocked here especially to go to its famed flower market. I went looking for some reminders of the fairs and the temple's history in 1984. I still remember the day, February first. It was one of those crisp Beijing winter days with a sparkling azure sky. Peaking in at every shop, buying a birdcage and eating some hot roasted sweet potatoes made a nice day of exploring with close friends. There were many grand residences with entrances high off the street and elaborate doors. I was told that the higher the entrance, the higher the status of the person who was living there.

In 1986, I was back on the *hutong* to call at one of those homes. I knocked with the large brass rings that decorated the bright red door. Two carved stone door piers, *mendun'r*, flanked the entranceway. Inside I found that it was a typical Beijing courtyard house with rooms facing a central garden.

This was the home of Aisin-Gioro Pujie, the younger brother of the last emperor. Drinking tea in his sitting room, he leisurely chatted about the friends who visited here from Japan. Around the room were loads of Japanese knick-knacks that the guests had brought as souvenirs. Yet there was not even one piece of decoration that would have connected with his Manchu heritage and royal past.

Out in the garden was a tree which he proudly pointed out. It was just a plain jujube tree, seemingly nothing special. Pujie, though, was eager to tell the story. He reminded me of the famous scene at the end of the Russo-Japanese War. The year was 1905. The setting was Lüshun, a port city on the Liaodong Peninsula of northeast China. This was the area where Japan and Russia fought a fierce battle to win influence in this part of East Asia. In the courtyard of the

Japanese Naval Command there stood a single jujube tree. Under that tree, the Russian General Stoussel proffered his sword to General Nogi and surrendered his forces.

This tree became famous over the years because it was in a line of a song about that war which became very popular at that time in Japan. "This tree," he said, "is the offspring of the famous jujube of Lüshun." Pujie had been given a seedling from that very tree which he later brought back and planted in his Beijing home. It thrived and now dominates the garden.

Three o'clock. It was time for him to go on his daily visit to his Japanese wife, Hiroko-san, in the hospital. This had been an arranged marriage from the so-called Manchukuo days when his brother Puyi had been made the emperor of that puppet government. As he stood to leave, Pujie called for the cat. He carefully hid it in a bag of food he was bringing for his wife. "They don't allow pets there," he smiled sheepishly, "but my wife is so happy to have her cat for even just a short time."

He stood in front of the red door, bag in hand, a fine old man and an adoring husband. Behind him was the jujube tree, its ancestry confirmed, a small reminder of his Manchu homeland.

# Trees Left at Former Imperial Villas

## Rare Trees of Diaoyutai State Guest House

Over the centuries, imperial detached palaces gave the emperors a bit of freedom from the stuffiness of the court and today great trees are still associated with their locations. Diaoyutai, the State Guest House of China, was at first such an imperial lodge. At the site of the original Diaoyutai, Fishing Terrace, the ancient water courses still weave through the garden. First used by the Jin emperors in the 12th century, it continued to be a retreat for the emperors in the Ming and Qing periods when the Manchus had it rebuilt.

On one glorious April day, I wandered in the back garden where flower petals and willow kapok fluffs covered the time-honored ponds. By the hillock of the original lodge site I found one 800-year venerable pine tree with a strong thick curving trunk that has probably been around since the earliest royal fishing trips. As I looked at the weeping willows by the water's edge, I thought, was this where the emperor sat?

There were more unique trees nearby standing in the grounds of the guesthouse's most famous restaurant, Yangyuanzhai. One is a small leaf Chinese hackberry, one of only two in Beijing. Its bark, in some places, has a rippling

like elephant's skin. True to its name, the leaves do seem small in comparison to the bulk of the branches. They murmured quietly in the wind. In the same garden, a pair of catalpa trees were blooming with light pink flowers for the first time in five years. It was a rare encounter indeed!

## "General in White Robes" and "Shading Marquis"

The Jurchen rulers of the Jin Dynasty made their central capital in the area that is now the southern part of the city of Beijing. These semi-nomadic peoples who wandered through the spotlight of history have left their legacy in numerous gardens and lakes they created for their country villas. Feeling confined in their formal palaces, the pull of the northern forests beckoned them back to their roots, and as often as they could they left their stifling thrones for places where they could relax. The closest villa was the Daninggong built in 1179 at what is now the Beihai Park.

What had once been a small island between the northern and southern lakes, is now a hillock fortress, known as the Tuancheng (Round City). It had been part of the earlier villa. The proof was in the trees. The "General in White Robes" is an 800-year-old lacebark pine that reaches high above the crenellated walls of the fort. Its title was bestowed upon it by the Qing emperor Qianlong in the 18th century, who

ing pine supported by an iron pole. It looks like some ageing duke, posing in a sophisticated stance, leaning on his cane. Perfectly manicured, the pine is of a rare variety with three needles in the group, instead of the usual five. Emperor Qianlong supposedly rested under this big tree. The light breeze and the shade cooled him off. Pleased, he named it "Shading Marquis." But these days the tourists hurry past the two trees in oblivion to the nobility above them.

## Old Soldiers Never Die, They Just Fade into Pines

The nurturing of pines, especially lacebark pines with their white bark, seem to be particularly associated with imperially sponsored temples or tomb sites. Driving on roads outside of town, I always have a look around at any place that has these white-barked trees or groupings of drooping pines, for they were definitely planted to commemorate a certain place or person. Once I catch a glimpse of such trees I have an irresistible urge to find out what they are hiding.

At the foot of the Western Hills in Hongqi Village is an unusual grove of almost one hundred of these trees. Both times I passed there in the 1980s and the 1990s were rainy days and the front gate was closed. But that did not deter me. I found a back way in by passing through

recognized its radiating power and paid due homage to it.

Another equally ancient tree is a thick bend-

a vacant farmer's yard.

This was Song Tang, Hall of Pines. It was deserted. It was silent. But there was movement of a sort. In the mist and light rain those clusters of white-barked trees made me feel as if I were at a ghosts' cocktail party.

The ghost of Emperor Qianlong should be among them, for this is where he rested after watching military exercises nearby. Originally the site of an old temple, the emperor had a fine marble hall built here in 1749 as his villa. It faces east toward the practice battleground and preserves a large stone stele inscribed with Qianlong's own seal. It seemed completely abandoned. Yet, for a flicker of a moment, I had the vision of the powerful emperor at his leisure, seated and looking across this forest of pines; these ghosts were his soldiers standing at attention.

## Unforgettable People
# Trees Ascribed with Human Emotions

Mr. Zhang Baogui is one of Beijing's well-known tree researchers. Tape measure in hand, Zhang has explored trees in every corner of the city in his spare time for almost 20 years. A humble man wearing his tidy blue "people's uniform" jacket, but when it comes to trees, Zhang speaks his mind. He wants many people to know about Beijing's living treasures and his excitement is quickly contagious. I am indebted to him for his generous introductions to his many "silent friends."

Zhang talked about the Dragon Claw scholar tree in the Imperial Garden of the Palace Museum, as the largest of its kind in the city. He had measured the trunk at 3 meters around. This twisted mass of branches creates a grand canopy. Great scholar trees like this one are a specialty of Beijing. They, along with the cypresses, were the imposing trees of choice for imperial gardens as they match the grand architecture.

He pointed out cypress trees that had been joined as pairs, symbolizing a never-parting couple, or others that had been splayed to form the character for man and gave off the appearance of holding hands or an embrace. Zhang mentioned that the last emperor and his wife posed for a still photo before the "Lianlibai" (joined cypress), the symbol of everlasting love. From this research, Zhang learned that people attached human emotions to various trees. Sometimes it is love, but the trees have also been thought to show the traits of anger or vengeance.

Look at the trees inside the compound of the Confucius Temple (Kongmiao), noted Zhang. This was also an imperial space, as recognized by the yellow-tiled roofs due to the high rank given the sage by generations of imperial respect. The most famous tree here is one of the cypresses, with

heavy knobs protruding from their hardy trunks. It is situated just to the west of the steps leading up to the main hall where many ceremonies took place in honor of the great sage. The tree's legendary title is the "Tree that Got Rid of Evil" because one of its branches knocked off the hat and humiliated a bad official. The nearly 700-year-old tree was thus thought to be able to tell the difference between loyal and treacherous persons. "That amazed me!" wrote Zhang. "Trees were ascribed with strong human emotions."

Indeed, his stories made me take another look at the magnificent trees within the Imperial Garden. The gardeners' caring hands over many hundreds of years have shaped tree branches, bolstered trunks, coaxed bending angles and pampered them to

be the finest trees of the empire. In front of the hall dedicated to the deity of water, a lacebark pine curves to an almost prone position as if it were kneeling before the shrine. Not so aged, but equally unusual, is the Dragon Claw jujube tree whose tight curled tips are like whimsical amoebas of bark making modern art against the autumn sky. Their emotion? Just playful and mischievous!

# Grave Markers

## Shimmering Trees Illuminate Tomb

It's not easy to always gain access to the remaining tomb sites left around Beijing. But their existence is marked by a grove of formidable trees. The sarcophogi may be in ruins, but the trees around them will surely keep up appearances.

Lacebark pines led me to the Ruiwangfen (Prince Rui's Tomb). This grave compound of about 4,000 square meters is dedicated to the grandson of Qing emperor Jiaqing. His father's tomb, also called Ruiwangfen, is located further south. But the tomb I visited is situated on a backcountry road within the grounds of the Research Center for Fruit Trees of the Beijing Forestry Department. It is now very easy to find. The western fifth ring road zips right past it. White-barked pines clustering around the grave mound are like tall candles on a birthday cake.

They are visible from the wide six-lane highway.

On my first visit to the site, Mr. Wang from the Research Center took me around to see their work in the fruit groves and then inside the burial place. The way up to the tomb was lined with sturdy pines and accented with an equally massive stone tablet set on a large stylized dragon base. Built in 1851, a towering rust-colored wall encircled the compound. The prince had been sick and left no direct descendents, but his place in the royal family assured him of a fine structure for the afterlife.

The Beijing Mi Di Music School now uses the remaining hall still covered with distinguished black tiles lined with green. Little else is left, except for several broken marble slabs of the sepulcher wall lying covered with weeds. The underground chamber was robbed of burial treasures early on and has since been used to store pesticides. Yet the glory is in the trees, those eighteen shimmering white-barked pines continue to ensure this prince his legacy.

*Unforgettable People*

# Caretaker of the Yuling Tomb, Ancient Pines and Almond Blossoms

It was January 21, 1995. That afternoon, we drove out of town north to the Ming Tombs. Seeing the old villages brought back glimpses of the Beijing I knew from previous visits here in the 1970s and early 1980s. We visited Yuling Tomb, set right up against the backdrop of the encircling hills. As we drove up the cobblestone road, the tall pines bending over the tomb came into view and the gatekeeper, our friend from previous visits, "Lao (old)" Xu, appeared at the entrance to greet us.

We could always find him in his field on the west side of the road leading up to the tomb or walking with his black horse. Whenever we called him from a distance, "'Lao' Xu, we've come back!" he would drop what he was doing and joined us for a chat. Xu would usually defer by sitting at a distance while we ate. Together we would walk around the tomb and he'd explain the history as he knew it. After all, his village has been the protector of the tomb for several centuries!

Those were the days when my dog Nike could run free on the grassy tumulus. It was about the only spot in all Beijing where I dare let her go without her leash. From the turret we looked down into the expansive valley of the Ming necropolis.

That outing brought back memories of our frequent visits in the early 1980s when foreigners had limited sites where they could venture outside of Beijing city proper. The Ming Tombs were one of them. So we came here a lot in all seasons. The spring view from the ramparts of Yuling Tomb is really spectacular. The usually stark landscape of the Ming valley, is transformed into a sea of pale pink and white blossoms of apricot, pear and almond trees.

I have another memory of a freezing day in the winter of 1985, with three families together eating boiling hot soup in the semi-enclosed area of ruins that had once been the sacrificial hall. This protected us from the biting cold wind. We were gradually warmed up enough for a hike around the tomb following the deep red walls with their broken yellow tiles. This was a ritual we have done on every visit. There is something so protective and private about these walls.

Coming to this place always equaled an outdoor picnic. We arranged broken marble stones as

within four months. The man who was emperor twice died at 38 years of age, buried with his two empresses.

When we go back there, I never fail to photograph the pines with their long sleeve-like branches slanting towards the stele tower in a natural deferment to the spirit of the twice-enthroned emperor. Xu has since retired but he's often in the fields with his black horse. And we still greet him, "'Lao' Xu, we've come back!"

picnic tables and continued to come here at all times of day and night to eat and sing and even dance, until the area was blocked off completely in 2001. I never thought of this as desecration of the tomb area, rather a celebration of this solitary place with the marvelous ancient pines.

I fell in love with the site even before I researched the history of the grave and the emperor entombed there. In fact, he was unique to be emperor twice. "Lao" Xu roughly filled me in on the details. Emperor Zhengtong, who later became Emperor Tianshun, reigned from 1436 to 1464, except for the period 1449-56 when his brother reigned as the seventh Ming emperor. While he was taken prisoner by the Mongols, his brother assumed the imperial mantle, and even after his release was held prisoner for six years by his own people inside the Forbidden City. No wonder when Zhengtong's supporters finally got control again, they turned with a vengeance against the sick brother, de-throned him, and banished him to a humble grave near the Western Hills. Yuling mausoleum was supposedly built

# Nicknames

## Shrine of the Black and White Dragons

At Xiaweidian Village two important roads intersect where the Yongding River cuts through the mountains of Mentougou District. A small dilapidated shrine stands on a hillock above this juncture. It is practically overpowered by two 800-year-old cypresses that have grown together as one, their branches spreading out over the crumbling walls in all directions like the flaying arms of a giant octopus. The villagers named them the Black and White Dragons. They were believed to be dragon spirits who could give protection against the whims of the river below.

I stopped a man with a long white beard. Mr. Liu said he lived most of his 90 years in the village. Except for using a walking stick to keep his balance, he was perfectly spry. Puffing on a short brown pipe, he proudly noted that the river used to be much wider and very much of a menace. "We came here a lot to give offerings to the spirits of the temple. But there was no particular festival," he went on. "We all went to the festivals at Miaofeng Mountain because it's so close. The monk had a place in the village, but he changed

his profession after we were liberated in 1949."

Together we climbed up the weed-covered stone steps that led up to the one hall. Paintings faintly colored the rafters and even some wall paintings left a faded impression. Liu said, "Before the 1960s, they were very clear and beautiful, but the kids, our kids, scratched them all up!" The trees were much older than the temple. Deep grooves made patterns on the darkened bark. Liu turned toward me with a toothy grin and pointed to one large stump of a branch. "It was hit by lightening just this summer." Some people must still believe in the trees' power as there are offerings and spent incense inside this Shrine of the Black and White Dragons.

## "Brigadier General" and the Shepherd's Family

Changping District has a rare "qingtan" wingceltis tree that grows above the village of Tanyucun, meaning Wingceltis Valley. Although the bark is famous for making high quality *xuan* paper, I could tell at one glance it was a tree I'd never seen before. Mottled bark and a hollowed-out trunk pronounced it antique. In some places it takes on a resemblance to *Taihu* stones with exotic holes and rough surfaces. The roots spread as thick vines rippling over surrounding rocks like a cascading waterfall.

Newer generations of these wrinkled trunks shoot up beside it similar to flourishing bamboo. And from these newer trees, some probably over 500 years themselves, branches go out in every direction competing for sunlight. This compound of related and connected trees gives such an imposing image that it has been named the "Brigadier General of Beijing", also because it is thought to be the second oldest tree in Beijing. Those extending trunks are as if a group of

officers have gathered as comrades to the senior general. It is a mystery, though, as to why this unusual tree was planted here about 1,500 years ago.

I went back there again in the wintertime. With the trees bare, the discoloration and peeling of the bark was even more pronounced. And the older tree's branches clearly reached nurturingly over the younger trees like a mother's arms reaching over toward her children. I spotted a small shrine on the hillock behind it, its single hall recently decorated with red New Year's trappings. Inside, I was impressed by the rough and naive clay sculptures of Guanyin (Goddess of Mercy) and two attendants. They were draped with fresh yellow capes. An offering of ripe persimmons and burned incense spoke of recent prayers before them. This is not a formal shrine, but it has a deep religious aura of the humble yearnings of those who believe in something greater than themselves and have a heart of gratitude.

Down in the village, Yao Jingquan, 83, was eager to tell what he knew. Dressed in a green people's jacket with brass buttons and sporting a fur cap, Yao said that the trees were there first, then there was the village, named in fact after the trees. He didn't know who planted them, but the seeds were probably from the south.

He invited me to come to his house and chat. His home was a simple single courtyard of stone and earthen walls. The winter sun, though, gave it warmth and I sat in their living room drink-

older scholar tree." Yao added, "The *qingtan* can only grow at that location. It has something to do with those rocks." It seems they must grow in conjunction with the stones of the mountain. They have tried to plant the young shoots in soil but they all died.

The granddaughter Yao Chunyan said matter-of-factly that she would take me around after lunch. Her words were so straight and unassuming that I thought it would be offensive to decline the girl's warm invitation. Her father, Yao Changliang, 50, returned to cook the meal. He is a shepherd and to my astonishment, the sculptor of the Buddhist figures in the temple. "I am an unlearned man, but have faith, and have tried to do something with my hands to show respect. I can only work at night, so it took me about a month to finish."

ing hot water next to his 16-year-old granddaughter. Yao took off his hat, his bald palate shining, "I have been a farmer all my life." They don't have any particular festivals here, rather eight villages banded together for the yearly festival at Hepingsi (Temple of Peace) that also claims to be older than Beijing. Yao noted that it, too, has some very ancient trees.

"Nobody dared to cut our unusual *qingtan* trees," he continued, quoting an old saying, "Thousand-year pine, ten-thousand-year cypress, if you don't believe it, just ask the even

And in this very natural way I ate lunch with the shepherd and his family. I was deeply moved by their gracious hospitality. Moreover, I was impressed by shepherd Yao's yearning for good education for his daughter and his own spiritual commitment. Those sculptures came from the heart. They then served delicious persimmons from their cold storage. And I remembered the persimmons on the altar. Who planted the *qingtan* trees remains a mystery, but the moving force behind the Guanyin temple was clear.

## "Brother Trees: Cypress Embracing Pagoda Tree"

A special nickname is given when two different trees grow together. There are many such interlocking trees in the Greater Beijing region and their name usually refers to one tree embracing the other. Tiantan Park has one cypress over 1,000 years in whose trunk a pagoda (scholar) tree has also grown for 100 years. Its nickname is the "Brother Trees: Cypress Embracing Pagoda Tree." Their companionship is one of brotherly mutual dependence. The existence of a number of equally old cypresses and junipers there suggest that Tiantan was also a special sanctuary even before it was designated as the Altar of Heaven under the Ming regime.

It was below these cypresses that my family had an evening picnic with friends in the late summer of 1986. The party continued long after dark. Unknown to us, we had been locked in. As we rushed around from closed gate to closed gate many of us were resigned to spending the night there. In fact, it was a gorgeous evening with full moon rays striking the deep-blue-glazed circular roof of the Hall of Prayer for a Good Year, so we went back to partying in the cypress grove that stood like tall phantoms joining our festivities.

Around midnight though, someone had finally found a guard who would let us out and we left almost reluctantly. Since that time night floodlights have been added to give brightness to the hall and old trees, but the shining of the natural moonlight of that one evening filled me with awe for the shimmering azure tiles and the mysteriously looming shape of the "Brothers" who had kept us company.

# The "Curling Dragon" Pine and Palace Chestnuts

On one extremely hot September afternoon, I found two trees with special nicknames at the Yanshousi (Temple of Extended Life) on a hill above Heishan village. The temple, being restored by three monks, dates from the Ming Dynasty, but the two pines are decidedly older. One is more than 800 years called the "Panlong Song", Curling Dragon Pine, because of its swirling gnarled branches. The "Fenghuang Song", Phoenix Pine, growing more than 500 years on a nearby slope, has branches curving upwards as if in flight.

In the temple compound, the Yanshou spring flows out of a carved dragon's mouth. The water supposedly has special healing properties because it has passed through rocks deep in Heishan, Black Mountain, which is the backdrop to the temple site.

Lining the path going up the mountain to the temple are groves of 500-year-old chestnut trees. They are referred to as the "Palace Chestnuts" because during the Qing Dynasty all their chestnuts were harvested as tribute to the emperor. A local farmer remarked, "Today they are all exported to Japan. We can get 8 *yuan* a *jin* (500 grams), and I can harvest 800 *jin*. But tell me, how can I export directly to Japan? I hear they sell many times over that in Tokyo!" Those "*Tenshin Amaguri*" (Sweet Chestnuts from Tianjin) that sell at the railroad stations in

Tokyo at 1,000 yen (80 Chinese *yuan*) for 500 grams is an amazing markup. They leave through the port of Tianjin but, in fact, many of them are these "Palace Chestnuts" from the Black Mountain Valley.

## "Jujube King" of the Fast Food Court

Xidan intersection is one of the busiest in Beijing. It is also one of the trendiest with many shops catering to the fashion-conscious youth of the city. On an unusually warm February day I wandered in the hustle and bustle of a chaotic maze of small shops known as the Big World Nationalities' Marketplace. Only when I looked up did I realize that I was standing in the midst of a former princely residence. The room interiors had been gutted, cubicles created, and it was transformed into a makeshift department store.

Shoes, jackets, sweaters, sunglasses, etc. were piled for sale. This is where the young get their discounts. The courtyards in between the halls had also been converted into outdoor stalls. One whole wall was covered with *faux* Red Guard green knapsacks complete with a decorative red star. Nearby an outdoor café served a limited selection of Chinese fast food like pancakes and noodles. Unexpectedly, there in the midst of cluttered white plastic tables and grimy umbrellas I found a sturdy mature jujube tree that in the past must have had the courtyard to itself. It was unmistakably old, more than 500 years. A plaque beside it gave it a bit of authenticity and protection, declaring it to be the "Number One Jujube Tree of Beijing." I was struck by the contrast between the weathered tree and the young culture swirling around it.

This used to be a guild hall from the 15th century for the citizens of Changzhou city (Jiangsu Province), a place where they could stay in the capital and take the tri-annual national exams. Then in the mid-17th century this became a princely residence, E'fufu (Mansion of the Son-in-law). It was the home of Wu Yingxiong whose wife was a daughter of the emperor. Their political marriage was arranged to keep an eye on the strong Wu family and keep them loyal to the Manchus. Wu's father, Wu Sangui, was the soldier who allowed the Manchu troops to pass through the Shanhaiguan barrier into the capital region and overthrow the crumbling Ming Dynasty. The residence later became an academy for the children of the Manchu bannermen and in the Republican period, it was a Mongolian and Tibetan school.

Underneath the wizened boughs of the old tree, two young girls hawked *tanghulu* candied haws and strawberries on a stick. For three *yuan* I got the haws. I am addicted to these fruits of the winter scene. It made me feel a little better about the state of the jujube tree. At least people pause to look at it while they are eating!

*Unforgettable People*

# Coal Salesman Recalls Potholed Route

A bumpy dirt road winds back through Gaojing Village passing a small temple compound. Three scraggly cypress trees jut out over the wall. One tree has already died. The others are pathetic, with dusty drooping leaves. Its gate was locked fast but peering in through a crack I could see a fierce dog guarding the shambles within. The deserted Cuiyun'an (Green Cloud Retreat) was a far cry from its former self. Its neighborhood was overpowered by the nearby electric power plant. On that sweltering hot day, July 3, 1997, the smoke from the three tall smokestacks hung heavily in the atmosphere.

Standing shirtless by the doorway of this simple Ming Dynasty hermitage was former coal salesman Bai Lianji, age 70. He was eager to talk about the past. "This was all our village," he

said expanding his hand around the vicinity. "But the power station took over the land. They gave us a little money."

"I remember there was a pagoda with an inscription," he rambled on. "This was the monks' graveyard for the superior Fahaisi (Temple of the Sea of the Law) up the road." Bai still recalled the last monk in residence. He turned and pointed out the

old cypress trees. "I've looked out at those trees almost every day."

"You name it, I've done it all!" he declared, "Farmer, merchant, worker and member of a people's commune! But I was basically a coal delivery man."

"I used to drive a horse cart to Beijing every week. That's more than 20 kilometers to Fuchengmen Gate. The roads were really bad. Lots of potholes and rocks, I had to be very careful. It took me two days to do the round trip. Never rested or missed a delivery," he recalled. The price was 40 yuan for a ton in the 1950s. Now that's more than 200 *yuan*.

"One of my customers was a minister of education in the Republic. Then there was the Japanese Occupation. After the Eighth Route Army took Beijing, the authorities of Zhongshan Park wanted my coal." Bai stopped his story long enough to re-tie his pants' string. "I also took coal to the home of an artist on Nanwei *Hutong*." He still remembered his delivery routes.

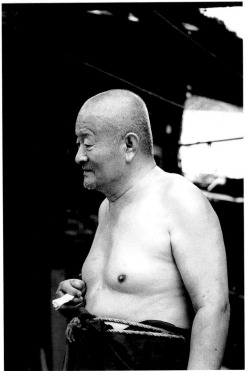

"Foreigners couldn't come out here like you did today. I'd have had to report you. But I knew an American named Fu. Sold him coal, too. And you know that Catholic cemetery? I sent coal there." He stopped and laughed. "No, not to the dead, to the caretakers!"

Bai doesn't sell coal anymore. He lives quietly between the three chimneys and the three dying cypress trees, remembering the importance coal used to have in every Beijinger's life.

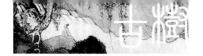

# Decorating Trees

## Good Luck Charms and Prayers Adorn Temple Trees

The Eight Grand Sites of the western hills have inscriptions and legends going back to the seventh century. Several of the temples are home to trees proving their ancient origins. Reminiscent of tree-cults, these trees sometimes are dressed up with prayer papers as pilgrims make this part of their rituals.

Two 800-year-old ginkgos dominate the courtyard of the fourth site, Dabeisi (Temple of Great Mercy). I climbed the hill on an icy day to inspect the extent of decoration to the trees after the Chinese New Year's holidays. And it was quite a festive air with little red lanterns tied with a wish to every available bough and twig among the hundreds of auxiliary shoots. They are like aged Christmas trees bedecked with ornaments all year round.

Further up the hill at the sixth site, Xiangjiesi (Temple of the Pilgrimage Boundary), I found its famous heavy set pine, the Dragon Pine, to be void of any adornment. It wouldn't look right to put fancy dress on such an elderly and distinguished "dragon." Rather the celebration was going on before the main hall in the back courtyard. There, two sal trees, or "seven-leaf tree", said to be planted over 1,000 years ago by

the founding monk of the temple, have all the attention. Unfortunately, one of the pair has deceased but its mummified carcass still gets homage paid to it from visitors acknowledging the fragility of life.

As noted earlier, the sal tree is one of the Bud-

dhist holy trees, venerated because the Buddha entered nirvana at Kushinagara in northern India under twin *sala* trees. They bloomed at that instant, so the story goes, and the nearby forest turned to white like a flock of cranes. But these trees here were instead covered with red "flowers."

For five *yuan* one can buy a red strip denoting prayers for various purposes. There was long life, marriage, good health, etc. I chose the one for increased intelligence and wrote my name at the bottom. Grabbing one outstretched branch my prayer strip joined the myriads of dreams asked of the divine sal tree.

## Holy Tree Wears an Apron

A bright red apron tide around the trunk of a tree towering above its surrounding village, was what caught my eye. Immediately one knows it has a special meaning for the people who live in Xiezishi Village in the north. This particular setting of the

mountain village with one thick straight pine that grows above all else and decorated with its bright red cummerbund, had fascinated me every time I passed here. I knew that it must mark the site of an abandoned temple, but it wasn't until January of 2003, that I finally decided to prowl the village paths until I got the story. Light snow lingered on the ground, but Mr. Zhang Shixin, 72, who was born and raised here was out sunning. He called the tree a *shenshu*, or supernatural tree.

With a trunk more than a meter in diameter, it is probably 1,000 years old. "That tree used to have many branches swinging way out from the trunk. No matter whether there was a wind or a breeze or not, the tree always had a deep 'whoo-whoo' sound as the branches swayed. When we heard this we knew that the tree had a special spirit," recounted Zhang.

At the base of the tree three incense burners and piles of small rocks as offerings show that the tree is considered holy. On lunar New Year's Eve and fifteen days later, a festival is celebrated around the tree. After prayers to the tree, there are *yangge* dancers, stilt walkers, paper boat dancers and firecrackers.

Zhang squatted on a stump and told another story of local lore. One villager in past times climbed the tree and a cut a few of its branches. That night he had a terrible back pain and could never stand again. Mothers tell this story to their children, warning them that this tree should never be cut. They say, too, that the sap runs

red as blood, further proof of its peculiar entity.

But years of drought have affected even this grand tree. Many branches have dried up and died. The eerie "whoo whoo" noise is heard less often. "There used to be a shrine to the mountain god behind the tree," explained Zhang. "We villagers fought off the attempts to cut down this tree when they were building the road through here in 1968. They killed so many old trees, but nobody was going to touch our special tree, and we defended it." He proudly looked back at the Holy Tree.

Zhang went on, "The red cloth? That is tied there for a special prayer. People put a new one on it when the tree's spirit is called upon to help them. Not just the people from our village, even neighboring villagers come here to pay respect." They say that one woman walked from Shandong Province to find this tree which she claimed was reflected in her water basin. She just followed the shadow until she reached here.

The name of the village means a stone with an unsolved riddle. Zhang said that he had seen the stone, about two meters square. The stone had a handprint and a horse's hoof mark. One line of characters went across the stone, but nobody was able to read them. Even experts from universities were unable to decipher the markings. So it is the Riddle Stone, pronounced as "Xiezishi." The stone was buried under the small village reservoir for safekeeping.

Like many similar mountain villages, their residents are depleting as the young move elsewhere for work. Their 60 households rely on hill haw fruit and almonds which they sell for a meager income. But all is not grim here. Even though it is just a humble mountain village, they have a very distinguished tree, one that they boldly fought for, and one they continue to revere as the spirit of their home.

## Tie a Red Ribbon on the Old Scholar Tree

The Taoist Dongyuemiao (Shrine of the Eastern Peak) is well known for its New Year festival. The grand slanting "Shou Huai", Scholar Tree of Longevity, in the courtyard is wrapped up in colorful ribbons, each attached with a name of the devotee. Another

### Shrine of the Eastern Peak

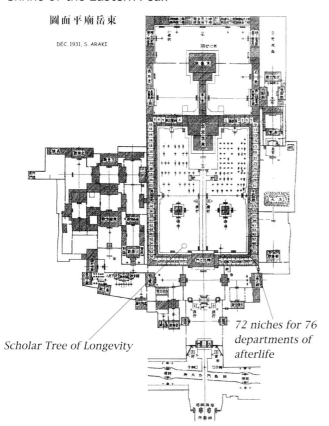

圖面平廟岳東

DEC. 1931, S. ARAKI

*Scholar Tree of Longevity*

*72 niches for 76 departments of afterlife*

custom is to walk clockwise around it three times, perhaps earning a longer life or gaining points for the hereafter. And it does exude a kind of mystique, not just with age, but with its association with Taoist mysteries. The tree was there predating the shrine, nurtured by the founder of the temple in the early 14th century and cared for over the years by twenty generations of holy men.

I was there on the second day of the lunar New Year of 2002. Crowds jostled to make their way to and around the tree. It was such a pleasure to be allowed on the grounds. For two decades I had tried to get into the shrine precincts in vain. The halls were occupied by the security police until around 1998. I always thought it was appropriate to have the police there because of the 76 departments of Taoist afterlife, each one with a judge, depicted in the 72 niches along the corridors. They were a kind of moral guide to encourage good behavior. In the old days there was also a visual portrayal of the punishment in hell for those who dared bad deeds.

To me, the most frightening of these tortures was the one for the woman who refused to give her mother-in-law the warmest spot of the family "kang" (a heated earthen bed), so she was sentenced to slowly being roasted alive on the "kang" of hell. I hope I always gave my mother-in-law the most comfortable seat around the Japanese warm table. Just in case, I made several extra rounds of circling and tied a red ribbon on the tree.

## Listening for the Orchestra in the Sky

Song Qingling's residence in central Beijing is a well-preserved garden created as a princely estate in the Qing period. The grand "Phoenix Scholar Tree" stands proudly in the front garden where Song, the wife of Dr. Sun Yat-sen, used to relax under its elongated branches. In the center garden is a pair of crabapple trees that have spectacular blooms in the springtime.

The garden is also home to a large band of pigeons. One knows without even seeing them. It is that eerie high-velocity electric wire sound that punctuates the air of Beijing's neighborhoods. Most people are unaware of this particular sound unless they know this special orchestra in the sky comes from a flock of pigeons groomed with whistles in their tails. It's a very popular custom, especially of Beijing.

Over centuries the raising of pigeons – trading them, grooming them, fitting them with whistles and competing with them – has developed into an honored past time of retired men. But even Song Qingling was a pigeon connoisseur and there are photos of her feeding her flock. One might think pigeon raising would have died out after the Cultural Revolution or after the demise of one-storied houses supplanted by apartment complexes, but no. It is in fact making a comeback.

Zheng Zhanjun, 51, an otherwise average worker tending the grounds of the Song Qingling home, becomes passionate and erudite when talking of pigeons. Even in some of Beijing's most desolate days in the 1960s, when food was scarce and pigeon-keeping was frowned upon as "bourgeois", Zheng shared his food and foraged for rice and grass to keep a few birds alive.

Zheng showed me the coop and pointed out the beaks, forehead, tail and feathers as the distinguishing features of each bird. "These nose feathers, or 'feng', meaning phoenix, show good breeding," he added. In total, he has 12 varieties of pigeons, each type with its own unique coloration. They all have nicknames: "Plum Blossoms on Snow" are birds with a red-brown head

on the white body; "Ink Ring" birds have a black ring of feathers around the neck; and all black pigeons are called "Crows."

Zheng's birds also fly in chorus. Pulling out three different bird whistles from his pocket, he demonstrated how they fit on the 6th feather of a bird's tail. He then coaxed the birds out of the wire-mesh coop and pushed 60 pigeons in the air, waving a bamboo pole topped with red rags to keep them flying. "I never feed them before flying," he said, "because some lazy ones wouldn't be bothered to get up." As they whirled upward, Zheng's symphony came to life.

To get the birds to return, he sent up a few of their comrades that had remained perched on the roof, letting the others know it was time to come home. The flock circled several times to check it out before touching down on their special landing spot – a set of one yellow and four green tiles. They were like airplanes looking for their tarmac and even the make-shift bird coops jutting out from high rise apartments have markers so that the pigeon flocks can still find home.

Outside of the city in Qijia Village lives master pigeon-whistle maker Wang Xuezhang, 52. I visited him there in his workshop. "There are basically two kinds – the *xiao* bamboo whistles and the round *hulu* made of small gourds," Wang said. "The taller the bamboo stems, the higher the pitch. Gourds give a deep sound." Different notes are created by varying the size and the number of holes, the latter producing a full harmony. With calloused hands that are evidence of his 30 years of work, he takes a knife and cuts slits on a slight curve of a bamboo whistle. "It takes me a day to make the plain whistles, but seven to ten days to make a gourd whistle with three slits."

He handled a tiny gourd, shaving and polishing it until it was almost transparent, then put it on a heater to dry, making the beginnings of a whistle that is thin and lightweight. Almost like a mouth organ, Wang's greatest masterpiece has 15 tones. "But I keep the best ones as models," Wang told me as he compared it with the first one he made at 15. Whenever a flock swoops past in flight, Wang listens carefully to hear his many-toned whistles add their deep harmony to the "orchestra in the sky."

# Trees in Jeopardy

## Tree Silhouettes Linger from Vanished Courtyards

Work continues through the night. Old courtyard houses have been razed and only the trees that once stood as part of the gardens cling to their spot, awaiting an execution or perhaps an inclusion in the modern city plan. As the destruction and construction continue, there have been some weird landscape scenes. Free standing persimmons and jujube trees without their quadrangle confines, acacias every so many meters, one can look across the homeless lots and envision the old neighborhoods.

I walked into one area slated for redevelopment in 2002. Construction lights made the remaining trees appear as ghostly silhouettes on a big modern building already standing next door. I was actually there in the nick of time. One small hall from a former temple clung to its position at a corner of the lot. Its owner was not eager to move. He was the son of the last monk who married after Liberation in 1949. As the fourth son, he was "Xiao Si'r" (little fourth), and the people in the neighborhood referred to him since childhood as "Fourth Son of the Old Monk." He was reluctant to move away as his frail mother still lived there, but his house was the last holdout on the block and was under great pressure to evacuate.

Fortunately for me, "Xiao Si'r" was able to point out the last bits of the Tietasi (Temple of the Iron Pagoda) before it evaporated. "Look at that stone," he said of a slab with some carving on it. I also made note of a base stone, part of the original wall and several wooden pillars.

Using old maps, I had actually searched for this place several times to no avail. In 1986 I went all around it by bike, but a factory unit blocked entry. One street had actually cut the temple grounds, leaving tree vestiges in an apartment complex. Neighbors recalled that there used to be a small iron pagoda on top of a high brick base. It was pulled down in 1968. Standing now in the background is a towering office building with a large antenna on top. I note that as the "new Iron Pagoda."

In the old days, a Spring Festival Fair on the premises was famous for its kite sales. Others remembered the mummy of a well-respected monk that sat in one of the former halls. "We were just kids then. We ran in and stole the embroidered shoes from one statue and took turns touching the 'Buddha.' It was soft." Some say it was the plaster-covered remains of the second son of Ming Emperor Yongle that used to be enshrined there, fittingly clad in yellow robes.

In the summer of 2002, the last vestige of the temple, the house, was torn down leaving only one tree with a tenuous lease on life. "Fourth Son of the Old Monk" and his mother moved to the eastern suburbs. At least out there nobody will call him by his embarrassing nickname.

## Dead Trees aside Urban Cowboys

Huang Village has been overrun by migrant workers. They rent rooms from Shijingshan District and each compound seems to represent some faraway village of another province. What was once the Dacisi (Temple of Great Benevolence) now houses residents from a village in Henan Province. Everyone from this village except the elderly appears to have taken up a new life in Beijing. When I first went there, they asked me if I had ever visited their famous Shaolinsi Temple outside of Luoyang. And when I answered in the affirmative, they were very pleased, and welcomed me into their compound.

It was such a relaxed friendliness among the people living there. As the lowest paid workers in the city, they bonded with each other to make ends meet. The children were neatly dressed and clean. In fact, they were lining up to get their annual shots provided by the district. The compound was full of bicycle carts, their beasts of burden for hauling away trash from construction sites. Motorbikes were jammed by the doorway. These hustling migrant workers were like urban cowboys with a frontier spirit.

Behind their carts stood two tall marble tablets. The man in charge of the compound volunteered to clear away the junk on the surface so that I could read them. The steles were resting on turtle bases now sunk in the ground. Other residents helped by using a cloth mop to wipe off the dirt. It was clear that this was no ordinary site. Inscriptions declared this to be the place of the eunuch who was in charge of the imperial horses. Eunuch Lu Yongshou had chosen this site, a place known as "Five Flower

mind the trees. They did, though, agree with me on the importance of protecting the two steles. After all, the stones proved that their temporary home was the final resting place for the master of the palace horses.

## Fireworks and Sign Language

Two weeks before the Lunar New Year in 1997, the main street of Sanhe City was crammed with shed after shed, cart after cart of firework stands with rockets, incense sparklers, or just fire crackers. Since fireworks have banned in Beijing, one has to go to rural parts of the city or to the neighboring province of Hebei to purchase and explode them. Like driving out of a dry county and being met by liquor stores and bars, likewise here one knows immediately that one has crossed the border.

One vendor offered a special of three packs of one hundred crackers on a string curled into a ball for 40 *yuan*. With names like "Flags of Fire", "Falling Moons" and "Double Kicking Feet", it was a seller's market. Even professional fireworks could be bought. "This bomb is just like the aerial display they had at Tian'anmen Square five years ago," one lady boasted. "Just one hundred *yuan* for thirty seconds of light!"

Interspersed with the fireworks stalls were sellers of New Year's pictures. Most of their wares were spread out on the ground. There

Garden", to build a temple in 1605. It had once been a grand place of three courtyards. Now it's a dusty shanty town.

Two cypress trees and the two tablets stood before what had been the location of the main hall. On my first visit in 1996 these trees were a fitting backdrop to the steles. It was a strange sight among all those closely packed dwellings. Yet on my second visit in 2001 both trees were merely skeletons. Totally dead, their branches jutted out, standing with their permanently naked arms as sculptured monuments. Perhaps this was a natural passing, but with all the clutter around them it seemed more like a double-suicide. The itinerant workers were too busy to

were at least four different pictures of Mao Zedong flanked by auspicious couplets in bright red, showing the side of his face with the characteristic mole on the chin.

Just north of all this activity is the quiet Lingshan Village. A five-storied octagonal brick pagoda stands on a hill. This is the Lingshanta, Pagoda of the Spiritual Hill. A man with a large box on his shoulder was descending the hill. The wooden box had fine brass fittings and assuming he was going to town to sell it, we asked if we could buy it. He made a guttural sound and soon a woman helping him explained that he couldn't speak. Through his own variation of sign language we were told that he wouldn't sell his box because it was very important to him.

Then we asked about the local history. Using sign language the man began a story, which he obviously felt very strongly about. His hands waved around and he made many movements with his head. The woman helped to translate. He gestured with a thumb up, a point to the chin and a rolling of the eyes back around their sockets ("At the time of Mao Zedong"), he opened his eyes even wider and threw out his chest ("a high cadre came"), his hands made a wide circle and then a chopping motion ("and he cut down the giant ancient tree here"), and then with a flurry of motion he related how the tree had been the protector of the pagoda and the village for centuries. Since the tree has been cut, the *fengshui* (geomancy for good fortune) of the village changed and they have had bad luck ever since.

He is the caretaker of the hill and the pagoda. Daily he takes his box up the hill and then back to his home in the village. He opened the brass locks to show the contents: all trash and bottles, cans and candy wrappers picked up from around the hill. Recycling these gives him a bit of income. The fun of the New Year fireworks on Lingshan Hill will mean little to him, but plenty of trash to put in his box.

Up went the box on his shoulder and he was off, leaving us with the impact of his powerful communication, his feelings over the loss of that tree.

## Haunted Temple Spirits

Visiting Xiantai Village one early spring day, I could see the high reaching branches of old trees long before I could spot any temple-style roofs. They drew me into the village center where a wide-open space spreads out before the entrance gate of their local temple. Fengxiangsi (Temple of the Flying Phoenix) is being repaired and village signs are even advertising it. Foundation stones suggest the size of the original temple layout, which once had seven halls. Now only one hall with two flanking rooms remain. The original temple, it is said, supposedly goes back to Tang times, perhaps 1,200 years old. Judging from the trees, this could be true.

These two veteran cypress trees in the courtyard, though, are in trouble. Half of the branches are dead, appearing like some spirits coming back to haunt their surviving brothers. The villagers have paved the compound in their zest and maybe the roots of these once robust trees are suffocating. Deep wrinkle lines in the exhausted bark show that they are obviously weakened, but they are not completely signed off. Still, they survive as dignified living ruins with their strange limbs rising above the surrounding village homes.

# Flowering Fruit Trees at the "Ryukyu Guest House"

In ancient times, the Ryukyu Islands, today's Okinawa prefecture in Japan, actively traded with East and Southeast Asia. Items like Chinese raw silk and Japanese swords exchanged hands with the help of these Ryukyu entrepreneurs. Even when they were under the control of the Shimazu clan in southern Kyushu, the Ryukyu kingdom continued to trade with China.

It was customary for states bordering on China to send missions bearing tribute; a common practice of China's interstate diplomacy. For almost 500 years after the 14th century a tributary relationship existed between the Ryukyu kings and China's rulers. While they were on these tribute trips, the Ryukyu envoys brought back highly prized Chinese silks to Japan.

Tribute bearers visiting the Chinese capital in the late 18th century stayed at a hostel set up by the government in the southern part of the city. This hostel, the Huitongguan, was actually the official Qing Dynasty State Guest House for over 50 years. Located on a narrow street called

Nanheng Street, the layout of the quarters remains intact as it was when the Ryukyu envoys stayed there.

When residences for foreign dignitaries closer to the palace became cramped, the government looked outside the Imperial City and requisitioned former military barracks from the earlier Ming period, Bingmasi (Horse Calvary Department), and refurbished them for official guests. Two main halls and a number of side halls still stood when I visited the place in 2001.

Mr. Song Shuze has served on the premises in one capacity or another for over 50 years. He explained that delegates from

Ryukyu, Burma, Korea and Viet Nam all stayed here in Qing times. Later on, in the 20<sup>th</sup> century, Japanese military police and the Nationalist army also occupied the place. After 1949, it became a foodstuff distribution center. Song remembered the main gate, but it was torn down in the 1970s. "This was done so that delivery trucks could get in," he said.

The architecture is far superior to the ordinary homes of the neighborhood. "Come into this hall," he beckoned. A wooden panel still graces the whole side of one wall. At the top, intricate carvings of floral designs are mixed with the carvings of fish. Noted Song, "This is the place where the Ryukyu visitors stayed!"

Song spends his days tending plants, especially roses. But he is particularly proud of the trees gracing the four courtyards. "In the spring neighbors wander in to enjoy the flowering fruit trees." Song said, pointing out mulberry, persimmon, ginkgo, pear and crabapple trees. Two giant scholar trees that must be 500 years old dominate the front hall. Their thick branches almost cut out the sunlight.

In the small west garden an antique water cistern with lotus patterns stands forgotten under an unusually large crabapple tree. Song said that the tree overflows with fruit in the autumn. Most importantly, the tree was supposedly planted by members of a Ryukyu delegation when they were living here.

"If they ever restore this place," said Song, "they should tear up all the cement and expose the original stone walkway." He said he had heard rumours the street will be widened and that "some of those trees will have to go soon." That means that the crabapple, planted by Ryukyu emissaries 200 years ago, as a symbol of friendship, may not survive for long.

# Planting of New Trees

## Ancient Poplar Symbolizes Family Pride

When Mr. Cui Zongxu retired from his job at a bookstore on Beijing's famed Liulichang antique street, he bought a humble country house in a village south of the city so he could grow his own plants and trees. But it was not to just putter around a garden. No, Cui, 77, has something else in mind: growing a certain kind of poplar tree, which he will plant to restore his family graveyard in central Hebei Province, 200 kilometers south of Beijing.

The family mausoleum, he recalled, used to be grand, with a marble entrance gate. Encircling the plot were groves of a variety of poplar called *gu yangshu* (old poplar). The cemetery was ruined when soldiers camped there. Its marble was removed to build roads and trees felled to make beams for a bridge. "Those poplars were majestic, and even in heavy rain, they would protect people from the elements," Cui said. Ordinarily, fast growing trees such as poplars were used for shade and wind breakers lining roads. Yet this precious variety of poplar has a strong association with grave sites and some can grow to a height of 15 meters or more.

Cui was determined to grow and replant the trees to restore the atmosphere of his family graves. When he contacted the Department of Forestry, he was amazed to discover that the largest of this kind of poplar in the Beijing area was actually in his district. It appears even more gigantic because it grows on top of a six-meter-high dirt mound, the size of three tennis courts, once the site of an ancient temple. Now young army recruits practice marching under the canopy of its expansively extended branches. The tree is more than three meters in

circumference.

A local resident of Dalangfa Village, Mrs. Wang, 60, was caring for her grandson who was playing at the foot of the great tree. She had stories to tell. She called the tree by its local nickname, "Daqing Yang" (Poplar of Great Brightness), and said it stands where the back courtyard of the temple was situated. "Monks used to live here," Wang said. "It was turned into a school after Liberation. I studied here."

Cui figured that the poplar must be about 800 years old. "Most poplars in Beijing," he explained, "are *baiyang*, white poplar (aspen) varieties. This type though has darker bark." The male tree sprouts the *longxu*, "dragon beard" catkins, which hang from the branches before the leaves come out. This was obviously a male because the furry *longxu,* looking like tiny kitten's tails, lay on the ground. A metal plate was nailed to the tree identifying it as #0444, a badge of distinction. In front of the dirt mound, stones had been arranged to spell out the tree's honorary title, "Bravest Poplar of All." Fingering a "dragon beard", Cui looked up at the tall tree, "These are just like the trees I remember around my family tomb. I am now growing them to plant there."

Looking out over his private nursery filled with the poplar saplings, Cui started chatting about his ancestors then opened a sketch of his family tombs of over 1,000 years. The ornate marble entrance gate stood high above the grave mounds. A grove of tall and thick poplars sur-

rounded the plot. He said he hoped to rebuild the site, first by planting lots of poplars. He realizes it will take centuries to attain the girth of their predecessors. But at least the trees will restore respect to his ancestors and give him peace of mind.

# Cherry Trees and Other Saplings

Tree planting as a ceremony is the symbolic acknowledgement of the need to improve the environment as well as a ritual of visitors or to mark special occasions. In Beijing, planting of cherry trees at the Yuyuantan Park has commemorated the normalization of relations between Japan and China in 1972. Since then, many varieties of cherry trees have been planted around the lake. These new trees, planted at one of the ancient water sources of Beijing, represent a celebration of the renewal of beauty. I marvel at the masses of people who walk along the banks at cherry blossom time. Not just the loud party goers who stake out territory for night time bashes like in Japan, but true flower lovers, admiring and touching petals, are photographing themselves before each plant. Another image is the fishermen who sit calmly below the branches, the blossoms scattering on them and the lake on a peaceful afternoon.

Planting at designated sites near the Badaling Great Wall is an attempt to stave off the desertification of the area. In the fall of 2002, for the 30th Anniversary of Japan/China Normalization of Relations, 13,000 Japanese participants together with locals placed seedlings into the soil as a confirmation of peace and friendship. We all hope that succeeding generations will be able to see a grand forest there.

## "Paulownia Lane"

One of my favorite tree streets in Beijing is the one I've nicknamed "Paulownia Lane." For a brief week in late April, these trees are filled with bunches of almost transparent purple flowers the shape of tiny soft trumpets. And that is the time to go slowly down Chegongzhuang West Road, alias, "Paulownia Lane." It wasn't until I began to read Japanese literature in translation that the reference to paulownia kept popping up. I could never visualize the trees because I had never seen one.

In Japan paulownia is known as "kiri" and the tradition goes that a "kiri" is planted when a girl is born so that when she is married, a fine dowry chest can be made from its wood. The mark of the Japanese foreign ministry is the stylised crest

of a paulownia leaf.

Thus, I just had to plant one of these trees when I moved to Beijing for the third time, and this time with a big garden. The gardeners encouraged me by quoting a Chinese saying, "If a house has a paulownia tree, it brings good luck," and assured me that the tree would come that night. I was puzzled by all this. Why did it have to come at night? Was this another superstition having to do with luck? No. They had ordered, to my surprise, a full-grown tree, and could only be transported along the roads after 11 p.m.!

Planting was a serious ritual, with clean shovels adorned with ribbons, a red carpet and readied small piles of dirt for easy transfer. So we all bonded, the Chinese gardeners and my family and friends, in the planting of this tree, put out

among some trees planted to mark the occasion. Another stone is a memorial to an outstanding person, Sun Pinghua, who devoted his whole life to the promotion of friendship and exchanges between the two countries.

Local resident, Li Yuanhai, 55, knows the history better than anyone else. A director there since the young age of 33, his broad face broke out into a warm smile when he recalled the

of sight of the formal Japanese style garden in the Ambassador's residence, but close to where I could see it from my room. And I was sure it would protect us like a talisman, especially when it is adorned with almost transparent purple trumpets.

earliest years of the commune. This village lying northwest of Beijing was selected, he said, because it was close to the city and that the proximity of the Agricultural University ensured that the farmers had good advice from expert horticulturists. "Even though the commune was relatively small," he continued, "we were successful in agricultural output."

## Peach Groves to Hi-Tech Landscaping

In the heyday of communal living in China, the Dongbeiwang People's Commune was tapped to play an international role. It was named as the China/Japan Friendship Commune in October 1978 to commemorate the signing of the Treaty of Peace and Friendship between the two countries. A stone marker still nestles

In those early years, Japanese dignitaries visiting Beijing were often brought out to see the commune. Japanese school children took part in the annual sweet potato digging day, one of the few places where they could touch the lives of ordinary Chinese. The commune also had "the first fishing pond in Beijing," noted Li. "Another one of our early business attempts was making baseball gloves for Japan, but the currency controls in China at that time made it hard

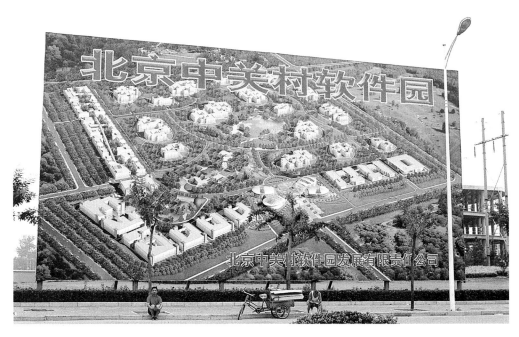

to make a profit."

Vinyl greenhouses introduced from Japan drastically changed vegetable production. In the late 1980s, the land was a sea of plastic coverings. Greenhouse vegetables became a cash crop. The revolutionary idea of a commune had been replaced by the free-market principle and a policy of more openness. When Sun Pinghua, President of China-Japan Friendship Association, guided our family around in 1996, the name had already changed to Friendship Farm. The local farmers began to concentrate on fruit orchards that require less work and much less water than vegetables. Peach groves were everywhere.

A bountiful crop of large succulent-looking peaches were still being picked in 2002, as Li explained to me the future plans. "It's been already four years since the Beijing University Biotech research center was built on one plot here." Dongbeiwang Village is on the western edge of Beijing's elite development, the Zhongguancun Hi-tech zone.

Turning onto a newly constructed avenue going north, it became clear that the place was already under transformation. In front of two recently cleared fruit groves stood billboards mapping the software park to be built here soon. A commuter train stop was under construction nearby. Li was animated as he discussed all the new projects.

The farm has now graduated officially to corporation with its new emphasis on intellectual technology and business development. Down go the peach trees and up go the tidy office spaces of a "silicon valley." However, these new subdivisions are being given modern landscape beautifications. The trees here are a new gang for Beijing: not for fruits and nuts, not for sacred sites, not for kindling, not for imperial gardens, not for tomb markers; but simply for decorations enhancing contemporary structures. Dongbeiwang went from commune to peach groves to hi-tech in 20 years.

# Environmentalists Passionately Work for Change

Liang Congjie and his wife Fang Jing are passionate environmentalists. Liang and Fang founded the Friends of Nature, China's first NGO, in 1993. Just being with Liang is being with history. His grandfather was the famous reformer of the late Qing period, Liang Qichao, scholar and political activist who was in exile in Japan for almost 14 years. His parents were China's first scholars of architectural history. Liang acknowledged his inspiration from them. "The main thing that I learned from my parents was a sense of responsibility. Someone has to do something, instead of just complaining."

Sitting in his small office with hand-me-down furniture, he continued, "I claim myself to be a concerned citizen. The environment's getting worse and worse, but I never thought that we laymen could do something in this field. I knew about NGO's promoting environmental issues in other countries, but I didn't know whether or not that was possible in China. So a few of us got together and took a chance." Fang Jing added, "We were approved by the government in 1994 and since our emphasis is educational, we are affiliated with the Ministry of Culture as the 'Friends of Nature'."

On the walls are pictures of recent projects such as the campaign to save the rare snub-nosed monkeys of Yunnan in southern China. "Look at this school reference book on the environment." He showed me "The Green Handbook." "We helped to get this published and will try to get this in as many libraries as possible."

In 1997, the two of them talked about their recent tree planting in the desert areas. "Last year we put in 2,700 trees in two days. What we've learned is that it is easy for people to destroy nature. Overgrazing in just 30 years destroyed the land we went to, but when we try to restore it, it's so painstaking. More than planting trees, our main purpose is to educate," related Liang. He got out the pictures of the volunteers. "This is a hard lesson, only when you go and actually plant does the message really go into your heart." He continued, "Every year for the past six years Japanese volunteers have been planting in Inner Mongolia, but no Chinese ever volunteered to go help out in

that part of the desert. It's a shame! Our group is the first of Chinese volunteers there." Several families also took part in the trip, donating not only their trip expenses but also paying for the seedlings. It was really a new phenomenon at that time in China.

Since then their Friends of Nature projects have expanded greatly. Their focus is local environmental education. Often they bring whole classrooms to the students in the form of "learning cars." The volunteers know that protecting the environment is more than just a few trees, it is fostering the understanding of the balance of nature and human life.

One day at Liang's apartment, he presented me with his father's *A Pictorial History of Chinese Architecture*. Liang Sicheng and his wife Phyllis Lin (Lin Huiyin) were graduates of the University of Pennsylvania who returned home to be China's first architectural historians and passionate preservationists. Liang's discovery in 1932 of the long forgotten Dulesi (Temple of Solitary Joy) was his first find as a serious scholar. It dates from the 10th century and has a giant standing eleven-headed Guanyin (Goddess of Mercy), the largest clay figure in China, being about 20 meters high.

In winter time, I set out on the road going east of Beijing about 100 km to Jixian Town with a copy of Liang Sicheng's original drawing of the Dulesi temple in my hand. I found the temple mostly dismantled for a massive reconstruction project. I remembered Liang saying that it was the large brackets and wide overhang of the roof that helped his father identify it as a Liao Dynasty structure. Dulesi has been there for 1,000 years together with a thousand-year cypress. They withstood wars and earthquakes.

Climbing up the scaffolding as high as the roof level, it was exciting to be able to peer into the skeleton of this magnificent edifice and see markings on beams left by some of the original artisans. There in the center standing tall in the void was the colossal Guanyin. Only the main beam of the roof ridge was still in place.

When I returned again in winter, 2001, I found the temple all put back together. It was beautifully done and kept the old flavor and colors wherever possible. Alas, the thousand-year cypress, as old as the Liao Dynasty temple buildings, had not withstood the construction work. Its withered trunk stands as a sculptural symbol of our need to be careful of these relics as well. Calling for the protection of such living treasures, as well as cultural heirlooms, as in the commitment to saving the environment, is what the Liangs have done in their family tradition.

# II. Stone Reflections of the Past

Those old stones "are all silently telling you or even singing out to you the unbelievable changes wrought by time." (Liang Sicheng)

# Introduction

## Energy in Stone

**M**uch of the legacy of Beijing's ancient sites remains etched on stone tablets, columns, sculptures and even stone halls. These stones are the reposito-ries of ideas, history and art. They are full of energy of the past. Motifs from ancient times live on. A poem inscribed on a tablet keeps its meaning. The face of a Buddha maintains its serenity. A stone temple preserves its sanctuary.

Stones also have energy as they are filled with the minerals of the earth and reflect the rays of the sun. Mountains and hills form an arch across the top of Beijing where there are many rich marble and granite stone quarries. Interesting rock formations, some as individual giant boulders and others as beautiful arrangements of rock, decorate the hillsides.

Numerous villages of Beijing are made completely of stone. From slate roofs to walls and foundations, all the materials have come from the mountains beside them. Millstones or hearths of stone were commonplace, as well as stone spring covers, aqueducts and troughs. Stone tombs range from massive imperial structures to simple graves marked by a single rock. In the hills around the city are traces of stone routes and pilgrim paths. The stepping-stones are worn by footsteps; old roadways have ruts worn by carts over the centuries. They all carry the warmth of human endeavors.

The long tradition of inscribing events on stone has helped preserve true historical records as almost every stele has a date that can be identified. I have come across hundreds of slabs during my explorations. From them I found details of the background of the place, like other names for a temple, or who gave the money for a certain repair and the extent of imperial patronage.

Explorations to find lost temples often brought me to places that no longer have any semblance of the past. But I was usually able to find leftover carved pieces of stone that gave at least some clues to the place's history. It ensured me that my search was at the right location. For instance, Beizheng Village once had a thousand-year pagoda. It had cracked during an earthquake and revealed one marble and two clay pillars inside its central core. These were put in museums for safekeeping, but the pagoda itself was crumbling and thus destroyed for safety reasons. Trying to verify its original location seemed almost impossible because the area had been cemented over. However, a few young boys pointed to a piece of a stone pillar thrown away at the roadside. Only one word was legible. That was *ta* (pagoda). Villagers were surprised that such a fuss was made over it. That bit of stone, though, suddenly had meaning and energy.

On another occasion, I was out with my photographer friend,

Kosima Weber-Liu, looking for bits of history on a bitter cold day around the outskirts of southeast Beijing. Kosima, always concerned with the environment, surprised me by driving on a dusty street under construction with giant pipes waiting to be placed underground and large trucks jostling with horses and carts. Finally before us stood a lonely pagoda, but the canal in the background made it even picturesque. A stone plaque identified it as the Pagoda of the Buddhas of Ten Directions. Several broken tablets lay scattered around the base. These inscriptions were a clue to its past: the pagoda was dedicated to a Ming Dynasty Zen monk from Shaanxi Province. Another tablet told how the emperor stopped here and drank water from the river. Unexpectedly, this place took on a new dimension.

There were more tablets in the fields and as we sat there reading them, a local man of 70 with thick glasses stopped to help out. The man proudly recounted the temple's history, even though it had disappeared long ago. He talked on and on, making it into a beautiful mirage before our eyes. In the meantime, I had kicked the dirt off another stone tablet. A wonderful carved smiling face materialized out of the dust. It appeared to give a laughing welcome to this site. Yet the face also seemed boastful that they, the stones, had survived.

The following encounters are all results of the endurance of stone and what it helps us to learn about the past and our habitat here in Beijing.

This selection of stories often touches on how stone relics have been carefully preserved by people in certain communities. Another thread is the tradition of stone cutting and carving on the one hand, with the importance of protecting stones in their natural setting on the other. It is a dichotomy that must find a balance.

# Early Morning Dew from the Thunder Roaring Cave

The dew sparkled on the ancient stone steps and a palette of many colors radiated from the surrounding stone mountains as I made my way up to the sutra caves above Yunjusi (Dwelling in the Clouds Temple). It was going to be another hot summer day, so I went for an early morning climb. I have come to this temple almost 20 times, but I never fail to be impressed by the determination of the long succession of monks to preserve their Buddhist classics which they etched in stone for posterity.

During my first visit to Yunjusi in the summer of 1985, a gatekeeper named Wang took me around. "At the time of founder, Jing Wan, around the beginning of the 7th century," he instructed, "Buddhism was facing one of the first waves of persecution. Even the emperor withdrew his support and had ordered the closing of many temples all over the country and destruction of scriptures. To protect the holy texts from oblivion, Jing Wan chose to hide in this remote mountain area and leave Buddhist teachings for future generations engraved on stone slabs." His project was continued for 1,039 years, spreading to nine caves and involving sixteen generations of monks. It is the world's largest stone tablet library.

Yunjusi had six compounds, each built on a higher level up the mountain. In 1935, Japanese scholars who published their research and diagrams in the *Journal of Oriental Studies* ("Toho Gakuho") investigated all the compounds in

detail. But tragically, the whole monastery was caught in the crossfire with Japanese troops during the war and everything was destroyed except the North Pagoda. At the time of my first visit, that was the only edifice standing at the former temple site except for a few smaller stupas. "Digging through the ruins," Wang continued, "we found the stone scriptures in secret caches in an underground room underneath where the South Pagoda had once stood. There were more stuffed in the caves on the mountain, hidden by piles of debris." It was a treasure-trove of over 14,000 slabs.

Wang led the way up the jagged rock path. It was already boiling hot and no shade at all. After

40 minutes we finally reached Jing Wan's cave, the Leiyindong (Thunder Roaring Cave). Four stone pillars with intricately carved small Buddhas stood in the center. But the real treasure was on all the walls where the first sutras were carved in Jing Wan's own calligraphy. I tried to visualize the monks gathered here meticulously digging and carving for hours and days on end, over so many years. Scrambling up on the hill above the caves, I found a small stone tower. This was made to commemorate the Tang princess Jinxian who helped arrange for the carving of more than 4,000 Buddhist sutra scrolls on to these stone slabs. These became invaluable in the history of Buddhism.

I have continued to visit Yunjusi since then and have watched with admiration as they have rebuilt the temple just as it was diagrammed by the Kyoto University group. The sutra slabs found under the South Pagoda have now been reburied in an air-controlled underground museum. There is even a gondola to the caves! But I prefer ascending the familiar way, over the time-worn stones and watching the shimmering dew glistening in the early morning light.

## Quarry of the Stone Mansion

An old Chinese proverb goes, "Live by the mountain, eat the mountain." That is just what Shangshifucun (Upper Stone Mansion Village) has done over

the centuries. Their rock quarry is deep and wide. Left along the edges of the roads are the villagers' creations: massive stone mortars and grinding stones of their prized "douqing shi" (bean-green stone).

"This is an incredibly strong stone, but when polished has the smoothness of human skin," pointed out stonemason and head of the mining company, Gao Yuyun, 46. "It is not for delicate carving as white marble. No, this green stone is chosen for its power." Gao continued, "Our stone was used to make the Marco Polo Bridge some 800 years ago!" He explained that in recent restorations to the bridge, he was asked to provide the stone. "You can see it lining the most important stress points in the arches."

The quarry is some 1,000 meters east of the village. I had been poking around taking photos of the stone mortars when a stocky man in rough working clothes came out startled to see a foreigner in his factory compound. I told him that I was interested in the history of stone making of this village. It turned out that I said the right thing to the right person. Gao welcomed me to his office. This humble mason was in fact quite proud of the contribution their stone has made to architecture around the successive ancient capital cities built at Beijing.

He is also helping in the reconstruction of many important buildings. Column bases and stairs were being prepared for a restoration in the Fragrant Hills. "Qing Dynasty annals refer to our stone as particularly prized." The ma-

sons of previous generations made stairways for the Temple of Heaven, bridges for gardens, and door stones all over the city. Thus, the term *shifu* (stone mansion) was bestowed on the village.

He took me to see what they call the Japan Well, dug during the occupation. The well naturally was lined in this strong stone. "95% of all well stones in Beijing are Shifu Village stones," claimed Gao. In the quarry itself, workers were busy dislodging large slabs from the mountainside. They don't use dynamite and carefully cut out the stone using traditional methods. "The stone has no contamination. It also doesn't take in water. That is why our mortars give fragrant grain. They are in demand all over China," he explained.

We were standing in the midst of rock piles in the shadow of the Cuiwei Hills. Gao pointed out places cleaved by his forbearers and ancestors of many villagers. Long iron picks and poles handed down from generation to generation lay neatly by the rocks. "You are certainly the first foreign woman to ever walk here," he noted with a large grin. He then recounted a story about a little one-roomed stone temple by the road.

Once in the remote past, about 35 stonecutters were digging deep into the mountain when an elderly man with a long white beard appeared before them. He told them about a wedding feast in the village and encouraged them to join in the festivities. So they lay down their tools and walked down the hill. But in the village,

nobody knew anything about a party. Instead, at that moment, they heard a thunderous roar. The whole side of the mountain had caved in. Realizing that the old man was surely a mountain saint, they built a little temple to thank him and pray for continued protection in this dangerous line of work. To this day, nobody has been killed in the quarry. The mountain saint also seems to have ensured that there is an almost endless demand for Shifu Village stone.

# Tracking Jesuit Tombstones

A book from the 1920s mentioned a village called Zhengfusi (Temple of Real Fortune) in western Beijing where the temple and its surrounding fields were bought by foreign missionary Jesuits in 1732 to build a country house and burial ground. Although much was destroyed by the Boxer Rebellion in 1900, at least 60 carved tombstones of the French missionaries and other converts remained until the mid-1920s. These stones, most about two meters high, were embedded in the walls of the compound or scattered in the overgrown cemetery.

Notable Jesuits among the buried were Gerbillon (1707) who helped the Chinese conclude the Treaty of Nerchinsk with Russia in 1689. There was also Atiret (1768) who painted the portrait of Emperor Qianlong and Amiot (1793) who helped the same emperor correspond with Voltaire. Many were given imperial favor and their tall headstones were decorated with coiling dragons.

When I went searching for this place in 1985, it was unlikely that anything survived, given the civil war and then the Cultural Revolution. Finding the village was not hard. It is on one of the roads to the Summer Palace. I wandered about and discovered the former temple site (used as a factory), remains of the sturdy stone wall and even a roadside post with an inscription *Tianzhu jiaotang* (Catholic Church). But when asked about the tombstones, the locals seemed not to know anything. Those big hunks of marble could not easily disappear, so I continued to snoop around the village. At last a middle-aged woman, who after first denying that anything of the sort existed, gave a puzzled expression. "Well, there's a large stone in my latrine, it's part of the wall over there. It has some carving on it."

One wall of the latrine was indeed a large white marble stone. Alongside the weathered Chinese characters seemed to be a Roman script. Then I noticed the cross carved just below the curling dragon. The lady was surprised to see someone taking pictures inside her outhouse!

Further down the road were some broken marble slabs resting against a house. She pulled them back to reveal the underside that had writing with Chinese on the right and Latin on the left. Not too legible, but I could make out some of the words like "Mathematician", "Consecrated", "Mission", and "Domini Finis." Villagers crowded about and pointed to a dirty sidewalk. Some brought out brooms and swept it clean. There lay an almost perfect stone with very legible writing in Chinese and Latin. It was the tomb of one Frenchman ("Gallus") of the Society of Jesus named Joannes Baptista Thierry. He was born in 1823, came to China in 1842 to work in the Vicarage of

Peking. "Requiescat in Pace (rest in peace)," it said. The Chinese version added that he died of disease at the age of 58.

In 1995, I returned to the village. This time, however, the stones were nowhere to be found. The villagers reported that the stones had been taken away by truck. They didn't know where. One man, Mr. Zhao Encun, 73, invited me to his house where his wife and family were having lunch. Religious pictures decorated the walls. Over the bed was a large cross. Zhao said, "Our village has 100 families, of which 30 are still Catholic. We go back many generations. Our families were all converted by the Jesuits and we have kept up our faith. Every Sunday we attend mass at the Southern Cathedral. It takes us most of the day." When asked about the stones, he simply said, "They were taken away."

It took me another year to find them. Exactly where they should be: the Stone Carving Museum of Beijing. Standing in two neat rows were the stone steles from Zhengfusi Village. Many were badly worn. Under a coiling dragon on the top of the tablet was a cross. It was the tombstone stele of Joannes Baptista Thierry, the one the villagers swept clean for me in 1985. Recalling the faces of the Catholic families of the village like Mr. Zhao, it was clear that using the gravestones as they did had not been desecration but a way of protecting them out of admiration for the Jesuit fathers. The villagers had cared, after all.

Now they are under the watchful eye of veteran archaeologist Wu Menglin, 65. She is a sweet and diminutive lady, but she has lots of perseverance and knows all about the stones of Beijing. Having graduated from Beijing University in 1961, she had to pursue her career during some of the most difficult times of modern China. But she was determined to research and protect what she could of the myriads of tablets and stones with historical meaning around the city. She made sure that the Jesuit, Lazarist and Dominican gravestones have been given the dignity they deserve. These thirty-six 200-year-old foreign missionary tombstones, with Chinese and Latin inscriptions under crosses and dragons, now stand in a row together as they had in the former Catholic graveyard. "Rest in Peace."

# Beijing's Ancient Stone Villages

## Villages with Special Characteristics

**B**eijing's villages all have their own special history and characteristics. Some originated as coal mining or trading villages. Others quarried stone for a living or sold kindling. Some functioned as post towns, guardians of tombs or defenders of mountains, rivers

and canal crossings. Villages also grew up around important temples or tea stalls along well-traversed roads or pilgrim paths. Imperial order founded villages to serve as builders of forts or to produce pottery and tiles. This great variety in the rural scene around the capital reflects not only the diverse geographical landscape, but also the importance these hamlets had in the history of Beijing.

The villagers have kept the continuity of their community. They have preserved their stories and passed them down as oral history, built and rebuilt their homes and have perpetuated crafts and special livelihoods. Their tradition of co-operation in digging wells, repairing roads and guarding trees at their sacred sites was essential for their community.

As stone has been the predominant building material, most villages have kept their ancient layout. In the mountainous areas, villages like Cuandixia and Lingshui in Mentougou District have stone homes and walls maintained over 500 years. The Village of a Pair of Rocks not far from them even has a house built on top of a giant boulder.

Although only 23 families remained when I walked along the narrow stone passages of the Cuandixia Village in 1996, it had the structure of its village from Ming and Qing times when more than 100 families were mostly involved in the coal trade. It was a strange experience to peer into the abandoned courtyards. Most of the families are surnamed Han, so it wasn't surprising that a Mr. Han took me around. He showed me an underground storage for food, deep wells, secret rooms to hide cash and a stone-grinding wheel in continuous use for over 400 years. Faded revolutionary slogans reminded him of his own participation as a Red Guard in destroying the village shrines. Since then, the exodus to find jobs elsewhere has left a complete stone village frozen in time.

Beijing's oldest stone dwelling is thought to be Guyaju in Yanqing. There, on the side of a mountain face, are about 100 small caves that formed an early town, complete with meeting places and shrines. Stone pillars and stone hearths remain but not much is known of these stone dwellers. We can see, though, that they had social organization, a hierarchy and a defence system against intruders.

Mobeicun (Stone Engravers Village) in Fangshan District also has a long history. This is where the stones for the famed stone sutras of Yunjusi were quarried and many engraved over 1,000 years. In the village center is a neglected temple, Stone Engravers Memorial Shrine, dedicated to the stonecutters through the ages. In 1997 only one hall was left and it had a hole in the roof. A factory used the temple grounds where workers polished and dyed stone tiles. Their quarry still seems to produce adequate supplies. One former engraver, Mr. Zhang, 80,

boasted to me of their special stone, the White Cloud Stone, which is almost translucent and has a natural lustre. And yes, he thought it was fitting to have a shrine to their profession, to the myriads of unnamed craftsmen, and that it should be repaired. The annual village festival on the 19th of the second moon, he noted nostalgically, once honored their stone engraving tradition.

Just west of the city is Black Rock Village. I've visited there a number of times, most recently in the spring of 2003, the day before the SARS alert for Beijing was announced. It was a carefree morning and I was driving some friends on an excursion around the Shijingshan District. My fellow explorers were amazed that we could find such a well-preserved stone village in this close proximity to urban Beijing. Many old homes with slate roofs and aged scholar trees face the village's three roads: upper, middle and lower streets. Located along a way that leads over the Western Hills into the Beijing basin, Black Rock Village was also a coal depot. A young boy jumped on his bike to guide us to a massive stone, three times the height of the red van parked beside it. This was the "Black Rock." Such a singular giant outcropping must certainly have been impressive to the locals in the past. Why else would they name their village for it?

Today villages and their traditional culture face various challenges for survival. But as long as the stone structures endure, the outer shell at least will leave an impression of the past.

## Passageways to a Walled Enclave

Once when driving along a country road, I spotted an eight-meter-high stone wall curving in a wide circle. What is this? I was incredulous to see such a site rising out of this flat plain west of the Yongding River. This was Changlesi (Temple of Invariable Happiness) Village referring to the Ming Dynasty temple where a community of retired eunuchs lived as monks. Inscribed over the eastern stone gate is the remaining half of a couplet in praise of these palace eunuchs. It reads: "Big Loyalty, Always Constant, Good Reputation, Forever."

A retired gatekeeper, Zhang Huishun, took me around. The temple's main hall, though still standing, was in pretty bad condition. One of several broken steles told the story of how retired eunuchs came here to live out their days and were buried in tombs also within the walled enclosure. Zhang proceeded along the stone path to the northern part of the village.

Two broken brick tombs constructed as domes sat amidst overgrown weeds and persimmon trees. Some village children were teasing sleeping bats within the broken vaults. These were the only remainders of the former eunuch

graveyard. One was the tomb of Wang An, "in charge of attendants and ritual clothing at the imperial palace." Most of the marble stones covering the three-meter-high mausoleum had fallen off exposing the brick interior, but there were a few finely carved stone roof and tile designs still decorating the outside.

Behind them the wall makes a wide arc dwarfed by rows of looming peaks in the distance. A convenient crack in the wall allowed another access into the village. Seen from afar, this setting appears like it was 500 years ago: a special walled enclave for eunuchs!

# Picks Ring by the Pagoda of the Jade Emperor

The Gaozhuang villagers are all certainly in the stone business. In fact, the whole valley reverberates with the sounds of their work in the quarries. Standing on a small hillock topped by a hard bed of large boulders, Yuhuangta, Pagoda of the Jade Emperor, is the symbolic protector of this village of stone-cutters.

Large boulders are being wedged out of their once comfortable nests and with rudimentary tools are dissected into more manageable stones. Veteran workers stripped to the waist take their time at this exhausting labor. With their hammers and picks they chip a bit and rest and chip a bit and rest. Other sites are deep chasms in the earth and only the rhythmic sound of the cutters' blows acknowledges their presence. Sputtering noisily, tractor lorries crisscross the hillock on makeshift dirt tracks as they cart away these stones for carving or to be crushed for other uses.

The stone cutters have come dangerously close to the pagoda itself, slashed scars define the boulders remaining under its base. One peasant woman tending her flock of goats seemed impervious to the other activity around. She knows that the pagoda won't really be put into danger, for it has stood there 1,000 years to help the village families. Local legend has it that a high official visited the site in ancient times and remarked on the good *fengshui*. To insure further good luck he instructed villagers that a pagoda made in the name of the Jade Emperor would suffice. So they built this octagonal, seven-storied pagoda and carved an image of the Emperor inside the marble door. With the great demand for the high quality of stone these days, it seems that the luck still holds.

137

# Caves and a Cave Digger

Deep in the mountains around Beijing there are a number of natural caves. Some of these were adapted as Buddhist temples in the tradition of early Buddhist communities along the Silk Road. At one grotto, a former convent from the 11th century called Chaoyangdong, Cave of the Morning Sun, I found the remnants of painting on stucco, once a part of a Buddhist image. A stone base below these pieces confirmed that it was indeed an ancient altar. Peering out from the cave entrance, the view of the mountain ranges was the same for the nuns who lived here 1,000 years ago and I could appreciate their precious seclusion.

Further south, the trail to Lianhua Mountain's Shengmishitang (Stone Hall of Sacred Rice) used to take four hours one way. Now locals have restored the old Taoist retreat for a scenic zone and have carved a road into the remote mountains. But even so, from the foot of the mountain, it took me almost two hours of climbing to reach the famous cave. Legend has it that a starving young monk boiled the stones he broke off from the cave's wall and they cooked up into rice. The impressive thing about the cave, though, is the incredible panorama of the surrounding peaks.

It was dark by the time I had finished exploring the many shrines and grottoes. I began to panic. The park was not as yet officially open and the place was deserted as laborers had already quit work. I fortunately found two men on duty, Mr. Dong and Mr. Zhang, who offered a surprising solution. They threw on a switch and instantly a heavenly runway of little lights appeared out of the blackness. I rode down in what I felt was their enchanted cable car with what appeared to be a large sack of rice.

Another cave, Kongshuidong (Cave of the Water Opening), isn't on a high mountain, but it's also not easily approachable because it is in the precincts of a factory. However, a kind guard let me in. The cave is actually the source of a spring, while built on top of it is a solid stone hall, Wanfotang (Hall of 10,000

Buddhas). When I first peeked in the dark and musty room, I couldn't see anything, but little-by-little the walls came alive. A congregation of Buddhist figures etched in white marble focused with a magnetic energy on the central Buddha. This carving is known as the "10,000 Buddhas Assembly for Teaching", one of the great treasures from the Tang Dynasty in Beijing.

Yunshuidong (Cloud and Water Cave), in contrast, is actually a deep cavern with several large halls. Located not far from the entrance is a large Buddha in bas-relief dating from the 11th century. Worn down over the years by the dampness and polished to a fine sheen by the soot of incense over 1,000 years, the strength of this image defies its age. It reminds me of similar Buddhas seen at Balinzuoqi in Inner Mongolia and in a cave at the Panshan area east of Beijing, both from the same period. The temple standing in front of the cave is home to a number of monks from Anhui Province who all wanted their photos taken. They were so interested in knowing my income and how much my cameras cost, but had little to say about the fine Buddha I had just seen in the cave.

I also visited a cave of a different sort when searching for the 12th century Yuzhuang pagoda. It is perched up on an inaccessible cliff. While wandering around the base looking for a way up, I came across a blind man, Ma Sanbao. He took me into his humble home and seemed to trust me enough to talk about his own project. He mumbled, "I've been making grottoes. Small caves. Shrines for the Buddha. They're hidden under the pagoda."

"Come, follow me!" He shuffled around to the back of the house where he unlocked a makeshift door leading into the side of the cliff. Inside it was totally pitch black, which obviously didn't matter to Mr. Ma, and I followed him groping along the wall through the damp maze. "Here they are," he boasted, but I couldn't see anything. Then I remembered my flash camera. With each flash I could make out three small caves where Mr. Ma had carved altars with his own hands and placed Buddhist figures. Room one was dedicated to the Buddha, with a number of fat-bellied "Laughing Buddhas" assembled on a rickety table. Room two had only statues of the Goddess of Mercy. Another cave had a mildewed chair. The fourth was still being dug. There are no inscriptions, nor murals, but the simplicity of Ma Sanbao's caves had a piety unto their own.

# Surviving Steles

## Emperor's Memorial to the Bell Martyr

Just west of the Bell Tower in central Beijing is the Temple of the Bell Martyr on Small Black Tiger *Hutong*. The alley winds twice and becomes very narrow. In a corner, a small temple with glazed roof tiles set it off from neighboring houses. This shrine was built to revere the soul of the girl who according to legend helped her father in the early 15th century forge the great bronze bell for the Ming emperor Yongle.

The tale was probably promoted over the centuries because this was the foundry district where so many bells were cast. Her story is also one of filial piety. Failures in casting were severely punished. After the girl's father had several unsuccessful bells, she finally leapt into the boiling bronze ore and the last bell turned out perfectly cast. Large bells were important to the power of the emperor, as the court was in charge of the time of the day. This famous bell was hung in the Bell Tower and rung at two-hour intervals from 7:00 a.m. daily and could be heard all around Beijing. They say her cry reverberated in its echo.

In 1995, just a gate and one back hall remained of this unusual shrine. The gate was used for

## Tablet in the Pavement

The national flag flies from a pole as classes are in session at the local school in Xikaokaofa, a farming village in the eastern suburbs. Where the school stands on a low hill was once the site of a famous monastery of 1,000 years. Drying cornstalks cover the road in front. Walking up the gradual incline to the school grounds, I found an ancient stele, commemorating a restoration from Emperor Qianlong's time, embedded in the stone driveway. It was partially covered in cornhusks and on clearing them away beautifully carved dragons emerged from the dust. This denoted important imperial connections. But why here?

Everyone in the village was busy with the harvest, so they only had a little time to talk about the once famous Tiangongsi (Temple of the Heavenly Palace). They had heard stories that the Liao Dynasty emperor had come here for hunting and that nearby was an imperial campsite founded by the 12th century Jin emperors. The locals also told me about an old rumor that there used to be imprints of the feet of an empress dowager of Liao somewhere on the temple grounds. The place was, furthermore, renowned for its peonies, but they were all cut down in the Cultural Revolution, added one farmer. Another man remarked that the "Heavenly Palace" well is hidden under the school

storage, but up on the rafters were faint floral patterns. Across the small courtyard in the main hall, girls were assembling cardboard boxes for Chinese medicine. For these migrant workers from Anhui Province, this was not only their factory, but also their living quarters. Clothing was hanging from painted beams and walls were decorated with photos of fashion models.

One wall had a small inscribed stone. It was a memorial from the 18th century Emperor Qianlong praising the filial piety of the bell makers' daughter whose soul is in the bell. The sincere message of the emperor assures that she won't be forgotten. It's certainly not a bad place for a women's dorm. Perhaps these girls felt the protection of the Martyr of the Great Bell.

## Straightening out Slanting Street

The bulldozer fell silent after it scraped another large stone. In construction-frenzied Beijing, the rule is, check it out first and then continue digging. Sure enough it was an artifact and workers had to inform the city authorities. After sweeping the giant stele clean, it was clear that yet another treasure had been found. Within one hour, two more pieces of history had emerged from the shadows. The big jaws of the crane lifted the tablets out of the earth where they had hidden for decades. These stones shed important information on the neighborhood that was just about to be demolished.

History maps of Beijing show that the area was known as Slanting Street (Xiejie). Because most city streets form a checkerboard pattern running in cardinal directions, slanting streets are rare. Actually, this old street was known as "lower slanting street" because the street crossed south of the Ming Dynasty moat, to differentiate the street from its northern extension. Slanting Street had ancestral temples and guild halls. It was also called Street of the Soil God and, more commonly, Changchun (Long Lasting Toon Tree) Street. The bulldozers were brought in to straighten the street to fit the demands of modern traffic.

Why did it slant in the first place? In ancient times there might have been a natural curve

dormitories. These farmers will at least pass down the story of this secret water source, in case of a future drought. As we were talking, the students were let out of school and they blithely went down the hill treading on the stone dragons.

caused by a stream. Since buildings grew up along the bend, the street kept to the original shape. Most important was the temple at the north end, Changchunsi, built by the mother of the Ming emperor Wanli in 1592. It was a grand temple with numerous halls covered with imperial yellow tiles. It is said that the emperor's mother vowed to make her son a monk if he recovered from a bad illness. He did recover, but instead of having him surrender the throne, she built this temple and had a substitute take his place as a monk.

A short street of one city block, it was filled with history as the discovered steles testify. At the southern end was one of Beijing's most famous shrines dating back 700 years. Tudimiao, Shrine to the Soil God, was a tiny place of just three halls. It was believed that the last thoughts of deceased persons were transmitted to their loved ones through the medium of the soil gods. Even family members away from home who were having a crisis were supposed to be able to communicate via this god. According to superstition, the family members could go there like a modern-day Internet café and transmit and receive messages.

The shrine itself disappeared with the construction of a hospital in the 1950s. But memories of its famed monthly fairs were legendary and even today elderly people recall the great throngs of people along Slanting Street where the fair had expanded. The Tudimiao fairs were especially renowned for the flower and plant sales, for three days a month, on the 3rds (3rd, 13th and 23rd days). An old poem still harks back to the spirit of the area: "When the springtime of Xiaohai Lake is like a painting, let's go to the dawn flower market at Slanting Street."

North of the Tudimiao site stood a building with an unusually high entrance. This was the Zhejiang Provincial Lodge. Behind it the jaws of a large crane loaded newly uncovered steles onto a truck of the Relics Bureau. They commemorated the restoration of the lodge 300 years ago. A carved marble stele base was also found nearby.

Inside the remnants of the lodge were two large white marble drum-shaped door piers that had once stood outside facing Slanting Street and welcomed the out-of-towners from Zhejiang to drink tea or listen to Chinese arias. Mrs. Ma, 72, who has lived there for 40 years, lamented the passing. She was uneasy with all the noise of the equipment vehicles nearby. "I know I'll have to move soon, we all will."

The bulldozers went quiet again. Just behind the temple, an even more magnificent marble door pier (*mendun'r*) was uncovered by the jaws of the crane. It was a double stone door marker of the highest rank. Perhaps it once graced the entrance of the temple, or held up an ornate gate.

On the doors and walls of the neighborhood, the ubiquitous word *chai* (condemned) was drawn in white within a circle. All residents on the west side of Slanting Street had to get out. Where the Tudimiao and the Zhejiang lodge once stood is now a park. The imperial temple will be restored and the new wide and straight street bearing its name now runs behind it. A corner of Beijing history has been turned.

# Temple of the Cross

Deep in a valley west of Beijing is an ancient temple site that once had Christian connections. It is not easy to find because the road winds through a petrochemical plant and then goes by several coalmines. In the distance there are the extending branches of a large tree growing at the end of this valley. It is the site of a former temple that is now all in ruins except for the massive ginkgo tree that dwarfs two stone tablets standing side by side below it. The tree has been there for over 1,000 years. It is a quiet and special place. Only occasionally do hikers go by on their way to the springs on the hill behind.

I read what I could from the inscriptions. One Ming stele describes the original Buddhist temple from the Liao Dynasty built in 952. But it is the other stele that was conspicuous. In the middle of the coils of the dragons at the top is a prominent cross. Under the cross is the name Shizisi, Temple of the Cross. This place was in fact the remnants of a church of the Nestorian branch of Christianity on the site of the earlier temple. Nestorianism spread from Syria to China during the Tang Dynasty. The first official recognition of the religion was when the Nestorian Bishop Olopen went to Chang'an and made contact with the emperor to practice the faith in China. Nestorianism then spread to the Beijing area. The Mongols must have been open

to the faith, as Khubilai Khan's mother had been a convert. The "Temple" of the Cross is the only site left in Beijing, which verifies the existance of that sect.

The young Uighur Nestorian by the name of Rabban Sauma also once lived here. Around the year 1266 he arrived at the "Temple" of the Cross. This young friar, though, had a bigger role to play. After staying at the Mongol capital over ten years, he started out on a pilgrimage to the Middle East and Europe, making it as far as Italy in 1287. Although he died in Persia, the manuscripts of his travel records keep the story of the voyage of this "Marco Polo of East Asia."

There are other Nestorian stones at the Nanjing Museum and in Xi'an, as well as in Qingzhou. The simplicity of the vestiges of this Christian site, the trees and the stones, are solemn reminders of the monastic life of the friars of long ago.

## Stones Confirm Temple to Capital City-god

Hidden amidst new tall buildings around the Fuxingmen area, the Duchenghuangmiao (Shrine of the Capital City-god) is partly used for the offices of the Erlonglu neighborhood committee and partly for a paper factory. When I first explored its grounds in the 1980s, the local junior high school also was located here. Inside the paper

factory, there were tablets stuck in walls and one partially sunk in the ground. These are all imperial steles from the Ming and Qing Dynasties. The top of one tablet was inscribed with large letters, "Forever Flourishing." The site has survived but it is hardly flourishing.

Chenghuang (City-god) was an ancient deity of China, once the spirit of walls and surrounding waterways, that gradually became the protector of walled cities and was incorporated into the Taoist pantheon. It became the custom for honest officials after their death to be elevated to City-god status of each particular location.

This shrine, though, was more than just the local City-god once found in all cities of the country. This was the protector of the imperial capital city, built in 1267 in the southwest corner of the Mongol capital. It has had a checkered history and the identity of the god itself has changed, just as officials were also promoted and demoted with the times. The popularity of its fair in the fifth lunar month waxed and waned as well.

Fortunately, a slab at the front gate declares the one hall to be protected. As the capital is ever greater in size, thus the symbolism of the Capital City-god takes on even greater importance.

## The Buddha Footprints

Wutasi, Five Pagoda Temple, located behind Beijing Zoo, is also known as the Stone Carving Museum and has become the repository of thousands of stone monuments and steles collected from all over Beijing. These stones came from sites that were being cleared or that needed protection and have been brought to the grounds of this early 15th century temple. The temple itself is one of the finest examples of relief carving in the city. It is capped by five pagodas on the top to resemble the temple at Bodhgaya in India where Buddha reached Enlightenment. All over the exterior are exquisite carvings of Buddhist symbolic patterns.

The most extraordinary carvings are those

of the imprints in hollow relief of Buddha's feet, an early iconography representing Buddha before the human form came to be worshipped. I found out a lot about the symbolism of the *Buddhapada*, as they are referred to in Sanskrit, from a Japanese monk whom I brought to visit Wutasi in 1985. He was so excited to see these carvings of feet and eight Buddhist treasures. Usually, such symbols are placed on the feet themselves, but here they are put around them in a vine pattern. I had not known that this was the monk's special research, and yet I had brought him right to the spot!

I read of another temple in Beijing with a stone tablet of Buddha feet, but it wasn't until

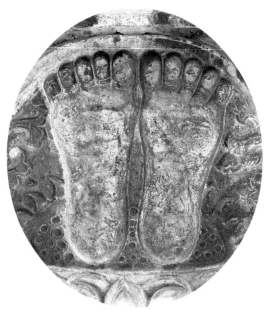

ten years later that I actually found the temple in the west part of the city. The five halls of the 14<sup>th</sup> century Baochansi (Temple of Precious Meditation) were nearly intact and used as living quarters. But the stele with the feet was nowhere to be found. Finally I asked my friend Liu Weidong, a cultural relics specialist at the Stone Carving Museum, if he knew where it was being protected. He indicated one tablet that was so badly worn that the inscriptions were almost illegible.

Liu offered to make a rubbing. "The history's written in the stone even if you can't see it," he added. So Liu and his coworker Guo Jihua taught me the art of making a stone rubbing. Liu said, "It's best if the stone isn't too hot as the paste doesn't adhere well." When he stripped the paper from the tablet, the impressions were much more legible than the actual carvings. "Here's your historical record," said Liu as he handed me an exact replica of the stele and the large Buddha footprints. The bottoms of the feet were covered with auspicious Buddhist symbols, including the pair of fish and the ever-turning wheel. The toes were decorated with fire and Buddhist swastika signs. I could make out a Buddha and two Bodhisattvas above the feet and two formal dragons on the crown.

This stele was made in 1592 during the time of Ming Emperor Wanli. It told the story of how the symbolism of such footprints came to China. When the Tang monk Xuanzang went to India, he mentioned seeing them on his travels as rep-

resentations of the Buddha image. Similar designs cropped up in Chang'an brought by travelers from the Silk Road. One design made its way to Beijing. The rubbing from the stone tablet thus yielded both history and symbolism. I felt happy to be going home with a pair of Buddha footprints!

# Memories of Festival for the Western Queen Mother

The third of March is celebrated in Japan as Girls' Day, but the festival's Chinese origins are obscured because under the lunar calendar, it occurs on the 3rd of the third month, making the two dates different. In fact it isn't celebrated in China at all anymore. It has been replaced by International Women's Day on March 8, as the female holiday of note.

There used to be a grand fair just outside the walled city of Beijing to commemorate the festival day of the Taoist Western Queen Mother. A large watchtower that used to mark the city's south-

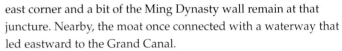

east corner and a bit of the Ming Dynasty wall remain at that juncture. Nearby, the moat once connected with a waterway that led eastward to the Grand Canal.

In the early 1980s a dilapidated little temple still stood across from this corner tower. A stone inscription identified it as Pantaogong (Palace of the Sacred Peaches). With one word on each stone, "Pan Tao Sheng Hui" (Pan Tao Festival Association) was written on slabs across the front of the building. Another sign denoted it as protected cultural property. Though just a small shrine, it was the center of worship for the Western Queen Mother.

When I went in for a look, however, I found it was jam-packed with brick shanties. Families from the nearby glass factory had taken up residence in two small halls around the courtyard. "Our fair was famous in Beijing. There were people coming here from all directions. But the Pantaogong is no more," an old man with cataracts lamented.

This goddess supposedly resided in the Kunlun Mountains of western China. The legend goes that a certain peach tree grew with a branch that extended for thousands of miles so that the Western Queen Mother could pluck peaches at her leisure. The peach is the Taoist symbol of immortality and the Queen Mother, the essence of the female life force. Once a year on her special day, supposedly all of the Immortals in Heaven went to her palace for a solemn feast.

It was hard to imagine that this tiny shrine was the site of one of the great fairs of Beijing. For the three days at the beginning of the third moon, girls used to do up their hair in coils, *pan*, corresponding to the shape of the special flattened peach, *pan tao*, as a sign that they were of marriageable age. The fair was also popular with the elderly women praying for long life. Sometimes the shrine also served as a women's refuge.

Today, only a large stone stele stands alone across from the watchtower. Just when I felt that all memory of the shrine had disappeared, I met Zhang Xiande. He is a scholar of cultural relics and a fine artist. Zhang has spent the last 50 years doing watercolor sketches and paintings of the now mostly phantom towers and gates of Beijing's historic city walls. "When I heard that another part of the wall was about to go down or that another gate was to be destroyed, I rushed out with my sketchbook and captured it on paper one last time." he recounted.

Seated around a table in his apartment, he showed me sheet after sheet of his paintings. When I asked Zhang how he got interested in painting gates, he replied he was born in the shadow of the Di'anmen Gate. "My house was right next to it, so I remember when they tore it down in 1954." Each painting had its story of Beijing's past.

I inquired if he knew anything about the neighborhood in the southeast corner of the city. "You mean near the old Pantaogong?" he asked, so I knew he had a story. "That big stone stele on top of the tortoise, you know, by the overpass. Well, it isn't in the original spot. They moved it west when they made the new road," he said. "I remember because the shrine gate was a bicycle repair shop in the 1950s."

Holding up his Pantaogong painting, he said, "One of the best things about this fair was its snacks. They had sellers with food stalls lining both sides of the waterways." The temple to the Western Queen Mother is long gone, but its tradition is preserved, in a sense, in Japan's Doll Festival on the third of March and in Zhang Xiande's paintings.

# Stones and Temples

## Stone Hall Set in a Peaceful Scene

The dirt road led through rock quarries and went past piles of cement dust where workers were busy breaking up stone mountains to provide construction materials for Beijing's booming expansion. It was almost impossible to think that a peaceful valley lies hidden behind all this mess just west of the city. My family certainly couldn't believe that I was actually taking them here for a picnic in this polluted air.

At one worker's camp I spotted a tall stone gate. A local man named Zhang said it once was an entrance to a monks' graveyard. It contained the ashes of clergy from the three temples in the valley. "The temples are now deserted," and he added that only a few people could live here,

as "the two wells just don't have enough water."

Beyond the stone gate was an unmarked path of stepping-stones winding through a crack between two hills. It gradually climbed upward following a dry riverbed. The noise of the quarries had vanished, the air was fresh. I caught my breath when I first saw the solitary stone hall, hidden in a crease of the enveloping hills. It was so quiet. Just the empty hall and a few stone tab-

lets here and there. This was Huanxiuchansi (Temple of Surrounding Beauty).

A pear tree in the courtyard was in bloom, its white petals falling softly on a stone stele beside it. My dog curled up by the stele and immediately felt at peace in the stone enclosure. The temple building, roof, and windows were all of stone. In the beamless hall, three niches were empty without any Buddhas. But detailed stone carvings framing the door and windows were full of religious symbolism. One can only marvel at the genius in the construction of this solid stone hall.

Reading one of the tablets, I learned that the temple was established in the 12th century by order of the Emperor. Another inscription described the construction of this hall in Ming times. But the best stele was one lying on its side. Somebody had propped it up with other stones and made the perfect picnic table. After lunch, we all took an afternoon nap, the best way to enjoy this peaceful scene, surrounded by beauty, hidden behind the curtain of dust.

## Stone Terrace to Honor "Big Black"

The patron saint of Mongolia, a lucky god of Japan, Indian Buddhism's revered black man, or the Hindu god Siva in disguise, are all attributes of the deity

Mahakala. What is a temple dedicated to him doing in central Beijing? *Heihu Fahu* (Black Pro-

tector of Buddha's Law), a frightening image with a skull necklace, is respected as a Buddhist guardian. *Mahakala* is the Sanskrit pronunciation, whereas in Japan his name is written as Big Black and is the lucky god for a rich harvest. Chinese also call the image Pudu (Savior of the Universe). Thus this former lama temple, just east of the Forbidden City, is known either as Mahakalamiao or Pudusi.

In 1985, while searching for this temple using a 1939 map, most people knew right away when I asked the whereabouts of Pudusi. The lanes in this area created a particularly confusing labyrinth. Finally, one old man pointed to a five-meter-high earthen mound, but densely built brick houses blocked the former entranceway to the temple grounds. Once a palace built in 1457, this place was also home of Manchu Prince Dorgon, regent for the early Qing emperor Shunzhi. Emperor Kangxi later converted the buildings into a Lama temple in 1691. A famous image of Mahakala was brought from Mongolia and enshrined here. It was clear that the Manchus were careful to include this symbol of the Mongols within their empire, in fact within the Imperial City.

The entrance gate, though architecturally intact, was a cluttered shop, with drying noodles swinging in the breeze. In the back one large hall stood alone. At that time it was used as part of Nanchizi Primary School. Piles of garbage practically hid the beautifully carved marble base of the building.

Back again ten years later I met a group of local elders sitting in the late afternoon sun. One lady said she had lived there for 46 years and remembered the black deity's statue and ceremonies on the 1st and 15th of every month. They all recollected two Mongol lamas who read sutras in Mongolian. It was just about time to close the school gate, but they let me in for a short look. The big hall was no longer a classroom and I was impressed by the massive strength of its wide bays and expansive roof.

One of the elders mentioned the legend of the builder who realized that he'd made a faulty calculation in designing the roof. In despair he saw no way out but suicide. That day their cook got sick and a strange man came to replace him. When the workmen ate the meal, they found it terribly salty. The new cook just repeated the phrase, "I put in too much salt." The builder got the play on words, a homonym meaning, "add an extra set of eaves." When the cook disappeared, they concluded he surely must have been the God of Masons, Lu Ban, giving them advice. Thus, there is a double roof support to this grand temple hall.

Now in the 21st century the temple has a new look. I was amazed to find the entire area in front of the hall cleared and turned into a lovely park. This setting accentuates the beauty of the high marble terrace with its elegant carvings. The temple of "Big Black" with its "extra set of eaves" radiates once more the strength of a protector to be reckoned with.

## One Stone Left on a Basketball Court

Shanguosi (Temple of Beneficent Fruit) was renowned as one of the ancient temples in the city, with references dating back to the 11th century Liao Dynasty. Its temple fair was the sixth day of the sixth lunar month, the same day as the annual washing of the imperial elephants in the nearby river. It became a custom to watch the elephants and then congregate at the Shanguosi.

I had read an account of a visit to the temple

in 1937 by Japanese archaeologist Torii Ryuzo. At that time a school was using the front part of the temple and he described the large backyard and exquisite main hall. A senior monk took him around the grounds. There his eyes focused on a *dhanari* stone pillar inscribed with Buddhist script. Torii was enthusiastic that this and another stone column with a carved *Yaksa* warrior were from the same Liao Dynasty. They were similar to other pieces of Qidan Buddhist art he had seen. The monk invited him for tea and, as they sat huddled around the stove, shared his admiration for the strong following of esoteric Buddhism in Japan and was hoping for a comeback of such mystical Buddhism in China.

In 1995, I went looking for what had become of that temple. The Guanxi Street Primary School continued to occupy part of the grounds. One of the senior teachers took me around . It was amazing when she declared that a carved marble stone, now holding up the basketball net, was a temple relic. It was a base, perhaps for one of the Liao stone pillars now long disappeared. She could remember the large wooden columns of one hall that had been used as a classroom. It was demolished in the early 1980s to build a new school building. The temple's front gate and Hall of the Guardian Kings had been a part of the watch factory next door, but they were taken down just the previous year. Two side halls still stood within the compound of the reception center next door. However, the exquisite main hall described by

Torii had vanished. Yet I felt satisfied to see the single stone left on the premises and I hoped the school would keep it as a token to perpetuate the memory and remind the students of this temple which Mr. Torii cherished so much.

# Double Ninth Climb to an Ancient Walled Monastery

It was the ninth day of the ninth lunar month, and according to tradi-tion it was the day to go climbing with family or good friends. An old temple in the western district of Mentougou was the destination for the day's adventure, but none of us knew the way from the base of Yangshan Mountain. Asking directions at the nearby Yingtaogou Village, one woman nodded convincingly in one direction and swirled her fingers in the air for the many turns we would have to follow.

Into this deep valley set among five peaks we proceeded along a path of uneven stones, slowly weaving up the mountain. High grasses impeded our movements. Finally before us loomed high stone and brick walls that encircled the abandoned temple compound. The way leading up to the entrance gate was so overgrown that we had to push away thorny branches and spiders' nests with our elbows and trample the waist-high weeds covering what had once been a trail.

Inside the walls almost nothing remained of the original Qiyinsi, Temple of the Secluded

Refuge. Two broken steles rested in the grass. Only the top part of a 12<sup>th</sup> century stele remained. We made a rubbing. Another stone revealed the history of the site as an imperially sponsored monastery with hundreds of monks under its roof. It was difficult to imagine because today it is so lonely and abandoned.

Behind the walls, we saw remnants of pagodas, the final resting places of former monks. To inspect these stupas more carefully, we climbed down the gully on the other side of the wall and crossed over to where they were clustered. Most were crumbled in heaps of brick and stone. Only two were left in good condition, one having a graceful curve like a bottle. We debated their heritage, were they from the Mongol period or earlier? But we came to no final conclusion.

Nearby, among the bushes, I was excited to find the narrow stone aqueducts, now dry, but they showed how water used to flow into the valley by

the temple from springs deeper in the mountains. So this was the water source that sustained this once great monastery and famed Jin Dynasty water courtyard!

Before going back down the mountain, we stood above the stone wall of the temple and loudly sang the popular song, "*Jiuyuejiu de Jiu*" (Wine of the Ninth Day, Ninth Month). It was a very memorable way to spend the Double Ninth festival.

## The "Topsy-turvy" Temple

The only time I saw the few remaining stones of Cihuisi (Temple of Compassionate Wisdom) was in August of 1986. The temple grounds were used for housing by the Beijing Paper and Clothing Factory. Yet the temple entrance gate still had the name carved in marble above the arch. A man of 77 years said that there were still some broken monks' quarters until recently. He recalled that one stone tablet was moved to somewhere near the Ming Tombs. Then he excitedly showed off a pair of marble stones used for the temple's flagpoles.

This was the temple that prayed for the souls of those who had worked at the Palace. In the back were the tombs of concubines, maids and eunuchs from the Ming Dynasty. Thus, another name for the place was the Palace Attendant's Slope. The man also remembered the graveyard.

There was another strange story about this place. A small white pagoda was built there 1,000 years ago by a monk in honor of a little spider who supposedly died just after bowing to Buddhist statues on the altar. There were many stone tablets surrounding the courtyard of the "Spider Pagoda" even in the 1920s.

However the people in this neighborhood of North Fuwai Street had yet another story and another nickname for this place. The locals referred to it as Daoyingmiao (Shrine of the Inverted Shadow) or fondly, as "Topsy-turvy." That was because light showing through a small hole in a back wall produced the up-

side down image of those standing before it. It was a popular superstition that this revealed one's future fate. New maid servants for the palace came here as a kind of initiation to see their reversed image and accept their servitude.

In 1986 there was no Spider Pagoda, just an entrance gate, one hall and several marble stones. One noticeable aspect was the low land of the backyard. It was almost two meters below the surrounding area at Ming Dynasty level. I looked for the former graveyard and found a crumbling wall, but no tombs. It was being used as a coal deposit for the paper factory.

That was the last look. The

road was later widened and the site is now a modern building. The low area has been covered with cement for use as a parking lot. I surmise that underneath will be found the remains of those Ming eunuchs, maidservants and even the lofty spider.

## Carvings at the Temple of Perfume and Powder

"This place used to be magnificent!" declared one local resident of Yongfeng Village in Haidian District. "We had large celebrations at festival times." At the time of my visit on a cold December day in 1995, the remaining halls were used by a furniture factory. This was Xiangyansi (Fragrant Rock Temple) where an interesting tree "*Huai bao yu*" (scholar tree embracing an elm) stood in one courtyard. More ancient trees graced the entrance.

In the front garden, many stone blocks were strewn about a large marble platform. These were remnants of stone windows and lintels and all were very finely carved. This was especially true for the stones that used to be set in the arches of the former entrance gate with three passageways: one for men, one for gods and one for devils. The carvings all had symbolic content. Some were parts of stories or allegories. Dragons, monkeys, men with strange-looking Arabic hats on donkeys and a variety of mythical beasts protruded from the surface of these stones. I was astounded that such high craftsmanship was to be found in this very rural place. It wasn't like the other temples in the hills where imperial camps sponsored temple buildings, nor was it one of the famous wealthy monasteries. This was just a temple out in the flat farmland north of the capital.

The history lay in the Qing period tablet now laying prone between two piles of wood. Supposedly Emperor Kangxi's Empress had an illness which left her deaf. But while riding in a palanquin she passed this temple and could hear prayers and music. The Empress in gratitude gave money for temple restorations from her own make-up stipend and the temple was renamed as Xiangfensi (Temple of Perfume and Powder). It also explains why such a place

could afford these elegant stones. Thus this seemingly simple temple was actually once on a grand scale of five courtyards and in charge of 72 other branch temples in the area as well.

When I returned to look for the place several years later, I found the neighborhood to be part of the fast developing high-tech zone. I feared that the temple couldn't possibly still exist. But there was the compound standing as before. Wang, the caretaker, was determined to have the place restored. There was not much he could do about the demise of the grand scholar and elm tree. The pair had died due to neglect in late 1990s. However, the fine stones that I had seen before were all neatly stacked to the side.

Mr. Wang commented on the carvings. "They were made from the heart of deep belief. Can't do that today, even when making an exact copy, the faith doesn't come through." These carved stones certainly would be the showpiece of a refurbished temple, if they can manage to match all the pieces.

## Stone Pagoda of the West Yellow Lamasery

I finally got into Xihuangsi (West Yellow Lamasery)! For two years I'd been repeatedly turned away as it was officially off-limits to visitors. It hadn't occurred to me before to go through official channels. Luckily, my neighbor from the German embassy invited me to come along with their visit. There was a catch. I would serve as the interpreter.

When we arrived at the temple on January 20, 1985, four monks in deep brown robes waited for us at the gate. They were followers of the Yellow sect of Lama Buddhism. As they escorted us in, we were so excited that we forgot about any interpreting and all spoke Chinese. The temple was built in 1652 to welcome the 5th Dalai Lama to the capital.

What we had really come to see was not the halls but the beautiful white marble stonework of the famous pagoda. This uniquely shaped 16-meter-high structure, with smaller pagodas at each corner, symbolizes a mandala. It actually

serves as a stupa, but instead of ashes it holds the clothes of the 6th Panchen Lama who died of smallpox in 1780 while paying a visit to the capital on the occasion of the birthday of Emperor Qianlong.

The top of the pagoda looks like an inverted cone resting on an octagonal foundation and capped with what reminds me of a gold-plated lama's cap with long ears. The whole edifice then rests on a large marble mausoleum base. Every part of the structure is intricately carved with about 40 Buddhas and Bodhisattvas in their vari-

ous poses, scripture engravings and lotus designs. Around the base are scenes from the Buddha's life story. Each corner has an Atlas-like figure appearing to hold up the pagoda.

This temple was badly damaged by foreign troops in 1900 as Boxer groups had used this as a base. Fortunately, the pagoda with its hard marble stood firm against the intruders and only suffered a few chips. We offered incense and as we left, the four lamas stood at the gate, looking happy that we seemed satisfied. The supposed interpreter enjoyed the visit more than anyone.

# Temple Fair of the Medicine King Still Drawing Big Crowds

It was already 36 degrees, but the heat wasn't keeping people away from the Festival to the King of Medicine held in a poor suburb of the city's southwest. Large banners and red silk lanterns decorated both sides of Kandan Road leading up to a local shrine dedicated to Sun Simiao, the father of Chinese medicine or Yaowang (Medicine King) as he is affectionately known. It was his birthday, the 28th of the third moon, that year falling in mid-May. From the noise of gongs, drums and the yells of hawkers selling their wares, it was obvious the party was in full swing.

Sun Simiao, a collector of herbs and plants with medicinal properties, was a respected 6th century doctor who lived to be over 100 years in Shanxi Province. His healing powers were legendary and prayers in hopes of good health were asked of him by the emperor on down. More than 3,000 temples throughout China were dedicated to the Medicine King.

Following the founding of modern China, village temples such as this were put to other uses. These temple halls off Kandan Road, quite appropriately, were used as a traditional Chinese medicine clinic. Medicinal herbs grew in the front garden. Nurses then made a pharmacopoeia of these healing plants and packed them in glass bottles.

Several large stone steles in the main courtyards, although cracked here and there, served as a reminder of past festivals and successive repairs to this temple. On the festival day they were almost hidden from view by the crowds and temporary stalls. An actor sat placidly on one of the turtle-like stele bases. Many more tablets were packed side by side behind the opera stage. These tablets were mostly records of pilgrim associations of the past who supported the activities of the temple. But no one was paying any attention to the aged stones. All eyes were on the stage. A pilgrim association was performing its lion dance.

Recent repairs to the dilapidated halls provided the incentive to restore the birthday celebration, silent for almost 50 years. Entrance tickets of five *yuan* were sold by local police manning the entrance. A storyteller of *Layangpian*, a paper-slide picture show, called for passers-by to gather by his one-man troop performance. He charged one *yuan* to look into peepholes to view pictures that accompany his stories of ancient China. Wang Xuezhi, in his early forties, wore a Chinese-style gray gown, with the long white cuffs folded up. Pulling on one cord, he simultaneously banged a drum and a gong to get everyone's attention. With that he began a loud recitation of the day's feature, a story of the Eight Immortals. For the elderly folk in the crowd it was all familiar stuff. But the children were enthralled and pushed anxiously to get a seat to see the picture show.

Another favorite recitation was about the great feats of the Medicine King during his long life. In the story, the Medicine King was wandering the mountains gathering herbs when his donkey wandered off and was eaten by a tiger. The Medicine King, furious, called all the nearby tigers to force a confession. Finally one of them admitted to the dastardly deed, only to be forced to replace the donkey as the carrier of the doctor's packs for the rest of his days. And that is why there is usually a statue of the legendary tiger in every temple dedicated to the Medicine King.

As raconteur Wang's loud voice carried across the courtyard, people prayed to the new statues of the Medicine King and Three Officials in the back hall. The same stories were painted on the refurbished walls. All this was going on while the two side halls were full of doctors and nurses dispensing free advice to all comers during the three-day festival.

In the courtyard one peasant woman burned incense, prayed for good health, then approached a nurse to complain about her backache. She also took off a shoe and showed her foot problem. She wasn't totally relying on prayer alone. Neither did the Medicine King.

# Stone Bridges

## Mixed Feelings at Marco Polo Bridge

One of the most impressive stone structures in Beijing is surely the 12th century Lugou Bridge over the Yongding River. It is a symbol of the great engineering abilities of the Jin Dynasty. It also stands, as a modern monument, to the war between Japan and China and the horrible pain that the war inflicted on mankind.

The Jin emperor remarked about the beauty of the setting moon over the bridge and this became one of the "Eight Views" of Beijing. On moonlit nights the bridge's carved lions cast long shadows over the ancient stones marked with deep wheel ruts. They often switch their positions, so the legend says. It is a spectacle that has been seen on similar nights over the centuries. Gathering on the bridge at the time of the autumn moon, however, has become such a popular event that vendors line the roads and crowds pour over the bridge most of the night.

In the early 1980s, though, it was still possible to drive on the bridge. One day my family went to see this famed "Marco Polo Bridge." We crossed slowly counting the lions and naively planned to return by the newer bridge down river. Immediately after crossing the bridge, we were stopped by an army guard. Somehow foreigners were allowed on the bridge, but not permitted even a foot over the edge of the other side. It was a puzzling situation. After long and heated negotiations, we were finally able to do a U-turn and drive again over the 900-year ruts.

he built his temple and tomb for posterity.

His tomb, though, was actually built on top of a Tang Dynasty temple that became one of the favorite camp sites of the Jin emperors in the 12th century, Fayunsi (Temple of the Law and Clouds), also known as the Court of Fragrant Water. High walls of the prince's tomb, however, block off the entrance to the earlier spot.

## Crumbling Marble Bridge Makes Link with Past

The seventh son of Emperor Daoguang decided to leave the capital and retire at the foot of Yangtai Hill northwest of the city. He moved out to live as a monk avoiding the hysteria of Empress Dowager Cixi. In 1868 he chose a site with good *fengshui* surrounded by fine shaped pines and ginkgos. There

So it takes some determination to explore back behind the tomb. Following a narrow path to the east, I then clambered down a hillside into a thicket of tall pines growing in the wild, wondering whether or not history would hide from me today. But right away I came across a crumbled marble bridge resting among a dense growth of vines. The bridge maintained the connection with the past. Although I don't know exactly when it was built, at least it was earlier than the usurper tomb in front.

A local handyman readily unlocked the metal lid cover of one of the secret springs. I crept to the rim, saw nothing but black, yet could hear the deep tones of the seepage of water passing below. From there, stone aqueducts, legacies of the previous temple, continue down the west side of the walls. Just standing at locations such as these, one realizes that the shades of ancient sites can still endure, even when a newer structure goes on top.

# Beijing City's Only Pavilion Bridge

In rural Beijing there are still a number of gate-like structures, which serve as bridges over a road. Until the late 1990s there was even one in the city, in Xuanwu District. This was part of a small temple, Guanyinyuan (Compound for the Goddess of Mercy), which had halls on both sides, plus the little hall straddling the road. When I visited there in 1995, a school used the west halls whereas another work unit used those on the east side. The tiny pavilion bridge, or *guojielou*, just seemed to be on its own, in a state of decay, but it still had the roof over its head and calligraphy stones over the arch on both sides. The stone inscription facing south read, *jue'an* (awakening shore), a philosophical phrase.

The vegetable man said it first. "They are going to tear it down." He continued, "This whole neighborhood is going to be newly built." Well, I couldn't believe it.

There was this quaint road going under a unique temple. And here were children happily going to school.

The next time I went there, the school and its halls had completely disappeared, but the little pavilion bridge was still poised above the path, its bricks barely left where it had connected with the school. Yes, the whole neighborhood had been cleared, but there seemed to be some hope for the bridge. The demise, though, was swift. Before any thought could be given on how to incorporate this unusual piece of the old Beijing scene into the modern development, it was just whisked away. It was a lost cause. But I'm glad that I had the chance to take photos and in fact to have climbed up on what had been the city's only pavilion bridge.

## The "Three Step" Bridge at an Old Mountain Convent

An almost forgotten stone convent is nestled in the mountains north of the Miyun Reservoir. One has to climb over a mountain pass and skirt clusters of large boulders on the way to get to the terrace on an inner spur of the mountainside. Arriving there

is like uncovering a fine treasure. Chaosheng'an (Nunnery of Super Victory) has been there since the 11ᵗʰ century. Its very remoteness has helped maintain the genuine rustic atmosphere of an antiquated sanctuary.

The gatekeeper Mr. Gao unlocked the door to the two small compounds, accented by a few cypress trees and stone tablets. Gao said that there were more visitors recently since a Hong Kong businessman donated new statuary.

Behind the compound a footpath, first of recently laid bricks and then of the original stones, goes by a tiny altar to the local nature spirits of white and green snakes, and then leads up 100 stone steps to the Cave of Guanyin, the Goddess of Mercy. The path passes over a small bridge arched across a dry streambed. I liked this bridge a lot, because it was so short. Three steps up, three steps across and down three steps. This little bridge must have been more impressive in the past because scattered nearby are the stone posts and lintels that were part of a narrow

entrance gate for the bridge.

Diminutive stone lions had also once stood before the gate, but these have fallen over or been put along the sides of the path. These figures have been weathered down and now appear more like gentle frogs rather than dignified lions. It was clear from touching the stone of the bridge that the rocks used at this temple are easy to crumble and break. Made of local soft stone, the "Three Step" Bridge and its several frog-like totems are fragile remnants of the nunnery.

## Pilgrims and Beekeepers

Two straight cypress trees 20 meters high stand at the foot of an outstanding stone bridge, Wanshanqiao. This is one of the most picturesque bridges in the capital with an unusually high arch. The present structure dates from a repair at the end of the 15th century. From here pilgrims would begin the ascent up the mountain to the grand festival at Tiantaisi on the 15th of the third lunar month. One village elder remembered that there used to be throngs of people passing over the bridge in the past. Between the two trees, a stone Buddha stands to bless the passersby. But few visitors go along the road nowadays.

One hot July day, a family of beekeepers was camping by the bridge. Their tents crowded the

cypress trees and their boxes of bees cluttered what had been the pilgrim route. They had found one of the most comfortable spots for camping and used a nearby spring as their water supply. When I came upon their settlement, they were busy pouring honey into used plastic bottles. Opening one wooden crate, which functioned as a hive, the beekeeper proudly showed off the dark brown propolis that had accumulated along the top of the box. He scraped off a bit with a stick and boasted that he could fetch a good price for it.

Among the group one young girl was being schooled by her parents and she sat oblivious to the bees, copying sentences into her notebook. These beekeepers were not as uninformed as one would think. Their constant moving gave them a wealth of information about the whole region. Even these nomads from south China were very vocal in their opinions on international affairs.

Though this location seems ideal with the comfortable backdrop of the hill, very few people crossing the bridge, a tasty spring and even a Buddha for protection, they only stay a couple weeks at one location. The beekeepers planned to move their tents and bee boxes to northern Beijing the following week. As seasonal residents of the city, they are sure to come back on next year's circuit and camp once again at the fine stone bridge.

# Stone Animals

## "First There Was Stone Nest Village, Then There Was Beijing."

On both sides of the road near Shiwocun, Stone Nest Village, in southern Fangshan District are hundreds of artisans chiseling marble blocks. The whole area resounds with the hammers and picks cutting into large slabs of marble. Fine stone carvings have been made here for centuries. The boom of construction of Beijing has given a surge to their trade handed down through generations. Just north of the village is a deep quarry. The gigantic marble blocks are cut below and hauled up by pulley or by carts to be carried off to the carvers. Huge raw stones litter the land waiting for their designated function and design.

Today most of the statues are the ubiquitous pair of lions for the entranceways to hotels and restaurants of Beijing, but a few are making more artistic images of a religious nature or even of revolutionary heroes. By the side of one carving factory was a line of eight larger-than-life Chairman Mao replicas in different poses. The other most popular figure is Guanyin, the Goddess of Mercy, either standing or in meditation.

I walked up to a man in the middle of his work and asked master carver Wang about his profession. His ancestors, he boasted, carved for the Imperial Palace in Beijing. Those large slabs of white marble that decorate the steps and colonnades of the Forbidden City

## Forlorn Statue Marks the Former "Dog Temple"

Dogs have had a special place throughout Chinese history. They were mentioned as pets of emperors from the 8th century Tang Dynasty. Photos from the early 20th century show the Empress Dowager Cixi always accompanied by her favorite Pekinese, named "Peony." She supposedly had more than 100 Pekinese that wandered around the back halls of the Forbidden City. Court eunuchs guarded the pedigree of these dogs and traded among themselves. The dog of choice for the imperial court and monks was the yellow-haired Pekinese with a tail curled upward and a full mane, resembling a lion cub.

The famous Longfusi (Temple of Prosperity and Happiness) was known for its monthly fairs. More importantly, it was where Beijing's dog market used to be situated. Today, Longfusi no longer exists. A department store, Longfu Dasha, decorated with an ornate Buddhist gate, sits on the site and dogs are no longer sold in the nearby alley as before. Instead, dog markets have sprung up in rural Beijing. One is east of the city on a dusty country road. Open only in the mornings on the 4th, 14th and 24th of the lunar month, the market stretches for about a kilometer on both sides of the road. Dogs of almost any species are displayed from bicycle baskets or inside

were in fact quarried and carved here and then sent sliding along the ice to the capital in winter, he elaborated. Then he quoted the local saying: "First there was Stone Nest Village, then there was Beijing." Some say that stone carving has gone on here since Han times, making that almost 2,000 years.

Wang had just finished carving a Buddha figure and was now working on a medium-sized lion. I asked him where he would put the mouth. He laughed and said that they were all pretty much standardized now. "That's the way people order them."

locals remembered in their devotions here. While Erlang was one of many Taoist gods to whom you could pray for regaining of one's health, it was here that you could pray for your sick pet. The dog-saint, thus, was Beijing's sole animal faith healer. In olden times, people would come in with small wooden or plaster images of their dogs and place them by the altar in prayer. Now the forlorn stone figure by the sidewalk is the one reminder of the temple's presence. Pedestrians, unthinkingly, pat the top of the statue as they walk past.

cages roped on motorcycles. Pet goods are hawked from makeshift tables. A baby *Chiwawa* poked her head out of one car trunk.

Dogs once were such a part of Beijing life that there was even a place to go pray for their health. In an upscale hotel neighborhood stands a seemingly forgotten stone animal with a worn-down head. A shop selling lingerie is the present·storefront, but the back halls occupy the remains of Beijing's only "Dog Temple", as it was nicknamed. The temple was supposedly founded more than 1,000 years ago. Originally dedicated to the memory of the master Erlang, it was actually his pet dog that the

## Grins and More Grins

Situated in the southeast corner of Yanqing Town is a restored temple that dates back to the 13th century. Visiting there in 1997 before it was officially open was a memorable time meeting with many grins. On the front steps of Lingzhaosi (Temple of the Shining Spirit) were two stone lions standing guard with large toothy smiles. Usually these statues are complacent or even stern faced, never funny like these two. Perhaps it was this laughable welcome that helped one to ignore the "No

Admittance" sign on a rickety gate.

Inside the first courtyard were many broken steles. One in particular had two finely carved swirling dragons. Again, large toothy grins. And beyond that, too, a stele base with a weathered dragon head. He, too, had a smirk on his face. A row of lions collected from other nearby sites were also all smiling. The local artisans certainly had a tradition of happy faces.

Nobody seemed to be around. The side halls were filled with straw and farming tools. Most doors were locked. Inside the main hall, there was nothing but a few old lanterns. Yet detailed floral carving on the wood of the outside doors was evidence that this wasn't just some country shrine, but the most important temple of Yanqing. A bas-relief sculpture just below the side roof ridge is a curled dragon, mouth open wide, and again a wide smile. However, on the way out the caretaker had wakened from his nap and was staring out of his window, but this time no toothy grin.

## Door Stones Still Mark Rank Fifty Years Later

A group of American journalists who had been posted in China before WW II were invited back for a reunion in April of 1985. Among those invited were Professor Harold and Viola Isaacs. Harold Isaacs wrote *The Tragedy of the Chinese Revolution*, published in the 1930s, and his last book was *China Revisited, after 50 Years*, remembering back to

when he was a journalist in Shanghai. At that time he was friendly with both Song Qingling and novelist Lu Xun.

I took Viola out for a day of exploring to find some of the places she remembered from living here 50 years before. But first we went to Madam Song's house where the curator gratefully acknowledged the donation of dresses Madam Song had given Viola in their Shanghai days. We also saw the photo in which Harold had been reinserted (after having been paint-brushed out for several decades). This was a picture at the Song home in Shanghai with the hostess and guests Lu Xun, Bernard Shaw, Lin Yutang, Agnes Smedley, and Isaacs.

Trying to find her former home was rather easy because she remembered the name of her alley. I found Dayang Yibin *Hutong* on my map. It was in the Eastern District. We threaded our way through the narrow lanes until we were on her street. But which house? Things looked a lot different, so it took a while for her to get her bearings.

"I remember we were near the east end," she was beginning to feel familiar with the setting. "And the John Fairbanks (Professor at Harvard) lived a couple doors west of us. Their home was more elegant than ours. It had a higher step at the gate, and their stone door piers (*mendun'r*) were more intricately carved." The search began and we poked our way in and out of all the houses on the street.

That was the first time I ever really noticed the differences in door stones. Some were round, others square. A few had more elaborate carvings than others. But all were made of fine white marble and had an elongated slab at the bottom that went under the door to fasten it tight. This *hutong* was obviously a well-to-do neighborhood

in the past.

When Viola stood in front of one entrance, she felt something was familiar. She recognized the door piers. Yet peeking into the courtyard she found a lot had changed. It was filled with temporary brick rooms to accommodate many families in what had been a single-family compound.

We worked our way through the outdoor maze that had been a garden. At the far back, Viola gasped, "That was my bedroom!" Sitting outside the door were six young Chinese artists absorbed in sketching. They quickly welcomed us to their circle. A boy with longish hair who now lived in the room told her that he was 22 years old. At that Viola exclaimed, "I was 22, too, when I lived in this room!"

Going back along the alley, Viola could figure out the Fairbanks' house by counting the doors. And she had remembered correctly. The door stones were indeed grand, big circular drums with small lions carved on the top. It was easy to feel the home's higher rank even after all these years.

## Stone Sheep Guard Revolutionaries

At the entrance to the main hall of Baozhong Huguosi (Temple to the Greatly Honored Loyal Protector of the Nation) within the National Cemetery for Revolutionaries at Babaoshan were a pair of stone sheep. Most temples have lions as their guards, but here the sheep rested calmly in the peaceful courtyard. I don't know what the symbolism of this animal meant, but there was something soothing about their nature. Instead of fiercely guarding a hall or gate as most ornamental animals do, they are just looking forward with their feet curled underneath.

It was my first time to go in to the Revolutionaries Cemetery, so I went in all black clothes from head to toe out of respect for the deceased. I was looking, though, for older relics. The temple where the sheep were sitting was originally dedicated to a famous Ming general named Gang Tie who castrated himself to prove his loyalty to the emperor and was kept up by eunuchs over the centuries.

However, this site was even older as evidenced by ancient trees and an 11<sup>th</sup> century Liao Dynasty tomb nearby. This is another example of the continuing use of important localities. Places are rebuilt layer upon layer and given new names and new characteristics. Gardens were rebuilt upon gardens, temples upon temples and graves upon graves. The sites were determined by their *fengshui* for their best use. This one was for burial. So I walked in the cemetery of the recent heroes while thinking this was also going back 500 years, in honor of the Ming hero, and going back yet another 500, as a resting place of Liao nobility. And maybe close by there were even Han Dynasty tombs from 2,000 years ago. The place gives a good perspective on time and space.

There is nothing more inside the halls of Gang Tie's memorial shrine. The garden though maintains a feeling of antiquity because of the trees. Two stele provide written records confirming its history. But it is really the two wise looking sheep that lend a special dignity to the temple and its surroundings.

## Beasts of the Iron Screen Wall

The winter sunlight helped to lessen the cold of that January day in 1995. I was walking in the *hutong*s southeast of the Deshengmen Gate. It was once a neighborhood of iron foundries. One alley in that vicinity carries the name Tieyingbi *Hutong* (Iron Screen Wall Alley). In the back part of the alley were the remains of a temple, Desheng'an (Convent

of Righteous Victory). Old beams of the remaining halls kept the flavor of the place amidst the disarray of the crowded living quarters now occupying its courtyard. Yet the famed spirit screen that had once stood before it was nowhere to be found.

An old cigarette seller sat bundled up in an armchair where the *hutong* branched off from a busy street. I inquired after the famous Yuan Dynasty stone screen. At first he didn't know what I was talking about. But after reminding him that was the name of his alley, he remembered that the big stone, almost two meters high, was removed from here, but he didn't know where. Supposedly this stone screen had been at a Dragon King Shrine inside the

Mongol's capital city that extended farther to the north. Legend has it that it served as a protective talisman that would help the city keep down the winds and sand blowing in from the north. Later, in the mid-16<sup>th</sup> century, the stone screen wall was transported to this place just within the northern Ming city walls in order to ward off the yearly sandstorms hitting the new capital.

I went back again in 2003 to see what has happened to the neighborhood. Surprisingly, nothing has changed. Even the man in the armchair was exactly where he had been eight years ago. Only this time he wasn't selling tobacco, instead he has become a self-designated advisor on local lore, including correcting mistakes on the nearby recently posted sign telling Iron Screen Wall *Hutong*'s history. "That sign is wrong," he instructed. It should read, "The alley was named after the screen in 1911."

His home at the corner has given him a good perch to watch life go by. Wang Hengqi, 83, even remembers the gateway that used to stand over the *hutong* entrance. "There weren't many monks, just one or two even before Liberation," he recalled. Iron Screen Wall Alley, just over 200 meters long, goes north with a couple bends, and then makes a right turn until it dead ends into another alley to the east. The screen and temple used to stand beyond the first bend. An elderly lady neighbor chimed in that the dragon heads on top of the screen were knocked off to keep it from being sold in the

1930s. Wang invited me into his home where he proudly displays his collection of antique New Year's rubbings. I inquired if he now knew the whereabouts of the screen wall. "It was moved to Beihai Park in 1947," he stated, this time assured of his information.

The famed 800-year-old Iron Screen Wall can be found by a walkway at the northern edge of the park. This bulky slab of pumicite-stone has a reddish-tint giving an impression of iron ore. It is carved on one side with a strange whimsical beast, a Kylin or Chinese unicorn. It has hoofs of a cow, horns and scales of a dragon, and is set within an ocean motif. On the other side is an equally strange lion before a wooded background, with two cubs playing around its legs. Sure enough, the two top corners of the wall were broken. It certainly must have been highly regarded to have been moved two times. However, its powers over winds and sand seem dubious.

## Strange Lions of the Central Summit

The number five is important in Chinese cosmology. The Taoist Wuyue (Five Peaks) of China are the protectors for the whole country. Beijing, too, had its five protectors known as the Wuding, the Five Summits. All of these had shrines built in the Ming Dynasty dedicated to Bixiayuanjun (Lady Sovereign of the Azure Clouds), the patron Taoist saint of the city. She is believed to be the daughter of the central deity of Taishan Mountain, the Dongyue (Eastern Peak) in Shandong Province.

During the Song Dynasty, an emperor went to Taishan and gave her the regal title. By the 16th century, she was the most popular deity to be worshipped in many places in Beijing. As a kind of Mother Goddess, she was prayed to for help with childbirth and certain sicknesses. The 18th of the Fourth Moon is her feast day, so there were many festivals in her honor in the spring season.

But where are these temples of the Five Peaks today? To find them, I organized a group of thirteen friends to spend a day in 1997 exploring Beijing to search out the sites of these popular shrines. I called it "*Wuding Yiri You*" (A Day of Touring the Five Summits). This kind of pilgrimage circuit was in keeping with the old traditions when the faithful banded together and went from shrine to shrine. Our group was made up of people from different backgrounds and nationalities, all bound together in this quest, bringing their variety of expertise to help the exploration. By the end of the day we had found stone tablets, even some old buildings, at most of the sites.

One of the five, the Zhongding (Central Summit), had several stone objects, which were particularly interesting. The little shrine sits on higher land above a place known as the Grass

Bridge where several streams used to come together in Fengtai District. This once picturesque neighborhood is now cluttered with crowded housing.

One woman who lived on the premises said that her grandfather had helped in the reconstruction of the back hall in 1937. According to her recollection, an annual festival was held here on the 1st of the sixth month. "That was when the flowers around here, especially the lotus blossoms, were at their best." She pointed out some of the stones. One was almost covered in dirt and lying on its side. It was a commemorative stone by one of the temple's support organizations. Another large stele had unusual carvings of boy children all around the rim. It was inscribed in 1696 as "The Support Association of the 100 Children." Indeed, the group's purpose was to pray to the goddess for sons.

But it was the strange looking lion standing before the entrance gate that made this place so unforgettable. It was absolutely weird, almost like a cat with a long thin tail. Its mane came down in shoulder length waves and it had a strange face with goggle eyes and a funny goatee. It is one of the most novel stone animals of Beijing.

# The 32 Styles of Calligraphy inside a Giant Turtle

The village of Balizhuang underwent incredible changes in the ten years between 1985 and 1995 when the urban sprawl caught up with the countryside. Once it was a rural village 4 kilometers west of the former Fuchengmen Gate. By late 1995, it nestled alongside a wide expressway with the latest town houses, a modern high school, a beautifully land-scaped public park, and a variety of restaurants.

After all this modernization it is hard to imagine that anything could remain from the past. Yet on the east side of the canal running up to the Summer Palace and across from the tall Balizhuang pagoda is the little-known former temple called the Mohe'an (Retreat of Queen Maya – Buddha's mother). Built in 1546, as a retirement place for palace eunuchs, the compound was thought to architecturally represent a giant turtle and thus had good *fengshui*. The original hall at the back was the shell, the four stone towers at each corner were the claws, the front gate was the head, the inside transom being the tongue. Its founder Zhao Zheng was buried at the back. Over the years, it became a popular gathering place for intellectuals who extolled the beauty of the temple and surrounding trees in their poetry.

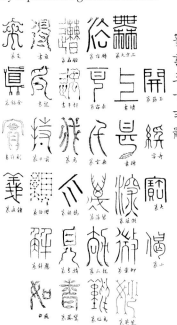

The temple now functions as the Balizhuang Primary School. A side hall on the east axis, in what was the teachers' room, houses one of the great treasures of calligraphy in Beijing. Embedded in the walls are unusual stone slabs with the Buddhist *Diamond Sutra* inscribed in 32 styles of seal characters. Among the different styles are the rarely seen *kedou wen* (tadpole) style and the *longshu* (dragon) style. Some slabs are now in the care of the cultural relics bureau and the remaining ones are covered with protective glass. During the

Cultural Revolution when temple scrolls and sutras were burning in the courtyard, then caretaker, Mr. Li Wencheng, promised the Red Guards that he would destroy all the slabs for them. Instead he hid them packed in mud. Li was still protecting the place on my first visit to the temple in 1985. He continued to be concerned about the safekeeping of "his" slabs. "How can we repair the temple? How can we preserve Mohe'an?" he asked.

The turtle-shape of the temple has been somewhat disfigured over the years. The main gate of the school has been bricked up, the turtle's tongue rendered silent. But the front courtyard still has the eyes of the turtle, the drum and bell towers. Before the front hall, stand two beautifully carved horse-mounting stones. These were usually placed outside by the street, but put inside if they are for use by ladies or eunuchs. In the second courtyard, the main hall rests on a high marble platform. Famed Ming period murals inside, though, were whitewashed and the coiling dragons that were once part of the sandalwood ceiling have disappeared. The whole compound is surrounded by another wall, which has the crumbling remains of corner towers, the once protective dragon claws. Li told me that many of the tower stones were used to build a nearby swimming pool.

At the back a white pine once grew on top of the eunuch's tomb, perhaps representing the turtle's tail. But the tree, related Li, was cut down in 1964 despite protests by the monk on the premises. The following year when digging to install an anti-aircraft emplacement, Zhao's coffin was dug up, but his mummified remains soon disintegrated.

In the late 1990s, teachers of the primary school were well aware of the buildings' legacy and knew they must guard the stone treasures. Someday, Mohe'an will return to its former shape, the claws of the turtle back in place, the tongue loose again! Scholars might gather once more to write poetry amidst the blossoms and appreciate the stones with 32 styles of calligraphy, grateful for their protection by Li Wencheng.

# Stone Paths

## Pilgrim Path to Peaceful Ruins

Stone pilgrim paths should also be considered as valuable cultural relics. Smoothed over the centuries, these stones still lead the way to temples in rural Beijing. Hidden deep in the Jincheng Mountains west of the city is the 900-year-old temple of Baipusi (Temple of the White Waterfall). It is certainly one of the most remote Buddhist sites in all of the metropolitan area. In the summer of 1998, the first challenge was just to find the

right track. Finally, one ordinary dirt road led into an ancient stone pilgrim path. Proceeding along up one mountain and then over another ridge, the sun reflected off the polished uneven stones. These worn stones, shaped by the footsteps of the faithful, gave such a deep impression of history. After walking for more than an hour, I was so excited when, at last, I spotted the temple's old pagoda in the distance!

This old pathway finally led to the ruins of the temple compound. Not much is left of historical interest, except for the fine brick pagoda containing the remains of the temple's founder. It was the return trip, though, that was unforgettable. About halfway, a sudden electric storm hit the area. I was on the top of one treeless ridge. Being the tallest object around, I was terrified. Lightening was crackling above and rain was slapping down on the stone path making it a slippery slide. The way up had been like a pilgrimage; the way down was a hurried exodus.

When I finally made it to a hamlet in the valley, it was almost night. I had become separated from my group and lost in a maze of small darkened alleys. Finally, I walked into a farmer's compound. Through the window I could see that the family was sitting down to dinner. So as not to shock them, I announced in a clear voice: "I am a foreigner. I am lost!" The family fortunately was quite calm about the whole thing. They laughingly accompanied me to where my friends waited on the other side of the village. I will always be in awe of this temple's ancient stone pilgrim path and the twists and turns of the village passageways at dusk.

## Stele Carved above a Precarious Ancient Road

Quite a few worn stone paths remain in Mentougou District. One such ancient road still winds its way high above the Yongding River. I found this place in 1996 after having read a newspaper article about Buddhist carvings on a hillside. When I asked local villagers about the where-abouts of these images, nobody seemed to know anything about them.

I kept asking around until finally one local man pointed to a large abandoned cement factory. The concave shape of the mountainside told of years of continuous digging. Camou-flaged in dust, I could barely make out four sets of inscriptions high up at the top edge of the quarry. It was necessary to walk through the pit, past rusted carts lying abandoned on narrow tracks, and climb through a lot of rubble. A sharp

incline led to a stony path that edged along the side of the mountain.

I met goatherd Wang, 60, taking his flock of 23 goats home toward Xishiguyan (West Stone Old Cliff) Village. He told me that some Buddhas were carved on the cliff face. It wasn't as I had imagined. There were three Buddhist images barely visible at the top of one inscription. Another stele on the mountainside recorded a 16th century monk's efforts to rebuild the bridge, which had collapsed. It also commended him for repairing this road.

When the river was fuller, the path may not have been so high up, but today it hovers dangerously as a ridge jutting out far above the wide riverbed. This old route was particularly important for many centuries to carry coal out of the mountains. Hoof print marks embedded deeply in the stones of the path are proof of the heavy loads on horses, donkeys and camel trains as they transported coal into the capital.

When you stand down by the river, it certainly is unthinkable that an old road still clings to that high crag. I later learned that villagers do know about the carvings. I just hadn't asked correctly. They call the place Shifoling, Peak with the Stone Buddhas!

## Stone Steps to Convent Hidden in the Corner

"Have you been to Galar'an?" That was the question I was asked several times when walking the mountains of the Fenghuangling Scenic Area in Haidian District. Galar'an is the way the locals pronounce the nickname for a small mountain convent secluded in a high ravine. That is what Galar'an means: Convent Hidden in the Corner. Not much is left there. But before the site was

visible, stones noted its history.

This nunnery, first known as Miaofeng'an (Convent of the Mystic Peak), was actually two caves and the courtyard below them. When I hiked there the first time it was all overgrown. A few stones lay where the buildings had once stood. In front of one of the caves, part of a stone Buddha lay on its side. Then I found narrow carved steps curving steeply around the edge of a gigantic, 20-meter-high boulder. As I clambered up 53 steps, I could visualize the nuns ascending to their hideaway, a small cave at the top of the great rock.

As is the way of many sacred sites in China, there is often a mixture of Buddhist and Taoist legacies at the same place. What once was

Buddhist became a Taoist sanctuary later on. The old convent was converted into the Taoyuanguan (Peach Garden Shrine) in the Qing Dynasty. It was well known for Taoist medicine, the priests having been trained as doctors. The Taoist halls are now in the process of being rebuilt. But the two caves are still dedicated to Buddhist deities.

The challenge of the tiny steps continues, and after climbing them you can confidently ask others, "Have you been to Galar'an?"

# Old Way to Temple of the Ordination Altar

Jietaisi (Temple of the Ordination Altar) is one of the main tourist spots of the Western Hills. Its giant five-meter-high marble ordination platform is one of the stone wonders of Beijing. Monks of northern China have taken their sacred vows on it for over 1,000 years. One can still follow the old stone footway along the gradual ascent up the hill from the road below. It took me almost two hours to hike it one brisk autumn day. Partway, the track goes by a cement factory and a dusty village. Yet here and there a few remaining gnarled pines helped mark the way. The route then passes through the village of Shifocun; named for the stone Buddhas carved on one hillside. These 22 images in small niches all date from the 15<sup>th</sup> and 16<sup>th</sup> centuries.

While on my trek, I met an 100-year-old

woman living in the village. In fact I was led into her house by her daughter-in-law, grandchildren and great grandchildren. She was lying on a raised bed beside a window looking out at the path below and wanted to talk with a foreigner. She recalled the throngs of visitors going up the pilgrim path to the temple, especially in the early spring. The elderly lady also told how the villagers had covered up the Buddhas with straw to protect them from being ravaged by Red Guards.

The pilgrims' path becomes quite clear when the stepping-stones take a separate way from the truck road. These worn stones prove the popularity of this sacred place. After a Ming Dynasty stone gate, elaborately carved with Buddhist imagery, the trail leads to the monks' graveyards. A group of stupas, under a forest of magnificent pine trees, lend dignity to this hallowed ground. One path ascends to the temple gate, while another track skirts the temple, and winds its way past caves and a Ming Dynasty stone pagoda until it reaches the Jile (Joyful) Peak on Ma'anshan (Saddle Hill).

I took a large group from the Beijing International Society there in 1997 to walk this latter path and have local experts explain the symbolism of the stone pagoda. But the top of the mountain was closed because of fire prevention season. We promised that none of us would smoke. Forty foreigners and three Chinese historians were determined to get to that Ming pagoda. It was our research! The lady gatekeeper

with the red armband was adamant, no entry. But then we spotted a few other people walking the hillside. "Oh, well, they will be fined," she said. The solution became clear. "How much is the fine?" So we were all fined five *yuan* and thus able to continue climbing to the pagoda and wander on to the end of the mountain road.

# Folk Sculptor Keeps Legends of Jin Tombs Alive

There is a striking starkness about the valley of Nine Dragon Mountain in the outskirts of Beijing. Nobody lives there. The last house is at the narrow neck leading into the valley, fittingly named Longmenkoucun (Mouth of the Dragon Village). Beyond that is a necropolis, city of the dead, covering 60 square kilometers. It is here that the tombs of Jin Dynasty emperors are located. The nine emperors of Jin (or Kin, dynasty name for the Jurchens of Northeast China) controlled half of China for 120 years from the mid-12th century, until they were eventually overthrown by the Mongols.

Nine ridges jut out from the Nine Dragon Mountain. Each of them forms a shallow valley which once held a tumulus of an emperor. The grand cemetery, though, is a ruin. It was destroyed by the Ming rulers in a particularly vicious act to violate the ancestors of their rivals, the emerging Manchu tribes.

The families who lived at the Mouth of the Dragon Village acted as caretakers of the valley. They have watched over the silent grass-covered stone tumuli and passed on stories by word of mouth through generations. Liu Shoushan, 56, is one such caretaker. He was born here. The family planted fruit trees in the valley and he is now a handyman for the archeological excavations now under way at the site. He also knows a lot about the tombs and the surrounding valley.

He explained that the Manchu emperors ordered two of the tombs to be restored, but even these have succumbed to the elements. Liu pointed out yellow roof tiles scattered among the weeds and a broken dome in the distance, "That was the grave of the grand ancestor, Emperor Taizu."

Liu followed a large herd of goats up a narrow incline. He had a story to tell at the top. The ruins here were not of the Jin Dynasty, but one tablet was to the brave general Yue Fei who fought against the Jin clan, and was purposefully built here to put a jab at the spirits of the imperial tombs. He clearly remembered a building with a large stone base. "But the local authorities tore it down about 30 years ago to use the stones to build the village school here," he said.

Liu's home is on the other side of a dry riverbed. He doesn't leave the valley often. He plays the *suona* horn and the *erhu*, but he is mainly a folk artist in his spare time. His passion is root sculpture, a traditional art of rural northern China. Although a modest abode, his shingled two-room house is crammed with wonderful objects of his creation. One by one he proudly brought them out into the sunshine. Some were like petrified *bonsai*, others were wild entwining and curled branches. There is so much movement and careful arrangement of the tree roots to make a sculptural whole.

Liu explained that he soaks the roots in water until they are soft. Then he arranges the roots in a design. They are placed between heavy stones and set for two weeks or so. Some of the roots get very thin with this pressing and make his sculpture all the more delicate and precious.

Holding up each piece, he talked about them as if each one was his dearest pet. "This is a rooster," pointing out a seemingly strutting bird formed by the root's curves. "And this is a monkey, isn't it?" referring to a particularly thick root with a top that looked like a mischievous chimp. Large loops of wood and branches made very modern designs.

His home offers a superb view of the Jin valley where the excavations are going on. Large segments have been dug up and some fruit trees cleared. According to Liu, many carved stone slabs have been unearthed, as well as stone conduits for water. But the stories protected by the guardian of the tombs and his marvelous root sculptures may be as important to the history of the valley as any ancient marble carvings.

# Buddhas of Stone

## Statues of White Water River

Most of the original Buddhist images from inside Beijing's temples have disappeared. However, there are a number of surviving ancient Buddhas carved in stone and in bas-relief on the facades of pagodas and on cave walls.

Baishuisi (White Water Temple) has Beijing's largest stone statue. It stands at 5.8 meters in a stone beamless hall in the hills beyond the Yanshan petrochemical complex in Fangshan District. The statue is of a wide-eyed standing Sakyamuni Buddha. He is flanked by his two main disciples. On the day I visited there, retirees from the Yanshan factory came to burn incense and relax in this designated scenic area.

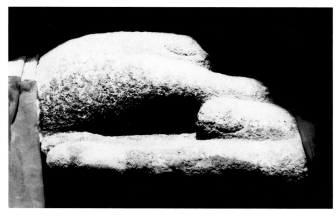

Inside the hall, plastic and fresh flower offerings were stuck inside used beverage bottles. Incense was curling up both inside and outside the hall.

This stone hall appears completely square from the outside, but the inside ceiling is formed like a dome, with bricks making a spiral to a tip at the top. No one is quite sure about the date of the statues. The locals believe that they are at least 900 years old. A smaller stone carving to the side seems even older because it is so worn that just the shape of a figure is suggested. While I was standing inside the hall, a beam of sunlight suddenly came in from the upper window and shone directly on the simple flat palms of the Buddha. I wondered if this phenomenon occurred daily, an arrangement by the architects to enhance the sacredness of the statues.

Mr. Zhang who had worked in the plant for over 30 years bemoaned the fact that the White Water River has recently become polluted and that fish have died off. I asked him if he knew of any other relics of the temple. He pointed over toward the railroad tracks running along below the temple. Several of the stairs leading up to the raised tracks were made from weathered stones with lotus carvings, obviously from White Water Temple. On a small broken piece of

stele lying nearby were the words "old temple." These finds: the spiral ceiling within the stone square hall, the bright light focusing on the Buddha's hands, and the bits of stone lying around, all added to the mystery of the place.

## The Great Stone Buddha Robbery

Perhaps the most valuable stone carving in all of Beijing used to be on the mountainside above Che'erying Village in Haidian District. It is a painted stone standing Buddha over 1.6 meters high and dating from the year 499 A.D. Asking the location in 1995 from local people along the way, I crossed through several orchards and continued to climb up the hill behind the village. At last I was directed to a farmhouse just off the road.

Nobody seemed to be home, so I just

meandered around to the rear garden. There was a strange edifice there, like an octagonal stone hut with a pointed roof. It seemed like something a bit European. Peering through a dusty window in the back, it was possible to barely make out the shape of the large stone figure inside. It stood on a high marble pedestal. When my eyes got adjusted I could see the beautiful carvings and soft drapery of the image. With a gentle archaic smile the large-shouldered standing Buddha looked out in a fixed gaze. One hand was pointed down and the other was bent at the waist. Both the protective backdrop of over two meters tall and the halo surrounding the Buddha's head were covered in intricately carved figures of small

Buddhas and celestial musicians.

As I was looking around, the caretaker, Ms. Zhang Baoying, came to check on what I was doing there. I asked her about the building and she told me that she was the fourth generation of the Yao families to protect this treasure. "That was why it wasn't damaged in the Cultural Revolution!" She talked about architect Duan Qiguang who went to France, and when he returned in 1927 he designed this protective case for the Buddha. Zhang came here in the 1980s when she married into the Yao family. So she felt it was her duty to also work to protect the ancient statue. "There was once a large temple complex here," she explained. There are theories that a prince commissioned this Temple of the Stone Buddha. At that time the Northern Wei Dynasty had a rich Buddhist kingdom with their capital at Datong. So it is reasonable that their control extended to this region.

I could only think of poor Ms. Zhang and the Yao family when I heard the news in 1998 that the statue had incredulously been stolen. Some thieves from Hebei came in the night with a bulldozer and truck, broke it into four parts and just whisked it away. The statue was later found and, though slightly damaged, was pieced back together. No more climbing through the orchards to the old site, as the stone statue is now protected at the Stone Carving Museum in the city. Unfortunately, the village lost its relic and the great stone figure had to leave its hillside after 1,500 years.

## Buried Buddhas Come to Life

The little village of Shifo (Stone Buddhas) in the far southwest of Pinggu County hasn't had too many outside visitors lately. But it once had a 9th century temple renowned for its stone Buddhist sculptures. The fact that these magnificent pieces of Tang art have survived the tumults of history is an amazing story. In 1952, the stone sculptures were buried by the villagers under the threshing ground. During the Cultural

Revolution, young people didn't even know of their existence. The temple had been a large monastery with three courtyards. But today it exists only as an illusion above the corn stalks drying on the open space where the temple once stood.

At first the villagers seemed puzzled when asked in 1997 about their temple and stone figures. They didn't even seem interested. Finally, a gray-haired lady came out of her door-

way and began to talk. Other elders gradually gathered and bit-by-bit the story came out. They said that the dilapidated temple had been torn down about ten years ago when they took the sculptures away. "No use having the temple if the figures aren't there," reasoned one villager. The stone Buddhas had been buried for almost 25 years as the locals had believed in their value and had felt responsible for them. They were brought out into the air again in 1978 and, one young man remembered, "They gave us twenty *yuan* each to help dig them out from the ground and then load them on trucks. We haven't seen them since!"

Glancing across at where the temple once stood, the villagers just shrugged their shoulders and went on their way. By the side of the nearby frozen pond two young boys were sitting on a large broken stone. Discernable below the boys swinging legs were lotus motif carvings and other decorations. It was the only stone left from the vanished temple!

The strangest thing was yet to come. On the threshing ground were piles of corn stalks drying in the winter sun. Yet it was still possible to see great gaps in the dirt where those Buddhas had once been hidden. The deep pits were testimony to the efforts of those villagers of the 1950s to preserve their special legacy. Looking at the pits made it even more compelling to search for their statues.

The local cultural relics department acknowledged that the statues were being protected.

There, under a shed, were the Tang Dynasty stone statues from the village. Stone torsos of two of the Buddha's disciples lay on the dirt. Nearby were two statues of Bodhisattvas seated on very fine carvings of an elephant and a lion. Even more impressive were the relief carvings of the animal keepers with detailed and vivid facial expressions. The seated Buddha, though, was missing. I asked around and found it several months later on the back porch of an archaeology museum some 20 km away. When put back together this full set will show the reason why villagers went to such efforts to save them.

# Oldest Standing Building in the City

Snarled traffic passes almost teasingly too close to the elegant Tianningsi (Temple of Heavenly Tranquility) Pagoda, Buddhist landmark of the 12th century Liao Dynasty's southern capital. Now partly encircled by a highway interchange loop in the southwest part of the city, this lonely sentinel seems to stand in defiance of time, as a reminder of continuity of 1,000 years and of Beijing's long history as a major cultural center.

The Liao rulers were particularly fond of this octagonal plan and set of thirteen eaves. One can still see dragons curling up the columns at each corner. The pagoda, almost 58 meters high, would have stood out then as it does now as an edifice evoking imperial spiritual power. Peering out from the brick facade are the guardian generals with their shouting open mouths and glaring wide eyes, calling for attention from passersby going too fast to notice them. Or are they angry at the chimney nearby that is taller than their pagoda?

While the temple compound was being used as a factory in 1985, I found it necessary to secretly crawl over huge piles of coal, just to get a good photo of the full pagoda. The first hint of change came eleven years later when neighborhood houses were being cleared away for a park. Shortly afterwards I was told, "There's a monk

back in residence." At last, a faint hope for getting closer to the pagoda! The monk was eager to oblige. And I was soon standing on the base of the pagoda staring face-to-face with the grand bas-reliefs.

Strong religious imagery is manifested in all the sculptured decorations. Especially beautiful are the graceful weatherworn Bodhisattvas. Their hands are captivatingly raised in prayer, their eyes look down demurely in forgiveness, but one disintegrating nose shows how fragile these statues are. Another five Bodhisattvas stand in a row, like a phalanx to protect the Buddha below. Pug-faced stone lions protrude from niches encircling the surface of the pagoda. These lions represent the "Solar Buddha" and thus have universal power as defenders of faith and to safeguard the site.

Tianningsi continued to be important throughout the later dynasties. In the 15th century, the powerful monk Yao Guangxiao, counselor to the Ming emperor Yongle, was the senior abbot here. During the following Qing Dynasty it was also used as a residence for scholars. Today, the temple is finally getting back some of its former space. Restorations began in earnest in 2002. It proudly remains calm in the midst of the frenetic pace of cars whizzing around it.

## Dancers on Stone Columns

Stone *dhanari* pillars found in Buddhist temple courtyards are made up of finely carved pieces of stone balanced on top of each other. They usually have a base of stylized lotus flowers and other portions decorated with Buddhist images and inscribed with religious scriptures. But what I have particularly enjoyed are the sections with animated carvings of dancers and musicians.

Beijing's tallest column supposedly stood over four meters in the courtyard of Shuanglinsi (Temple of the Twin Forests). An article by cultural relics expert Ms. Qi Xin in a scholarly magazine showed a faded picture of the stone tower in its original setting. I took the article with me when I drove several hours to the village of the same name far west of Beijing. But I was disappointed to find only a deserted compound with a stele and two abandoned halls.

In the 10th century this place was known as the Courtyard of Pure Water, but today pigs grunted from a makeshift sty in one of the halls. Trampling around the overgrown yard at dusk, I could find no trace of the famous stone column. A lady named Mrs. Shan who was walking up the hill had seen the stone pieces. The column, she said, had been taken apart because it weakened after an earthquake. The sixteen separated stones had been carted away. I later found the pillar dismantled into its many pieces in the Mentougou District Museum. Of all the inscriptions and carvings, though, what I found most interesting were the depictions of ancient dancers.

Another pillar on display at Jietaisi has Bodhisattvas etched on its six sides. One strikes a pose with bells in each hand. It impressed me with its similarity to the dances of the Shinto priestesses of Japan. The many dancers adorning the base of the 10th century Yunjusi pagoda

are also in a festive mood. These figures reflect the importance of dance in religion.

My friend from the Dance Research Institute, Professor Dong Xijiu, taught me how much we can learn from the ancient carvings. She pointed out that by looking at these dancers with their poses frozen in stone one could easily visualize the free lifestyle of the nomadic peoples of Northeast China who inhabited Beijing during the Liao and Jin periods. They loved to dance during their hunting on the grasslands. Looking at these carvings one can recreate the dances by assembling movements depicted on the pillars or found painted in tomb

murals. "We can see their unusual hats, tunics tied at the waist and high riding boots. They often danced in groups of three or in pairs," instructed Dong.

These chiseled figures allow us a peek into the celebrations of religious ceremonies, hear the rhythm of the drummers and feel the energy of the swirling dancers of ancient times. These aged stones give us a touch of their human spirit.

## Protecting the Buddha's Tooth Relic

Lingguangsi (Temple of Divine Light) is one of the eight temples of the scenic Badachu Park. It continues to be an active religious center. In 1997 the China Buddhist Association arranged for us to visit and view the famous tooth relic of the Buddha. It is housed in a rather new pagoda built especially to protect the treasure. The story I heard from a researcher made me appreciate the importance of the relic and why they had also chosen to maintain the broken Zhaoxian Ta (Pagoda for Inviting Immortals) in the temple precincts.

The Buddha's tooth relic was first enshrined in the original pagoda by the Liao emperor Daozong in the 11th century. The tooth's journey begins with the account that only two teeth of the Buddha Sakyamuni survived. One was sent to Sri Lanka and the other went first to Udyana in today's Pakistan and then was passed on to Khotan (Hetian) in Xinjiang. There it was found in the 5th century by the Chinese explorer Faxian who brought it back and placed it in a temple in Nanjing. Later the relic was transferred to Chang'an (Xi'an). Due to persecutions of Buddhism in the 9th century, it was whisked away to the safety of Northern China, finding a home in Yanjing (present-day Beijing) in the 10th century.

An aloes-wood box on which was written, "The Holy Tooth Relic of Sakyamuni Buddha", protected the tooth. This was sealed within a stone chest-casket and safely entombed under the base of the ten-storied pagoda built to glorify its treasure. Bas-relief carvings of flying *apsara*s, musicians and totemic masks, as well as bricks stamped with pagoda motifs, still embellish

its mossy facade.

Yet a sad irony of history awaited this pagoda. In 1900, the Boxer Rebellion brought the troops of Eight Nations to Beijing to protect their nationals and to fight against this anti-foreign movement. Indian troops were sent to this section of the Western Hills and in the course of the fighting, the upper stories of the pagoda were destroyed by Buddha's own countrymen. But the tooth was miraculously saved. Monks discovered the stone chest amid the rubble in the pagoda's basement. More than a half century later in 1964, a new 13-storied pagoda was built nearby the Liao ruins. The tooth is now encased within a glittering jewel-inlaid golden stupa.

After witnessing the afternoon prayer ceremony, then head monk, Yan Dao, explained the importance of the tooth. We took off our shoes and climbed the carpeted circular stairway inside the new pagoda to the second floor. Peering inside the small glass window of the golden stupa, we were amazed to see this gigantic 7 cm molar tooth. "They say Buddha was a big man and this confirms it," said Venerable Yan Dao. We stood in silence thinking of the miraculous survival of this relic through history. The tooth relic treasure continually attracts large groups of the faithful, who circumambulate both the old and new pagodas in a time-honored tradition of prayer.

*Unforgettable People*

# Monks Revitalize Ancient Music

Musicians carved on stone *dhanari* pillars and on facades of pagodas maintain the image of playing ancient instruments, as they would have been used in Buddhist rituals and festivals. One must go to a 15ᵗʰ century temple inside Beijing to actually hear the ancient tunes. Zhihuasi (Temple of Awakening Intellect) maintains its tradition of preserving Buddhist and court music.

The temple, though, was functioning as a light bulb factory when I first visited in 1983. Pressed between two crowded alleyways, the temple was surrounded by a high wall and definitely not

open to outsiders. Peering over the wall at the back, I could only see the wooden colonnaded porch of the second floor of the main hall with delicate lattice-work on the windows. Through a crack in the front gate, however, I spotted a pair of blooming lilac trees and managed to photograph several workers posing with them.

Originally this was the family temple of the eunuch Wang Zhen, Chief of Protocol to the Ming emperor Yingzong. Built in 1443, it became famous as a repository of ancient musical scores, which Wang Zhen introduced to the monks of his temple. They played a mixture of court, Buddhist and folk music, which evolved into a genre known as *Jing yinyue*, music that became very popular at court. To keep the secret of the music, each monk knew only the part for his instrument and passed that knowledge down to his student. This tradition of mystery continued for five centuries. Then the upheavals of the 20ᵗʰ century took their toll. The monks were dispersed during the Cultural Revolution.

I went back several months later. In my hand were photos of the workers and lilacs. That's when I got to know the restoration plans. Mr. Yang Wenshu, Ms. Xu Zhen, and Ms. Sun Suhua all had the daunting task of putting Zhihuasi back together again. It would take about ten years.

Mr. Yang instructed, "*Zhihua* was the eunuch's Buddhist name, meaning 'Awakening Intellect'." He also noted that the layout of the seven halls, though small in scale, went along the ancient imperial style. The black tiles also denoted a high rank. It is one of the finest examples of Ming architecture in Beijing.

In the summer of 1985 it had ceased to be a factory. I dropped by to see what was happening. They asked me to write an English sign advising visitors that it was not open to the public. Then I was given a full tour, a rare peek into the shambles of neglect this cultural treasure had endured. The Hall of the Scriptures was still occupied. Plates and towels cluttered the magnificent hexagonal scripture cabinet. On each of the some 360 drawers was a finely carved Buddha in relief. A wonderful cornucopia of Buddhist motifs were carved around the drawers.

The two-storied Hall of the 10,000 Buddhas at the back had a myriad of mini Buddha niches and storage space for over 5,000 sutras. Buddhist statues painted with great detail and even applied filigree stood under layers of dust. A visit to the second floor was weird. Here and there were death tablets of former monks of the temple. The ceiling had a large gaping hole in place of the famous sunken octagonal cupola, sold in the 1930s. In a corner were piles of cobwebbed cymbals and drums and other instruments, silenced for half a century. I thought at the time, would it ever be possible to hear them played?

In the summer of 1995, Zhihuasi was finally in pristine condition and I was invited to attend the graduation of newly trained musicians of the *Jing yinyue* music tradition. Sun Suhua took me to a seat in the Zhihua Hall. "Today you'll hear some melodies that probably date back to the 8th century, the music has really been well preserved in its original form."

The concert was performed by some of the former priests, the 27th generation of musicians, mostly 80 years of age. "They're living treasures," declared Sun, "we saved the music just before it almost went extinct!" These old masters were sharing their knowledge with students. The music began slow and gloomy. Nine musicians played an assemblage of flutes, small reeds, mouth organs, cymbals, drums and a nine-toned gong. Midway there was a quickening of tempo and the trance-like drone of the mouth organs was accentuated with the high pitch of the reeds and abrupt gongs. It finished with a slow rhythm, almost a dirge. We could actually hear the sounds of the flutes and drums, and know the tone of those unusual gongs, as they are set in the carvings of Beijing's aged stones.

# Stone and the Environment

## Rockeries

Stone has great value in landscape architecture, of course, as in the Japanese rock gardens or the use of the oddly shaped Lake Taihu stones in gardens around China. Rock appreciation in China has been around for a long time.

The rockeries at the Beihai Park are not just ornamental. Those unique rock sculptures have a story of their own. In researching the history of the Jin Dynasty, I learned that they were stolen in the 12th century from the Song capital of Kaifeng, at that time called Bianliang. A Jin Dynasty emperor took them as the spoils of war and added them to his Daninggong villa on the Jade Islet in what is today's Beihai Park. As a conquering tribe from the north, they were determined to match their capital of Zhongdu founded in 1153, with the sophisticated culture of the Song. Today these unique Lake Taihu stones still decorate the hill where the villa once stood.

The best-protected stones are on the slope behind the Fangshan restaurant. Normally I would just pass by a place like that, but the historical value made me give it another look. These porous stones, each having its own uniqueness, were assembled into this garden design more than 800 years ago. The cooks of the restaurant were sitting on some of the rocks having a smoke. They didn't seem to mind me climbing around and taking photos. Certainly they don't know these were stolen goods.

## Stones Mark Eunuchs' Paradise

Ming Dynasty eunuch Tian Yi was buried in an elaborate setting of stone tomb sculpture along the road of Moshikou, famous for the coal carrying camel trains west of the city. Larger than life warrior and scholar figures, a grand gate and tablet halls all of finely carved marble drained the funeral fund of the former head of protocol for the palace, Tian Yi, so that when he finally died in 1605, he was buried in only a simple dirt mound at the back. Later eunuchs, though, could utilize the same space and concentrate their funeral funds on just their own marble-covered tombs.

Another place closer to the city named Enjizhuang, Village of Imperial Favor, was also where Ming emperors gave land to retired eunuchs. The south part of the complex was a temple where retired eunuchs once worked as monks. In the back was their graveyard. When I visited the temple in the 1980s, it had become a rest house for army officers. Piles of cabbage and leeks covered the platform of the remaining hall.

The graveyard had also changed. It was a playground of the Haidian No. 61 Primary School. In 1985, a friendly caretaker took me to what looked like a park with two lines of pine trees. At the back was a mound covered with gnarled cypresses. This was the tomb of Li Lianying, the most infamous eunuch of the late Qing Dynasty, the favorite of the Empress Dowager Cixi. He died in 1911 at the age of 69, six months after

the Empress Dowager herself passed away. A trap door opened to a dark stairway. I followed the steps down to a damp corridor, but I only dared go part way. I saw no carvings, only slugs on the walls!

According to books of the 1920s, this site had already been desecrated by the troops of General Feng Yuxiang who smashed tombstones and cut down a number of the old trees. Yet the caretaker said most of statues and tombstones disappeared during the Cultural Revolution. At one time there were over 1,700 tombs from the Ming and Qing Dynasties, each with its own stone monolith, stone offering tables and incense burners. Supposedly, over 500 tablets remained in the 1950s, but I could only find a few.

Ten years after my first visit, the spot was totally unrecognizable. The land became the site for the 21st Century Experimental School and a tract of modern condominiums. One area, though, was left untouched. Li Lianying's tomb remained, with its pine tree walk and mound capped by cypresses. But no stone steles were to be seen at all and the trap door had disappeared.

One American teacher explained the situation. He pointed to a building where foreign teachers had offices and meeting rooms. It looked very swank. Actually, it was sitting right on top of what had been other eunuch graves and situated before the entrance to Li Lianying's tomb. This teacher, fortunately, protected a number of pieces of carved marble grave markers by moving them closer to the tomb. He recognized the need to deal with the altered environment and *fengshui* of the place. A mirror placed in the entrance, he was told, could ward off bad spirits. He knew they had better do something to pacify 1,700 eunuch souls. At least the voices of the happy children ringing in the air could give some comfort to those who never had children of their own.

## Sites of Silver Mountain

It is easy to see why the monks from ancient times chose Yinshan (Silver Mountain) as the site for a Buddhist monastery. Massive clusters of boulders and caves in the mountains also offered an unusual landscape. Three peaks rise above a cliff face, the color of iron, prompting the name "Iron Wall." Situated due north of the capital, the temple complex also fit into the overall scheme of the city's *fengshui*. The Iron Wall and its temples formed a protective shield against bad winds from the north.

Into this impressive setting add the work of monks who settled here from the Tang Dynasty. They built successive temple halls where flat land permitted. Like many other sites in the rural areas, they claim to have had 72 temples and convents. In the 1980s people were still growing crops around the pagodas. Stone steles and smaller pagodas were scattered about in broken

pieces. Still the setting was dramatic with the five Jin Dynasty pagodas standing tall amid the rubble of harvested fields.

Over the next ten years archaeologists gradually lifted the layers of history out from the earth in which they had survived below the ground. Foundation stones from the 12th century surfaced to show the layout of Longevity Temple, one of the great monasteries of the Jin Zhongdu capital. The digging revealed that the giant pagodas were actually built within the temple compound, as repositories for the ashes of the abbots. On a higher level above the temple, excavations also uncovered a stone platform where great monks once lectured on the scriptures.

Several paths around the central peak skirt huge boulders, some the size of automobiles; a small pagoda tops one while another has a carved Buddha. Others have small steps leading over their surface for the very bold. Looking down from near the peak, one can guess where the other temples might have been stood.

A local man, Mr. Liu, in his 70s, waved his hand pointing to a place beyond the hill in response to my inquiries about the remains of other sites. He instructed me to find a flat location below the Iron Wall and to look for a particular awe-inspiring boulder. If you also find a

spring, he advised, then you have likely hit upon the right spot.

Sure enough, Liu knew what he was talking about. In the shadow of a massive freestanding boulder at least two stories high, there was an area of land that had been used as terraced fruit orchards. But among the rocks of the terracing walls were carved stones from earlier usages. An old well, covered by heavy stone blocks, seemed dry, but water trickled into the nearby fruit groves. It was the runoff from the underground spring. This must be what Liu called Temple of the Iron Buddhas. But we'll have to see. The archaeologists must again sift through the lay-

ers to expose its past and lift its history back up to the top. But the big boulder was enough to convince me!

## "Be Careful of Stone-laden Trucks and Angry Mountains!"

Once these rural areas and mountains surrounding Beijing seemed so distant and expendable. Over the centuries rocks have been quarried to provide for building and rebuilding of the capital. Temple stones, steles, bridges, and images were all wrought from the neighboring mountains. But

as urban growth spreads out to these areas, there have sometimes been dire consequences for a number of the beautiful stone mountains and pathways still left around the city. This makes one wonder about what kind of legacy of stone will be left in the rural environs. Not just carved stones, but rocks and boulders too, are also deserving of protection under our environmental concerns.

One Sunday in the fall of 2001 our family took a drive north into Changping, getting off the expressway and weaving westward to the Baihujian (White Tiger Ravine) natural scenic area. It is a gorgeous mountain range and we looked forward to hiking in search of ancient sites in the area. Yet instead of an enjoyable outing, we were really shocked. We soon realized that was not going to be a nice quiet scenic walk in the fresh country air. We were barraged instead by the sound of rock cutters, not the chisel and hammer variety, but big machines on the move, big drills attacking stone boulders.

The beautiful ancient mountains were just eaten away! This range is particularly unique in its grand boulders and peaks of majestic beauty. But right here at the entrance to the nature zone, we were met with two mountainsides scraped away. In addition to the deep gashes on the mountains, boulders along the walking trail were cut open and carved away just like some slabs of meat. As we walked, trucks roared by laden with rocks from inside the nature zone itself. They sprayed us with fumes and dust while stealing

the soul of these gorgeous mountains. How could this happen?

Some say that a mountain or two will help the locals earn a living. These are the fine hard stones, a beautiful light brown hue, almost sandstone, that are being used in the new up-scale villas and expensive homes. But when will it end? Is there nothing sacred for future generations? How can one hide these gashes?

Walking out, we met a local resident and asked, "Do the trucks always dominate the road?" "Oh, come back in the spring," he requested. "The valley has beautiful flowers. The trucks will be stopped by then." "Oh, is that so?" I was amazed. He said that the dynamite blasting of the mountainside has been stopped. They were just taking away the already broken rocks.

And what happens next? No repairs? What about fitting the boulders still sitting there back into the crevices, back to the arms of the mountain, with some sort of crude cosmetic surgery? The man added that he loves this area and its beauty and he was saddened by what has happened, "sometimes we don't have enough power." At that moment an enormous piece of machinery turned the corner of the road inside the scenic area, like a giant orange praying mantis, the crane was tired from its day of rock lifting.

I went back again to the scenic zone a year later. Big machinery has stopped but the chipping goes on. The defaced mountains are a message for us to ponder on.

# Monumental Landscape Survives the Centuries

The mountains of Panshan on the eastern border of Beijing are famed for their five peaks, towering pines, large stones and natural springs. Once there were dozens of monasteries and convents, some dating back over 1,000 years. A grand garden once existed for the relaxation of imperial family members.

During World War II, the fiercest fighting against the Japanese occupying forces in the Beijing area took place here. The Battles of Panshan are etched in the minds of the elderly folk who still live here. In fact, that is the first thing they talk about when asked why all the monasteries on the mountain were destroyed. At the foot of the mountain is the Cemetery of Revolutionary Martyrs where school children learn about the war and scamper around a sea of large boulders known locally as the "anti-Japanese battle ground."

Many of the temple halls on Panshan have been rebuilt and designated as a tourist develop-ment area. Monks have returned and incense burns again before newly carved statues. Lying outside of the designated area, though, was another of the Panshan temples, Qianxiangsi (Temple of a Thousand Images). The name suggests it may have resembled a temple hall with many images standing in a row. There was a general belief among scholars in Beijing that nothing remains of this fabulous temple built 1,000 years ago.

It was really surprising, then, when a farmwoman announced to me matter-of-factly that her old abandoned family home was on the temple grounds. The woman, Piao Huiqin, 50, is of Korean ancestry. She had been busy sorting the family's crop of walnuts and dried crabapples in her front yard, but soon was leading me up a dirt track behind her present home.

After about 20 minutes the path wound its way around clusters of great boulders that covered the mountainside. Ms. Piao stopped for a moment and pointed to a faint figure scratched on the

surface. It looked like a standing Buddha. The next boulder had more faded ancient carvings. "They all used to have Buddhas or Bodhisattvas on them," said Piao continuing to climb up the slope. She said only about 100 of these fine line drawings could still be discerned. It then became apparent that each rock was in fact representing a Buddha or group of Bodhisattvas. She passed her fingers over the chiseled rock of another black granite boulder, "You can't see it very well, but you can feel that the image is still there."

These were in fact the thousand images and all the rocks together formed a giant outdoor temple of sacred stones. This monumental landscape is like some massive installation art. Yet the setting was marred by a number of boulders cut for stone housing blocks. With residential development creeping up the valley, it is in danger of falling victim to the modern age.

"There's where I was born," Ms. Piao said, pointing to a weathered farmhouse built amid the rubble of what had been temple halls destroyed in the war. "We had to move down to the village when the well dried up eight years ago," she added. A few scattered stone steles, one from 987 A.D., kept the written history of the site. Even though the halls were gone, the panorama of the hundreds of great rocks confirmed that the Stonehenge-like essence of the Temple of a Thousand Images was very much in place.

III. Nourishing

# Water Resources

# III. Nourishing Water Resources

No one lays flowers on the grave of water, for it is not here, it is gone. (R. Bly)

# Introduction

## Ancient Water Reserves

When I first came here to live in the 1980s, I had never thought of Beijing as a city of inter-connecting canals. I had never tasted spring water from the Western Hills. In those days, most deep-water sources were out-of-bounds; the canals clogged up beyond recognition. Rivers downstream were polluted, hardly an incentive to learn their names. But it is the very angle of water that allows one to understand the city's history and development. In my case, it was the temples and shrines that I was researching, which led me to study and explore their relationship with water.

As Beijing fights encroaching desertification and as the growing population increases its demand for water, the importance of the city's water resources has become a topic of great con-

cern to all. Obsession with water has been around since the time when Beijing first became a capital city in the Liao Dynasty. The Qidan rulers and the later Jurchen, Mongol, Han, Manchu and modern day leaders who followed have throughout Beijing's history of urban development tried to ensure proper water resources.

The Beijing plain was once a marshland left when the sea retreated from this region. Rivers are plentiful. But floods in the past were disasters, giving an impetus to build dykes for protection and shrines to calm the water spirits. The city grew around natural ponds such as Lianhuachi, and the city's central lakes were created by expanding the southern flow of the Gaoliang River.

Stone aqueducts siphoned off water from important springs in the Western Hills and from the northern Baifu weir, directing it into the capital. Spring water was prized and temples and imperial camps were built at their sites. Wells, too, were vital for they could be dug almost anywhere. So as the city expanded, these wells provided the growing population with neighborhood water sources. It is thought that the word *hutong* (alley) comes from the Mongolian word *hotlog*, meaning "well." Each lane had its well, thus *hutong* gradually referred to the alleyway itself. However, Beijing's well water was generally known for its bitter taste and a sweet mildtasting well soon became famous.

Canals were built to connect rivers, especially

the Yongding River, providing water for the moats and as transportation routes. The discovery of the remains of a Jin (Kin) Dynasty water gate in today's Fengtai District has helped us understand the sophisticated structure of these conduits. Water flowed through these gates into the Liangshui River, the Jin capital's southern moat.

Most important was the construction of waterways to connect with the Grand Canal to the

east. These provided the capital their link with South China for the supply of grains and silk. Coal, stones and lumber were also distributed along their routes. A number of these canals still exist and are recently being re-dredged. Leisure boats now ply their waters.

On the other hand, over development and exploding population has made the water situation of Beijing critical. A thousand years ago, the Beijing area was a lush forest. But massive logging over wide areas for the building of the Jin Dynasty Zhongdu and the following Mongol capital of Dadu, greatly affected Beijing's climate and water supply. Deep underground water reserves have been tapped over the centuries, but the water table has been sinking. In times of sparse precipitation, shrines to pray to the Dragon King for rain flourished.

By studying the historical uses of water in the Beijing area, we can better insure ways of environmental protection. The following encounters are how I have learned to appreciate these various water sources.

## Scouting Beijing by Rubber Boat

The story of the Empress Dowager Cixi going by boat to the Summer Palace was one of the first interesting things that I heard about the waterways of Beijing. But in the 1980s, most of the canals were poorly kept

up and seldom used. Large grates regularly stood as barriers, naturally collecting trash, making the route seemingly impassable. Most foreigners, therefore, were not aware that the city had connecting water systems.

I was determined, though, to check out just how the imperial boat entourages navigated those waterways. It seemed an elegant way to float through the city. All I needed was a boat. With the encouragement of friends, two rubber boats were contributed to this whimsical expedition and it finally got underway on a hot muggy day in June 1986. I had a map of sorts, but my idea was to begin at the center and find the connections as we went along.

The start was unusual. Our deflated rafts draped over the marble balustrades of a bridge within the Imperial Palace. It was a symbolic gesture of a take off along the Jinsuihe (Golden River) to connect with the surrounding moats. At that time the Jinsuihe had very little water. Moving to the moat off Zhongshan Park we placed our dinghies on the rented boats, but rowing was limited to a set area. It wasn't very elegant, but the high rusty red walls of the Forbidden City were behind us and we could imagine what it meant to get out from behind those walls.

From the moat, the waterway passed under a road so there was no choice but to take the boats and enter the Beihai (North Sea Lake) carrying them in through the east gate. This time we were determined to row our own boats. However, the

keeper of the boat dock wasn't happy as we pumped up our crafts to full size. We tried our best to explain that we just wanted to go straight across for research, not leisure paddling.

A group of our supporters pushed us off from the pier. The white pagoda's reflection shimmered in the water as our royal entourage of two rowed across the lake. Finally we felt we were on our journey. I

Summer Palace

I threw my head back and drifted, enjoying the great expanse of sky above. What a rude awakening it was to see the boat-dock man an-

Gaoliang Bridge

grily waiting with a policeman standing beside him! We smiled and waved. Fortunately, the policeman thought it was amusing and helped us on to shore. We lifted the wet boats on our backs and walked out. The boat keeper was certainly not amused.

Still lugging the boats overhead, we crossed the street leaving dripping prints on the pavement, much to the amazement of cyclists who came to a standstill. Our destination was Qianhai (Front Sea Lake). This time nobody stopped our launching. Paddling north for the Drum Tower, however, we ran into widespread webs of lotus plants covering the surface, becoming so entangled that it took an exhausting hour to get through. I am sure the royals must have had their passageway cut in advance.

The lovely arched marble Yinding Bridge crosses over the narrow neck leading into Houhai (Rear Sea Lake). At that time a grate

blocked the way. Out came the boats again. This time as we dipped into the water we were met with loud hoots from fishermen complaining we were scaring off the fish. By carefully circumventing the fishing lines, we did manage to row to the end where the passage was again blocked.

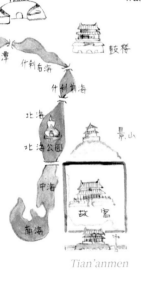

Tian'anmen

The next of the consecutive lakes, Jishuitan (Water Accumulating Pool), was a terribly littered pond then, so we had to exit early before we reached the old water gate by the hillock at the far end. I was saddened to see the beautiful landscape marred in this way. At this juncture we broke our journey, lugging the boats home.

We ventured out again the next day. My map showed the route of the canal going through the deep trench along the second ring road and making a hairpin turn through a restricted unit (now a route for sight-seeing water excursions). It resurfaced at the Gaoliang Bridge. Constructed by the Mongols and later restored, this bridge is an old landmark of the city. It stood next to the North railway station. High-rise apartments were going up on both banks of the Chang River, the name of this section of the canal.

Our boats launched from the grassy bank and we took off again going behind the Beijing Exposition Hall. Rowing west proceeding along the back wall of the zoo, an old village

spread along on the north bank. (It would later be replaced by today's aquarium.) Drifting by the Five Pagoda Temple, we saw piles of old stone slabs lying around before its front gate. West of that, we reached the well-known landmark, Baishiqiao (White Stone Bridge). A fisherman gave us friendly advice not to try to row under it.

From there the waterway cuts through Zizhuyuan (Purple Bamboo Park), an important ancient water source of Beijing. Long willow trees and bamboo thickets lined the canal. Today there is a modern lock that allows boats to pass through to the higher waters on the west. In the 1980s, though, several fixed locks guarded

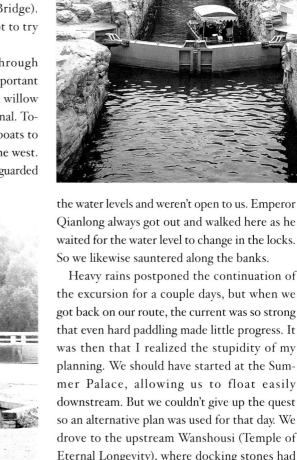

the water levels and weren't open to us. Emperor Qianlong always got out and walked here as he waited for the water level to change in the locks. So we likewise sauntered along the banks.

Heavy rains postponed the continuation of the excursion for a couple days, but when we got back on our route, the current was so strong that even hard paddling made little progress. It was then that I realized the stupidity of my planning. We should have started at the Summer Palace, allowing us to float easily downstream. But we couldn't give up the quest so an alternative plan was used for that day. We drove to the upstream Wanshousi (Temple of Eternal Longevity), where docking stones had allowed Cixi to debark here to spend the night. Our boats sailed quickly as we let ourselves be

taken along by the current in a reverse direction back toward the Purple Bamboo Park.

Skimming recklessly with the fast flowing water, we careened under the bridge of the Guangyuan locks, decorated with sculptured dragon faces, flood-subduing beasts, scowling down on us. My friend Michael Crook explained that dragons facing upstream are rather fierce, often with horns and a big snout. They seem to order the water to calm down. But the dragon on the other side has a different look. Usually with no horns and a very

short nose, this mellow beast facing downstream has a different appeal to the water, "don't go dry" it seems to beg. A little Dragon King Shrine stands close by, so one may offer prayers that the dragons keep to their duties.

Back to paddling upstream again, we went by the relics of Maizhong Bridge. Later, in 1999 a new bridge was built next to the exposed foundations of the old one. A 1639 stele once stood there. Part of its inscription reads as follows (translated by M. Crook):

> *Rowing the oar, we work our way upstream to the*
> *Western Lake*
> *A fresh breeze blows and all across the sky are clouds*
> *like wisps of silk*
> *What joy to see the crops on either bank a lush*
> *oil-green*
> *We pass repeatedly by stone bridges beyond the walls*
> *I ask you: could all years be as good as this?*

There was a lot of action along the banks. Some people were washing clothes, others fished with large nets, one young man was washing his trumpet, and a group of kids splashed around to avoid the heat. With the white stone balustrades now lining both sides, that kind of public use of the waterways has diminished. Of course in Imperial China, washing ones hands in the waters was even forbidden.

The waterway then meets up with the Miyun canal. Myriads of Peking ducks were being raised along its route. It seemed every village along the waterway in those days was in the duck business.

As the enormous hunchbacked bridge of white marble came into sight, many friends had gathered to watch the final leg of our fanciful journey. Cameras were clicking as we passed under the bridge and floated up to the grate blocking entrance into Kunming Lake. Everybody cheered, even people who didn't know us. For this was our destination and we swished about with a sense of accomplishment.

Our dinghies were deflated so as not to raise suspicions of the Summer Palace guards and we hung them over the railing by Cixi's famed Marble Boat. We looked out on the lake as she had done, enjoying the verdant images of the Western Hills.

The trip to find Beijing's old watercourse will always be indelible on my mind. Such a crazy adventure would never be allowed now because the canals are tourist attractions. But the trip by rubber boat stirred my interest in the history of Beijing's waterways.

For my 57th birthday party in 2001, I rented a dragon-style boat to cruise along the rebuilt

canal. Good friends sang and recited poetry against the background of *pipa* music. We passed the places where I struggled to paddle against the current fifteen years earlier. And I recalled as we drifted along the old waterway: "I ask you: could all years be as good as this?"

*Unforgettable People*

# Surviving Heirlooms of the Lakes of Sundry Temples

The Shichahai (Lakes of Sundry Temples) refers to three narrow and connected lakes in central Beijing. The place is popular for fishing and strolling along the banks. On this day in early June of 1997, dangling branches of willow trees almost dipped in the water.

At the very western end is a hillock with a small shrine commemorating canals, Huitongci. It is dedicated to the memory of the great engineer and inventor of the late 13th century, Guo Shoujing. Guo was also a water conservancy expert who developed the water system for the city, the then Mongol capital of Dadu. Barges used to bring rice and other goods from southern China via connected waterways from the Grand Canal into the Shichahai. It was a busy commercial center. But in the later Ming Dynasty the watercourses were expanded to make these small lakes look like scenery from South China with finely carved marble bridges. Homes for court officials and small temples were built around the lake.

The shrine is also a meeting place of the Beijing Shichahai Historical and Cultural Preservation Society. Zhou Zhongqing, Director of the Society, was in an upstairs room engaged in discussion with his friend, Professor Hou Renzhi, the renowned historical geographer of Beijing University. The talk of these two elderly gentlemen focused on Beijing's water systems.

Getting out the map, Hou pointed to the Shichahai Lakes and traced the ancient water course that flows from the north, "The canals have to make several turns to get the water flowing, because sometimes water has to cross higher land and without the momentum it would never make it down to the city."

He showed how the water of the Forbidden City is connected through this series of waterways, to Kunming Lake in the northwest. Spring water of the Western Hills used to feed into the lake from many directions. "There's even an ancient aqueduct out by the Fragrant Hills that brought spring water into the system. I excavated the site, and found the stone basins. This was once an important deep water source. Unfortunately it dried up."

Professor Hou, 86 then, lamented the growing difficulties of preserving Beijing's ancient water system. "Our water sources must be kept!" he exclaimed. "When they recently built the western train station, for example, I had to argue to preserve the nearby Lotus Pond. Well, I finally convinced them that the natural setting would actually enhance the neighborhood."

Mr. Zhou shares the concern with water, especially with regard to sustaining the Shichahai Lakes. He has been a leading crusader to preserve the traditional neighborhood of old courtyard houses, alleys and the once popular sundry temples. "No one can tell you exactly which of the many temples here were considered part of the original group." We went outside and from the hillock Zhou pointed out various rooftops; the temples' glazed tiles and architecture differentiated them from surrounding houses. Only the Guanghua Temple remains whole. The rest maintain only small parts of their former compounds. The Gaomiao (High Temple) by the hospital is a plastics factory. The Shichahai Temple is someone's house. Another one is a school for the hearing impaired. The #184 Vocational Junior High School is also on temple grounds. Zhou then pointed to a fairly intact temple next door. "That's the Shrine of Three Officials, it's Taoist."

Mr. Zhou recounted, "First the city walls right behind here were destroyed in the 1960s. Then in the early 1980s, this hill and the little shrine on top of it were torn down to make a subway station. It was a mess. Our neighborhood was changing so fast. That's when I started a campaign to see if the hill and temple couldn't be rebuilt."

"We were at the lakeside Roast Mutton Restaurant," recalled Zhou, "and ten of us wrote a letter to the mayor of Beijing. That's how this Society got started." Professor Hou added, "Mr. Zhou thoroughly researched the history of this place. Thanks to him everyone can enjoy this shrine and view from the hill."

The group acts as cultural watchdogs for the neighborhood. "We must begin with our own district. Each place needs a proper marker to identify its historical importance," Zhou said. These two men looked at each other in mutual admiration. They have seen so many changes in their beloved city. But they both are determined to keep pressing for preservation. I will never forget this day with these two distinguished gentlemen and the inspiration I felt from the dignity with which they shared their principles and knowledge. Finally, as Zhou Zhongqing nodded his head in agreement, Professor Hou declared, "We have to leave something, both cultural relics and good water, for future generations."

# *Dragons and Fengshui*

## Emperors Pray for Rain

Praying for rain was one of the imperial duties of all the emperors. The Dragon King shrine located on Huameishan Hill near an important spring was frequented by the nobility in times of drought. Built in the late 15ᵗʰ century, it received imperial patronage over many centuries to honor the spirit of the Dragon King and the water of its

Black Dragon Pool and three wells. There are four steles commemorating imperial visits. For me, one of the most moving steles is the 1798 one by Emperor Qianlong when he was 88 years old. That is because this tablet gives some personal insight into the imperial family and their responsibilities.

On this visit to the shrine he brought his son, the new Emperor Jiaqing, to teach him the importance of prayers at this site. Recalling his own

and prayed to show my respect for the Dragon spirit." It is rare for an imperial inscription to have such personal words. It is signed and sealed "Taishang Huangdi" (Emperor Emeritus).

Qianlong had his own way of dealing with a difficult dragon. He threatened the Dragon King with banishment to the northeast, and even removed his statue to begin his ouster, when rains finally fell. They both saved face

memories as a child, he told about coming to this place to pray for rain for the well-being of the nation. He remembered, too, that when he was a young emperor, he briskly climbed the three flights up to the Hall of Prayer to the Dragon King at the top. But this time he was elderly and a palanquin has brought him up here. "Even though I am almost ninety and tired, I felt I should come here." That year there were two rains, so he thought he didn't have to come. The stele notes the first two rainfalls amounted to six *cun* each. But the long drought after the 15th of the second Lunar month made it necessary to call on the good offices of the Dragon King for help.

"It is almost *Lixia* (beginning of summer)," he wrote, "and farmers really need rain." Thus he brought the new emperor to teach him the importance of this visit. In his words, "I told my son, 'You must take care of the farmers.'" Qianlong also added, "At the top hall I bowed

when Emperor Qianlong bestowed a high rank on him, entitling the temple to imperial yellow tiles.

I have visited this shrine three times over seventeen years, but it has always been closed to the public and there were no other visitors. Each time it was a challenge to convince the gatekeeper to let me in. I then could climb up the three flights and gaze down at the water in the Black Dragon Pool. But the Hall of Prayer to the Dragon King was closed with a heavy padlock. The water spirit, it seems, hasn't been given much attention lately, even during these years of drought.

## Exploring the Almost Forgotten Baifu Weir

Clear water rushes along the Jingmi canal north of the city. It was along these same canal systems that the Yuan Dynasty capital of Dadu received its water from a plentiful and clear spring, famed as the Baifu Spring. Mathematician, astronomer and statesman Guo Shoujing (1231-1316) created the system to meet the growing demand for water in the bustling new capital of the Mongols. The spring flowed out from a 150-meter-high hill on the plains north of Beijing. The canals that Guo designed for the Mongols continue to serve as conduits bringing water to the city, but they don't originate from this spring anymore.

Rather, Beijing drinking water flows from the Miyun dam much further to the east.

I was curious to see what had become of the famous Baifu weir in today's Beijing, so I headed for the village of Baifu in November of 2001, not knowing what to expect. All I knew was to look for two hills that stood next to each other on the plain. They are respectively the Dragon Hill, which contains the spring, and the nearby Phoenix Hill. One wouldn't take a second glance at these small hills unless one was purposely searching for the remains of their famous springs.

It now seems a forgotten place of history. A

① Baifu Weir
② Yuan Dadu
③ Yan, Old Capital
④ Grand Canal
⑤ Chaobai R.
⑥ Hun R. (Yongding R.)

high wall encloses the entire base of the tree-covered Dragon Hill. One gate leads to a deer antler medicine factory. Another old rusty gate leads to an abandoned summer villa. Trucks carrying gravel and sand from the adjoining pits encircled the hill with deep rutted tracks. It was not exactly the image of a lush spring.

The only possible entrance had to be that rusty gate. Standing before it I almost gave up the search, as the gate seemed so desolate and a fat lock and chain gave a finality of not wanting to open. Fortunately, a caretaker napping in the gatehouse was amazingly friendly and obligingly opened the creaky gate. Before he could change

his mind, I swiftly entered and took the closest track up the hill.

The path wound around to the northern side. There, almost forgotten in the midst of a wild overgrowth of grasses and trees, was the Nine Dragon Spring Pavilion. Poking out across the base of the pavilion were nine dragon heads of white marble, their open mouths the spigots for spring water. One could easily visualize how water had once gushed forth into the aptly named Nine Dragon Pond below. The Nine Dragon siblings, famous in Chinese mythology, all came together here. But they no longer spew out any water. The pond is now just a swampy

stagnant pool.

By the abandoned summer villa two stone pillars marked the path to the hilltop temple. I fol-

lowed it through a dense forest of pine and cypress. Wild rose bushes were blooming in the thickets. Slivers of prickly wild plants and thorns stuck painfully in my socks.

This Dragon King Temple of the Capital was where the commoners of the plains north of Beijing came to pray for rain. A small gate still has partial dragon-embossed tiles decorating its roof. Stepping into the abandoned courtyard, a few birds fluttered off and then it was quiet. Three standing tablets recorded this temple's important spiritual functions. The Hall of the Dragon King, covered by the wash of time, had

only a partial roof, but yellow imperial rank tiles hinted at better days. Inside, beams had fallen down in disarray. Faint wall paintings peeked through a veil of dust. The marble statue of the Dragon King was gone. Two old trees in front seemed bold as bodyguards because their strong condition was such a contrast to the broken temple.

With the desert coming so close to the outskirts of the capital, this spot seems all the more important as a symbol of how water resources were duly respected. Looking at the hill from a distance, it seems more impressive to me now, a place worthy of recognition. Keep a lookout for it when speeding toward Badaling Great Wall.

## Looking for Dragons on a Day of Mourning

Crowds gathered for the Lantern Festival in Yanqing, a town in the northwest corner of Beijing municipality. People from the surrounding countryside came dressed in their best clothes on this day, February 21, 1997. But the usual drums for the farmer's dancing and cheers for the stilt walkers were quiet. It was the 15th of the First Moon when Yanqing usually has its most important festival to commemorate the full moon at the end of the two week lunar Spring Festival. Yet everything was subdued, for this was the second day of mourning for Chinese popular leader Deng Xiaoping. However, the peasants of this agricultural and mining area north of the Great Wall came into town despite the cancellation of their annual fair. Milling around the streets or gathered in restaurants, the crowds seemed reticent. Nonetheless, hawkers were still pushing the usual New Year's fare of candied fruit. Paper lanterns and toy windmills hung everywhere. On one corner an entrepreneur captured the market in the sale of the round sweet dumplings (like the full moon).

A part of Yanqing's ancient mud wall still remains by the north gate. Just beyond that is a hillock with a small temple perched on top. It's dedicated to the town's protective deity, the Dragon King. Nowhere has desertification hit more harshly than Yanqing County. A dragon king here means only one thing: to pray for rain and plenty of it. One has to scramble up as many of the steps are missing. But bright red New Year's couplets around the gate signaled that it is not totally abandoned. The caretakers, Mr. Zhan and Ms. Zhang, are a couple who have both lost their right hands in mining accidents, but the disability has not prevented them from taking on this 15th century temple's restoration and decorating the place with their fine calligraphy.

The statues that had once stood in the main hall have never been replaced since they were destroyed in 1946. In place of the statues, the

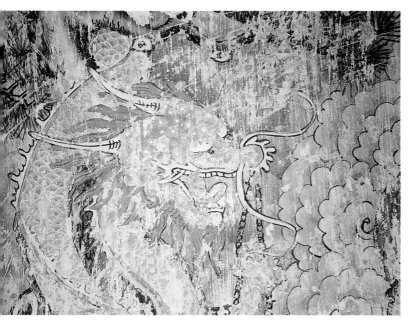

of Buddha, Confucius and Laotze. Mr. Zhan explained, "In China one is born a Taoist, is raised in the Confucian way and is dependent on Buddha for guidance to Heaven after death." He respects them all and studies their philosophies and prays to them respectively. Forty-year-old Zhan took up painting after quitting his job in a coal mine and sold scrolls to tourists at the Great Wall. But now he concentrates on being counselor to his community. "Many parents ask me to give guidance to their children, or others want advice on health problems." His serious demeanor quickly broke into an infectious smile. "I decided my road by myself and I study the three philosophies by myself. It is important to overcome the association with superstitions," Zhan emphasized, "We must share these philosophies to help the ethics of the people." They see the renewal of the Dragon King Temple as a benefit to their community. The Dragon King, in a sense, has become a symbol in the yearning for a better environment, for an assured water supply and control of water sources.

His wife noted that last year Zhan looked like a Taoist with long hair, but this year he shaved and is more Buddhist. Look for Mr. Zhan at the Yanqing Lantern Festival, he will probably sport a long beard to emulate, in turn, Confucius, or will he be a Dragon King?

couple have written the names of popular deities in large characters and let those represent the focus of worship. A candle and several sticks of incense burned before the words of "Dragon King" and "Heavenly Mother." Dragons outlined in gold curl around the rafters. Colorful wall murals depict the adventures of the Nine Dragon Kings. "It took us three days to clean the dirt off the paintings," noted the wife Zhang. In the courtyard, she pointed to gaping holes on the roof ridge where dragon heads once sat astride the tiles. "This place was almost totally wrecked," she stated flatly, adding cheerfully, "We'll restore it bit by bit."

In their apartment nearby is a large painting

## Villagers Still in Awe of *Fengshui*

A 1912 map drawn by a Belgian engineer, working railroad construction around Beijing, depicts the geological formations and cultural relics of a valley southwest of the capital. An interesting aspect of this map was the way the hillsides followed the meandering path of rivers to give Tiankai Valley a magnificent *fengshui*, or good geomancy. Since ancient times such land formations have helped determine good locations for building cities and tombs. The Tiankai River curves its way down from the northwest, crossing below Tiankai Village, said to be the only village with that name, as I mentioned earlier. The river then bends south after the Black Dragon Pool, where it passes through another village called Mouth of the Dragon Gate, and turns due east. The Shangfang Mountains form a protective barrier to the north for the perfect *fengshui*.

Chen Yushan, 64, born and raised in Tiankai Village, spun around on his motorbike and asked if he could help me. He's a business coordinator for the village, checking on properties and fixing up deliveries of goods for this community of 2,000 inhabitants. He was full of stories about the history of the valley.

"People who live here have the protection of the three mountains and the water doesn't escape," he lectured. This was in reference to the surrounding hills which form a small circle protecting an almost hidden valley with only three passes, making them feel secure. Unfortunately, the area has experienced six years of drought. The original riverbed is dry partially due to the dam upriver, ponds have shrunk, and some wells now barely reach the water table.

He led the way to the Big and Small Black Dragon Pools. "They're really low and so polluted," he explained, "It's not good for people, but our sheep still drink this water." He said locals mostly plant fruit trees, as they don't demand much water. On the hill above is the last impressive relic of the area, the Tiankai Pagoda dating from the 12th century. But it is now in a poor state of repair and badly weathered. "Archaeologists found a trove of Buddhist treasures under it in 1990," Chen continued, "including a large stone casket." It was Spring Festival vacation and many local children were climbing up the pagoda and exploring the interior where wooden beams and inner brick supports are exposed. "There used to be figures in the niches," Chen explained, "and there were carvings on the outside, too."

"Legend has it that Emperor Qianlong visited here," Mr. Chen related. China's famous 18th century ruler used the imagery of calligraphy to identify the Tiankai Pagoda as a brush, the Big Black Dragon Pool as the paper, and the hill on the opposite side as the ink stone. A small shrine dedicated to the Dragon King used to stand beside the river. Now there is only a cornfield. "During the Cultural Revolution, the images of the Dragon King and the stone stele were broken," Chen said. Only the ruins of the 800-year temple wall and memories of the four-day festival remain.

"See those two elongated ridges?" he asked, pointing. "They are imaginary dragon heads and guardians of our valley, but a developer from southern China came and cut the mountain for a new road. It ruined the *fengshui*." He added, "If this hadn't happened, there surely would have been a high official coming from our village."

Chen had his own theories about why the water table level has dropped. "In the old days, our dragons were partly submerged in water, and dragons have to be near water!" The eight wells dug near the village don't seem to have been enough. "We had to put rain water tanks on the symbolic dragon heads last year," he said in all seriousness, shaking his head.

Yet there is hope. "There are rumors that the new waterway bringing water from south China to Beijing will pass through here," Chen said enthusiastically. He knows that for good *fengshui* of Tiankai Village to return, the dragon heads have to be near water.

# Brick Pagoda Memorializes the Dragon's Tail of Beijing

Four giant ornate gates used to stand at Xisi intersection, one of the most historically important junctions in Beijing. The gates were torn down in the 1960s, but it is still a busy spot. Curiously, one aged edifice, an 800-year brick pagoda, still stands nearby. Hidden among a clutter of small shops and cramped housing surrounding it at the back, it is easy to miss the tower standing nearly 16 meters. Only by going through a nondescript wooden door and negotiating a maze of narrow alleys is it possible to get close to the pagoda.

It is practically overlooked except that the name of the nearby lane is Brick Pagoda Alley. This pagoda is actually the grave of the Buddhist monk Xing Xiu (1166-1246), also known fondly by his nickname "Wansong Laoren", Old Man of Ten Thousand Pines. He was an influential scholar and a leading philosopher of the Pure Land school of Buddhism. Xing Xiu had a reputation for mixing ideas from Taoism, Zen, Huayuan Buddhism and Confucian teachings.

Lian Chonghou, 54, his wife Ms. Yang Naiyun, 49, and their college age son live beside the pagoda. Lian was born at this intersection and has occupied his small two-room home for over 30 years. In a sense he is the ultimate Beijinger. He rolls his "r's", typical of Beijing dialect, and raises crickets in earthenware jars, a common pastime in days gone by. Even when the weather has turned cold, the crickets at Lian's house still sing. He has separate jars for each cricket and they are only brought together for a match. "The one who chirps is the winner," declared Lian as one of his crickets chirped loudly after a short bout with his challenger of the neighboring jar. But he raises them mostly just to hear their singing, rather than as fighters.

The window in front of their couch looks right out onto the

drab grey bricks of the pagoda. "When the devastating earth-quake in Tangshan occurred in 1976," he recalled, "the big ball on the top of the pagoda fell down. We all ran out to look and found lots of smaller balls inside." Lian and his wife know its history well. "The monk was the teacher of the great politician of the early Yuan (Mongol) period, Yelü Chucai," remarked Lian. Supposedly, when the monk died, Yelü had his mentor's ashes buried in this stupa in his own garden. The nine-storied octagonal pagoda soon became a landmark. It was known as an important part of Beijing's *fengshui*, representing the tail of the city's imaginary dragon, whose body was the walls of the city, the Golden River worked as veins to convey *qi*, the gates serving as the beast's eyes, ears and nose while the former Twin Pagodas were the horns.

The Old Man of Ten Thousand Pines insisted that a boulder be put under the central arch of the Marco Polo Bridge to keep the river from overflowing. This was done to symbolically quell the angry river demon. The emperor heeded his words and the monk carved a sword on the bridge's central arch inscribing the characters "Exterminate the Dragon Sword." The bridge has survived to this day.

Lian pulled up a ladder and climbed up onto the roof of one of the brick huts in the courtyard. Then he leapt across to the roof of his son's room, and in a moment he was standing alongside the second floor of the pagoda looking down. "All the neighbors once drew water from the well under this pagoda. There's a door on that side of the first floor, but it was locked up almost 30 years ago." Lian and Yang will have to move soon. The neighborhood is slated for development and a park is planned to surround the pagoda. Their house will be razed and the bicycle shop, bridal store and milk shop in front will be torn down, taking away the clutter of many decades. At last the pagoda representing the "dragon's tail" will again dominate the Xisi intersection, but the stories of its history will still need to be preserved by true Beijingers like Lian and Yang.

# Surrounding Rivers

## A River Town and Its Old Road

Sanjiadian, west of metropolitan Beijing, was once a well-known coal merchant's town. Located where the Yongding River comes out from its containment in the mountains and pours forth into the open plains, this small town has often been affected by the whims of the river. Main Street of the "old town", only 2 km long, begins at the river. When I first visited here in 1995, deep ruts scared the dirt road, but its recent pavement has brought a bit of respectability back to this community with a long history.

Beautifully carved doorways above portico-style entrances to a number of homes along the street speak of better times for this little town. As a large coal distribution center with more than 150 thriving family businesses, it was prosperous for more than 200 years. Coal was the gold from the mountains of Mentougou and the merchants of Sanjiadian were the middlemen, getting the coal transported into the city.

The town was not only once a center of trade, but also a way stop for travelers and pilgrims on the western highway to Beijing. This small hamlet provided temples where the pilgrims could offer prayers as part of their religious trek. Though no longer used as places of worship, they still keep a bit of the town's history.

The neighborhood association has its offices inside the Convent of the White-Robed Goddess of Mercy. The committee

head, a middle-aged lady, came with keys to open the locked gate. She noted it had been a hideout for one of the Boxer leaders in the 1900 uprising. "During its festival on the 29th of the second lunar month the temple grounds were once packed with visitors." The central hall was now decorated with "one child only" posters, quite appropriate at this shrine to the protector of children.

A stele at the back courtyard referred to the repairing of the road and the nearby bridge. The inscription from 1872 reads, "This road is important for the transportation of coal to Beijing for heat and cooking. Last year due to heavy rains in summer and autumn, the river flooded and the street was damaged in more than 30 places. Many people contributed to this reconstruction." One could imagine the quagmire caused by the flooding. Sensibly, the homes along the street all have high foundations.

At the western end of the street, at a crucial juncture of road and river, the Temple of the Dragon King has stood for centuries to placate the spirits of the often swollen and violent waters. It's a small enclosure of just one courtyard, but its guardian dragons on the roof, grand old tree and connected double gate made it unique at a glance. I got in from the back through a neighbor's garden and waited until the gatekeeper agreed to let me into the hall.

Inside were five statues, each representing an element: fire, water, earth, metal and wood. Mural paintings depicted legends of the dragon king and his siblings. Two stele inscriptions emphasized the importance of the shrine to the well being of the citizens. I asked the gatekeeper how the temple and statues had survived all the upheavals. He replied, "This place was the local headquarters for the water administration board for more then 100 years."

Sanjiadian is rich in historical sites, but they need attention. I hope that in the future some inspired urban planner will restore the stately merchant courtyard houses, keep the precious trees, open the temples and make the road of Sanjiadian a pedestrian walk through time. Don't worry about the river; the five dragons are still in charge!

# Vestiges of a Vanished Canal and River Dykes

S team was rising out from the giant water coolers inside the Shougang Steel Factory at the far west end of urban Beijing. On that June day of 1997, I was excited to get into this compound, not really to see facilities, rather to visit a small hill within its precincts, known as Stone Scripture Hill. Several temples have stood on top of the hill for centuries. An employee, Song Jinglun, took me around to see the ruins and one restored temple. But most importantly what I saw was the wide bed of the Yongding River far below. The fact that so many temples in the vicinity were built to placate the troublesome spirit of the river, testifies to its frequent flooding over the years.

Song pointed out the railroad tracks below. In fact, the tracks followed an old canal bed built 800 years ago in Jin (Kin) times. He explained that as the river comes out of its mountain gorge, it spills on to the open plain with a great force of freedom from its mountain restraints. The tumbling waters hit the first curve of the river with such a ferocity that the Jin rulers tried to harness this energy and siphon off the powerful flow into a canal leading into the capital and all the way due east to the Grand Canal.

This canal was known as the Jinkouhe, Golden Mouth River. We could see exactly where flood-gates had once controlled its passage. It was an ambitious project. But the slope down toward the Grand Canal was quite steep, the water flowed too fast, making it difficult for transportation. The canal rapidly silted up. It proved to be a failure.

Song, 50, who has written about this canal, told me that the river has had multiple names to denote its characteristics of the time. Once it was known as the Little Yellow River because it carried the yellow earth from Shanxi Province where it begins. It was not always so. In ancient times the river was clear. But over logging in Jin and Yuan times caused riverbanks to cave in, mountains devoid of forestation lost their soil, and the river became murky and full of clay. Its name was Hunhe, Muddy River. But the name that has stuck is a false name, given by a Qing emperor trying to trick the river into being what it wasn't. It was named the Yongdinghe or Eternally Fixed River.

We drove along the flood prevention dyke. It really surprised me because I hadn't realized how seriously Beijing takes its flood protection. The city was heavily flooded five times in the past and a lot of imperial attention was given to the building up of that east levee. One of the worst floods was in 1801 when it rained hard for over ten days. The banks broke and the suburbs were inundated. The story goes that court officials paddled in tubs to the Palace everyday for their official duties.

Repairing the breaches in the levee and dredging the waterways of silt has thus always been a

serious endeavor. Song noted that locals call the dyke "*shibadeng*" (18 steps ladder) for the way the stones have risen with the river. We climbed down the levee to inspect. Visible even now are large blocks locked together with iron butterfly clamps, many that have been there since Jin times. I found it interesting that the banks on the other side of the river weren't given so much attention.

Today not much water passes along the riverbed; it is mostly controlled by the Guanting dam on the border with Hebei Province. But the dam is 400 meters higher than Beijing and a disaster would be a grave threat. Every 200 meters along the wall there are markers designating

different units responsible for that portion of the levee, to bring sandbags if the water gets high.

For good measure though, Beihuizhimiao (North Shrine of Helpful Wisdom), another temple, dedicated to placating the river, still keeps its spot downstream. Song and I peered into its barbed-wired compound and could see the imperial stele on the premises. It used to have a bronze cow which acted as a kind of early warning system. When the cow gets wet, call for the sand bags!

## River Village Imposes Quarantine

Highway 108 in Fangshan District follows the Dashihe, Big Stone River. All along the way side roads were

blocked and villages cordoned off for no entry: the reason was SARS. On that day in the spring of 2003, more than 1275 cases of SARS were announced in Beijing. This caused a panic among Beijing's rural areas where the virus had yet to spread, but fear galvanized these peasants into a gut reaction to save themselves from this peril. For them the SARS slogan, "come together with one heart", had a special meaning. The heart is their village.

At village entrances serious guards stood sentinel by banners stating, "checking point to protect against SARS." But this is not the nonchalant atmosphere of the usual movements. The villagers were scared and protecting their villages

mountains, valleys and plains. This SARS epidemic made me appreciate all the more Beijing's natural setting and the usual hospitality of its villagers. It is an indelible memory of the Big Stone River.

to the utmost degree. They yelled, "Get out of here!" and "Don't stop your car!" Although this public highway was open, the villages straddling it were closed. Loud speakers were blasting SARS information. It was also telling people to stay inside and to not let anyone in from outside. But it was a lovely spring day and I had planned a picnic by the Big Stone River. We stopped where there were no homes to take a photo of the river. One villager from a hillside saw us and said "No photos!" We felt like outcasts.

Heilongguan is a slate-roofed village that has two temples, one to protect from floods and the other to guard the highway, both lifelines of the village. But today they wanted a different kind of protection; they didn't want the epidemic of SARS anywhere near them nor near their temples. It looked pretty desolate, except for the guards with red armbands. Fear was so very real in their faces like the fear of the Black Plague in the Middle Ages. Peasants fifteen meters away in the fields shielded their faces. Anyone not from the village was a suspect virus carrier.

In their justifiable tenacity in regards to this disease, they controlled access to the rivers and

## Fortification Defends the Upper Reaches of Yongding River

The Yongding River has always brought both nurturing and calamity to the people who lived close by it. But as I wandered along the river's meandering twists and turns near its upper reaches, this shallow stream seemed hardly threatening today. Yet I could make out markings in the rocky crags above, noting flood lines from times when the river had not been so calm in the past.

Water glittered as it glided swiftly below a precarious rope bridge. It was strikingly clear to the bottom, making it hard to imagine that the dam controlling the river up stream has been ruined by industrial sewage. Residents still wash in the river. They also go after small fish, cooking them in vinegar, so that even the bones are edible.

the river and the green of newly emerging leaves gave a dab of color against the dark brown cliffs behind them. A broken down little shrine got its name, Cypress Mountain Temple, from the time when cypresses once dominated the landscape. Now only one cypress is left in the temple's courtyard.

The river makes a bow-shaped curve at Yanhe town. From afar it is like some medieval castle town enclosed in high walls, except that it is a functioning community. The stronghold was constructed in 1578 to guard this important road along the river leading northwest out of the capital. Also, many lookout and signal towers were made to command the entrances to nearby canyons.

I climbed up the old wall above the village to get a better view. Modern pipes snaked along the top bringing precious drinking water from a mountain spring. But I was told that the taps open for only ten minutes twice a day.

From that vantage point it was easy to see how the river curves in from the northwest and makes a small turn north, before it travels southeast again away from Yanhe. The wider main street of town runs across from the west gate with smaller alleyways leading off from it. As I peered into courtyards surrounded by gray tile roofs, I could make out an old tree at the entrance to the schoolyard, noticeable by the national flag fluttering in the breeze. This marks the spot of the town center, once the site of a temple facing the village stage, now used for

These riverbanks were denuded of natural trees, felled over the centuries, so that much of the topsoil was carried downstream. Recently, however, young poplars have been planted by

storage. Not unexpectedly, Yanhe had more than its share of talisman deities to protect its citizens. The Dragon King, Black Dragon, Yellow Dragon, and a number of other divinities, all had their respective shrines. But they are now just things of the past.

Entering Yanhe through its main west gate, I walked along narrow alleyways lined with bundles of kindling wood. An 83-year-old local man named Bai, wearing a faded blue jacket, said he'd witnessed a lot changes. His ancestors were merchants. He pointed to a white marble pillar in the doorway and a small alcove once used for oil lamps, markings of a well-to-do home. Today the town has less than 400 families and they either collect firewood or tend orchards for a living.

Fruit grower Wei Lixin, 35, who raises Fuji brand apples, took us around and told why the south gate by the mountainside was no longer passable. Actually the north and the south gates were Yanhe's water conduits. "One year there was lots of rain," said Wei, recounting the village legend, "Water and earth were rushing through the south gate threatening to flood the whole village, when a huge boulder rolled down the mountain and shut the gate closed." This forced the deluge to curve around the walls and flow down into the river. The great stone saved the town. It is supposedly still inside the gate, buried in mud from that fateful day. And the crenellated town walls continue to provide protection. Wei noted, "People still climb up there whenever there's flooding."

*Unforgettable People*

# Revealing Recovered Relics

It looks like an ordinary field, but walking with archaeologist Su Tianjun, the bumps and deep holes in the ground near the Liuli River suddenly had meaning. Professor Su has been involved in most of the digs around Beijing for the past 50 years. These excavations at Dongjialin Village, close to the southern border with Hebei Province, were no exception.

We walked along the remains of an earthen wall from around 900 B.C., the capital of Yan during the Western Zhou period. Tombs of the leading family were discovered, bringing to light the sophisticated culture of those times. Su talked not only about the bronzes but also about finding remnants of their foodstuffs as well.

We went down into an excavation pit where Su explained the layers of civilization visible in the dirt. But what was most interesting was a nine-meter-long sewage canal that went from the "city" under the wall and out to a field where the waste was collected. Su, dressed dapperly, picked up a few shards and rubbed his fingers over the tiny groves on the baked clay. He passed them to me to do the same. Then he casually announced that they were perhaps a couple thousand years old.

Su has a wealth of stories. "Many of the eunuchs' tombs I excavated were along the Yongding River. They were buried with Buddhist rituals, entombed seated in jars." Their lost organs were replaced by sandalwood, ceramic or sun-baked clay copies.

When Su excavated the notorious eunuch Li Lianying's tomb, Li was found seated with a jade belt and ring, which were given to the Palace Museum. He was intact, not beheaded as one text declares. When Red Guards burned the house of Li Lianying, Su went later to try to salvage some of the treasures. He took the books and ceramics to the Cultural Relics Bureau.

He proceeded to recount another relic rescue not far from the Marco Polo Bridge. Wanfo Yanshousi (The Temple of the 10,000 Life Saving Buddhas) of Dajing Village was famous for its Ming Dynasty standing bronze Buddha. Su knew he had to save it from almost certain destruction during those harrowing times.

Try as he could, the eight-meter statue wouldn't fit into any conveyance. So he used a saw and cut it into three pieces, loaded them onto carts and pulled them across town to safety.

I tried to find the exact location of the temple. An elderly gentleman, Peng Yongzhen, working at a newspaper stand, mentioned that the new Asian Games soccer stadium was built on the temple grounds. I thought no relics could possibly remain. Peng gladly said he would show me there and quite casually got into the car. Outside the fence of the sports complex, he said, "There's the Buddha." I had my eyes focused near the ground. "Don't you see it?" But then he pointed upward... there it was, the great bronze statue of Guanyin, the Goddess of Mercy. Its elegant shape was clearly visible standing in the shadow of the stadium. I could not believe it! I drove fast past the guard at the gate. Nothing was going to stop me from getting in!

The statue's gentle round face is capped by an elaborate crown with three more faces. Of the original twenty-four hands only four remain but intricate jewelry and belt patterns on the ribbon-like flowing robes make it a gorgeous master-piece of sculpture and forging.

My guide recalled how local officials went looking for their statue after the remnants of the temple were taken down and building began on the stadium. "It meant a lot to our community, it was the symbol of our village temple." They searched and found it at the Capital Museum. Beijing authorities returned it all in one piece.

I climbed up on the cement base to get a closer look. There were the lines where the figure had been welded back together. It was almost perfect surgery. Then I told Peng about the tough archaeologist Su Tianjun and his determined feat in protecting their sacred image. Su, too, was happy to learn that the treasure was back intact. His exhausting work of finding and salvaging Beijing's heritage was well worth it.

# Lakes and Imperial Gardens

## Symphony on Ice

Lakes froze solid for several months during Beijing winters when we lived here in the early 1980s. Skating was a family affair and we regularly tried out different spots to appreciate the scenery and the surface of the ice. Beihai Lake was popular because it was easy to get to and they had night skating as well.

In those days it was still not easy for us to mix in Chinese society. But on the ice everybody was the same. There were elderly men who had skated there all their lives who happily gave us skating tips. And my son and daughter could casually meet Chinese children and enjoyed racing with them.

On the weekends, though, we often went out in our car to Kunming Lake at Yiheyuan, the Summer Palace. But only after all the crowds left on the last bus at four o'clock. This was before taxis were plentiful and before people had private cars, so the last bus was the only way

back to the city. We thus had all of the lake to ourselves. The sky in the last fading hour of light turned an almost navy blue as a backdrop to the temples on Wanshou Hill before us. Sunset beams created a colorful curtain over the Fragrant Hills in the west.

As we swirled about, the ice turned dark green. And from the bottom we heard repeated deep sonorous roars of ice hardening in the lower temperatures of dusk. Our blades sped swifter on the glassy surface. The great expanse of sky lay open and unimpeded, reflecting in the lake below us. And as it got colder the crackling roars of the ice quickened almost like a musical performance, made by the deep tones of striking a large gong, reverberating all around us. And we could hear it travel across the lake with each new contraction. It gave us all a sense of wonder.

But with the onset of global warming and urban development, Beijing has had higher temperatures in winter. Thus, there are fewer and

fewer days that are safe for ice-skating. The thunderous boom of Kunming Lake's symphony of the ice has softened as well.

## Water in Previous Splendor

Water was everywhere in the imperial Yuanmingyuan, Gardens of Eternal Brightness, in the 18th and 19th centuries until much of it was destroyed by foreign troops in 1860. One of the most magnificent fountains, the Grand Waterworks, was a water pavilion built in opulent western style. Now, except for a few lakes and canals in the central part of the partially restored public park, most of the waterways have dried up and the surroundings have returned to nature. A plan for rebuilding the entire area of the original landscaped gardens has recently been proposed and water will no doubt flow again through the dried lakes and streambeds.

During the time when the western garden of Yuanmingyuan was left to fallow, it was possible to wander around the grassy knolls and forgotten rockeries to imagine what had been there in the past. On several occasions I explored the area using old maps of the gardens to compare what they looked like in the 19th century with the present terrain.

On the map there was an image of a *swastika*, being a Buddhist holy symbol. This was once a pavilion designed in this shape in the middle of a pond. With everything overgrown, it was only possible to pinpoint this location by finding a clump of rockeries that the map indicated were nearby. Yet by walking in the dried bed of the lake now covered with weeds, I could find mounds of narrow earthen levees still set in the ancient stylized shape of the sun's rays, the bent arms rotating in the same direction.

Another former lake was easier to spot. A marble dock stands at the edge of what is now a large cultivated field. Several retired men seated on stone steps remembered when the lake held water. They used to fish here as youngsters. Some marble pillars stuck in the earth were survivors of once delicate arched bridges over the stream leading into the lake.

Following the map, I wandered to the north of this enormous complex. To my surprise, there stood the remains of massive earthen walls, some fifteen meters high. The dried-up deep gully of a former moat still runs along the outside.

Sometime later I discovered a copy of an 18th

century painting showing a full lake and the covered corridors of the swastika-shaped pavilion. It was only then did I understand the complete architectural setting. There were little wooden bridges connecting the ends of the pavilion arms so one could walk around to enjoy the water landscape without continually going back to the center. Also in the painting was one of the single-arched stone bridges where the water flowed on to the neighboring lake. It was almost as I envisioned it to be.

# Hot Springs, Cool Reflections

**X**iaotangshan town about 30 kilometers due north of the city is becoming a fast developing zone of resorts and weekend houses. Located at the foot of the Lesser Tang Mountains, two famous springs, the Boiling Spring and the Warm Spring, have gushed forth hot water since ancient times.

Even though I had driven through this town many times since the 1980s, I never had any inclination to try the waters until I was invited to go to the Jiuhuashan hot spring resort in January of 2002. There the warm pools are lined with rocks suggesting some outside bath in rural Japan. But the Japanese style *"onsen* culture" here really isn't the same because everyone is in bathing suits. Yet it is close enough.

The place has a long history going back to the 17th century, when the Qing emperors made use of the curative waters and even had a detached palace built on the premises. The Japan touch came with the war. Beijing was occupied from 1937 to 1945. The hot spring was taken over by the Japanese army and made into an Army Hospital. After the war the whole area was closed to the public. Only in the last few years was the spa reopened.

Two days before the lunar New Year, a light snow fell as I soaked in the springs. Firecrackers boomed early and lit up the gray sky. Tea was served by the poolside. The big rock has

the words "Yu Quan", meaning: reserved for the Emperor.

It made me think about all the changes that have taken place in China, especially in these last 20 years. Back in the early 1980s I would never have imagined sitting with Chinese friends in these surroundings. Mixing so casually in those days was still not accepted. I also thought about the long history of Japan-China Relations and how the two countries are today so mutually dependent.

My friend Sun Xiaoyan who was with me drinking tea in the hot spring pool also reflected on this. "The most important thing," she emphasized, "is mutual trust between the peoples, especially the younger generation." She also remarked that even though there are irritating noises made from both sides, that this solid relationship shouldn't head for a divorce.

In my mind, this method of communication, relaxing where emperors once soaked, is the best way of solving misunderstandings.

## A Spoonful of Water

Beijing used to be full of private gardens owned by the city's rich families and literati. One such garden, Shao Yuan or "A Spoonful of Water", was a small Ming Dynasty garden, now part of Beijing University. Dormitories for foreign students and professors there still bear that name. But the original garden has vanished. Some lotus ponds inside the west gate and rockeries and a small bridge, which have recently been restored, are sitting on top of the earlier garden. A fine scroll three meters long depicts this villa of 16th century scholar and

well-known calligrapher Mi Wanzhong as it was used to entertain Mi's friends who strolled on the meandering walkways by the ponds, rivulets, rockeries and pavilions that once graced this space.

Diane Obenchain, a visiting professor at Beijing University, arranged to have the original scroll photographed and precious copies made. Walking on campus with Diane is like walking inside the scroll. She can tell where everything once was. And she becomes particularly excited when standing by the former site of a pavilion; her explanation giving the land around the Shaoyuan Guest House a more distinguished appearance. According to her, the name of the garden came from the single spoonful of water Mi used to open a new stream. The name also suggests the garden's relatively small size and perhaps its shape resembling a dipper.

Mi Wanzhong, Diane instructed, created scenes in his garden using various water landscapes. Pavilions stood by water and willowed dykes, like fine screens, helped to separate these scenes. She took me to see the surviving relic of the garden, a massive upright rock, that is in the museum courtyard on campus. Then she unrolled the scroll, pointing out its prominent position of 500 years ago as it stood

in front of the pavilion.

For me, the Shao Yuan garden will always be associated with a humorous day in 1995. Once when I tried to enter the university through the west gate, the guard asked the name and address of the person I would be visiting. I was taking a guest to see the grave on campus of the famous Western journalist and friend of China, Edgar Snow. I kept repeating, "Snow", "Snow", but that didn't mean anything to the guard. He shoved a piece of paper in the window of the car and insisted that I put down a room number. He let me in after I had properly signed that Snow lived at the Spoonful of Water, underground at #B-01.

## Joyous Pavilion: Hangout for Actors, Revolutionaries and Poets

Taoranting (Joyous Pavilion) Park has been an important gathering spot since the 11th century when the capitals of Liao and the later Jin Dynasties were in the southwest corner of today's Beijing. April 4, 1997 was a glorious spring day with white almond trees, yellow forsythia and tree magnolias all in bloom. It was the Qingming Festival, the day Chinese go to lay flowers on their ancestors' graves.

A number of pensioners and workers had gathered to sing together in the park's pavilions. Accompanied by the strains of the two-stringed *erhu* and the rhythm of two gongs, a woman in her late thirties, took her turn to sing. Crowds gathered and applauded or yelled *hao*! (good), when she delivered a difficult passage well.

The park has a long history with Chinese traditional opera. Theaters of many provincial guild halls have been in the vicinity for several hundred years, making Taoranting popular with opera singers who lived nearby. Actors and actresses continue to practice their arias from early in the morning. Students from the nearby opera school can be seen doing martial arts.

Searching the western edge of the Taoranting area was a distinguished calligrapher, Mr. Yu Qilong, a former actor, who wanted to find a worn down temple where he had studied Peking Opera in his youth. Yu, 72, told how he was trained for the parts of the *Lao Sheng*, Bearded Man, role. This could mean anything from playing the roles of an emperor or a general to heroes like Zhuge Liang, a perpetual favorite. "We came very early on Sunday mornings to practice. There were about forty of us. We studied with famous teachers and saw well-known opera stars practicing nearby," he recalled. It is now the Beijing Institute of Kunqu Opera.

Yu's family is one of a distinguished line of calligraphers going back to the 8th century master Yu Shinan. "His calligraphy is carved on stone in the stele museum of Xi'an." Even though Mr. Yu studied at the French college in Beijing and at Jesuit Aurora University in Shanghai, he stayed with the stage and played with troupes throughout China. Yet a twist of fate took him back to calligraphy. "When France and China restored diplomatic relations in 1964, I was asked to teach Chinese culture to diplomats." The movements of the opera, though, are visible in his writing. When he does the strokes, there is a flurry of the wrists and a dramatic pose as he finishes up, brush lifted up in mid-air.

A small nunnery, Cibei'an (Convent of Mercy), sits on a hillock by Taoranting's lake. "That mound used to be the only high point in the city in ancient times where the common folk could go," said Yu. "At the popular Double Ninth festival, one is supposed to climb to a high place." For the ordinary persons, the Taoranting mound, which was higher than the old city wall, would do just fine.

From as early as the 12th century stone inscriptions showed the importance of the site. The Taoran (Joyous) Pavilion built within the convent compound in the late 17th century, was named for a line from famed Tang poet, Bai Juyi. One verse reads, "Ancient temple, people gone, yet incense envelopes it like a cage." Another proclaims, "Let's wait 'til the chrysanthemums are gold and our old wine matures, then we can get drunk and be joyous here together." Writing poetry here became a tradition and verses were written to acclaim the pavilion.

"Despite the poetry," added Yu, "the place really wasn't very beautiful in the past. Around the mound were graveyards and swamps. The lakes were really just stagnant ponds filled with reeds. To the south where the Ming wall and moat put it just inside the city, the backside of the wall was crammed with shanty dwellings."

The park temples and pavilions were also used as secret meeting places. In the late 19th century, reformers seeking change of the decaying Qing Dynasty held heated discussions here. The founder of the Republic, Dr. Sun Yat-sen, also attended gatherings in the park. Later, Taoranting was a clandestine rendezvous spot in the early Communist movement.

Today the park is beautifully landscaped and boats float on the lake that has replaced the swamp and smaller ponds. Leaving the park, Yu Qilong pointed to another small pavilion where an elderly man began an aria that Taoranting has listened to for ages.

267

# A Few Old Wells

## Courier Post Town: Stories of Wind and Water

**W**inds were blowing with a biting cold through the streets of the 800-year courier-post station of Yulinpu not far from the Great Wall at Badaling. In this rough terrain the old highway leading from the capital passes to Zhangjiakou in the northwest. One woman carrying water from a nearby well verified that this was indeed the post road from Mongol times. It was where the couriers with official dispatches rested or were exchanged.

A number of legends have been passed down over the centuries. One is the story of the old well of Yulinpu. When Emperor Kangxi rode north on one of his inspection tours, he rested here at Yulinpu to have a drink from their well. The emperor remarked on its sweetness and looked down into the well cavern. He noted that it was a *tong jing* (spring with moving water) and, thus, realized why the water tasted so good. Unfortunately, when people began using machines to dig wells wherever they pleased, the result was that the famous well dried up.

The village keeps its original layout with remnants of high dirt and stone walls still surrounding it on three sides. On the January day of my visit few people ventured outside as I ambled along the streets. Fine woodwork graced the porticos of several homes and gave a glimpse of village wealth in days gone by. One home with elaborate woodcarvings on window frames and door lintels served as the temporary palace where Empress Dowager Cixi stayed. People now living in

the courtyard say she was supposedly quite satisfied with her accommodations here.

A villager named Gao invited me in to his home to meet his family who were sitting on the *kang* after lunch. "Not much left," said Gao, 65, "they put a building on what used to be the post station, but there are some stones where they tied up the courier horses."

Close to the desert, with sand blowing in from Inner Mongolia, this place is in a wind pocket. Another story about Emperor Kangxi is remembered in a poem: "The emperor camped out here. A big wind blew in at night. In the morning there was nothing left of the fields."

Today there are many more donkeys than horses in Yulinpu. Donkey carts sit ready for harnessing on the streets, but they aren't for transmitting dispatches. Mr. Gao's grandson remarked that his junior high school has several computers.

Yes, this ancient post town with its earthen walls, deep wells and wind blown streets now has a faster courier: the information highway.

## The Whereabouts of the Discriminating Bell Temple

Following a historic Beijing legend isn't always successful.

Places have disappeared with a few leaving only a name to commemorate them. Sometimes it's a street name, or a bus stop name, or often a school may preserve a name from the past.

If you ask any cabbie in Beijing the whereabouts of Fenzhongsi, the Discriminating Bell Temple, they can immediately tell you where it is. For in their mind, this place is just an overpass at an important highway junction where Beijing's southern ring road has an exit to the expressway to Tianjin. But none of the drivers have ever been to the place where the temple actually once stood.

Fortunately, I went searching for the remains of this legendary spot in 1987, before urban development reached that part of the city. The story of the bell is as follows: The temple's bell was quite unusual. Its ring told each person a different message. Instead of just vibrations of a bell, people heard words instead, which seemed to suit their needs. For a lazy guy, it said, "get up," to one sad, it gave hope; to the tired one, it was a soothing lullaby. Being so discriminating

in its tone, the bell earned its nickname and thus the legend.

A bus stop name was what caught my eye. I wandered to the south where a map put the temple's location. It was in the midst of a farming commune. Irrigation ditches ran full of water dispersing it to a wide field. I skipped along the ditches until I came to a well that was the source of all the irrigation water. It had a pump and was dispensing the water in several directions. On one side of the well, a wall holding up the pump was bolstered by a carved stone stele commemorating a restoration of Fenzhongsi.

No temple, no discriminating bell ringing, but whenever I take that overpass marked Fenzhongsi, I recall the legend and remember the abundant water flowing out from the well, the last connection to its past.

# Seclusion Enables Survival

Following a fantastic curving road climbing high up on Baitie Mountain, one thing was certain: the villages seemed almost totally abandoned. Strange on this winter day to meet almost no one from one snow-dusted deserted village to another. One place had in fact caved in due to coal mines dug under the village itself.

The last hamlet up the mountain was the village of Lingyue Temple. The remaining halls of the old temple could be seen from a distance. Two towering trees, one pine and one scholar tree, dominated the scene. With a tradition dating back more than 1,000 years, this remote temple keeps its fine architectural design of the 14th century Yuan Dynasty.

One villager appeared lugging a dead tree up the stone-inlaid mountain path. He shrugged when asked why people have left here and cited poor transportation and no jobs as reasons why there are just three families left. But he added that at least there was a good well that provided plentiful water for the remaining residents.

Deserted narrow pathways cut between dilapidated homes. Most windows were broken. It was an all-monotone landscape. Here and there, abandoned tools showed years of hard labor. A finely worn grinding stone was no longer useful. Where neighbors had once shared chatter on the door stoops, a lonely silence prevailed.

I came across a group of donkeys that had taken over a vacated garden. They seemed free

to roam as they pleased. Soon they were on the move again, following in single file in the fading light. They congregated around the village well where the abundant water was free for the taking, as if they were the rulers of this discarded place.

Although the people leave, the donkeys, the flowing well and the tall trees have opted to stay. My lasting impression was that this remoteness had actually kept the place as a village museum.

## Lake of Ink Slab Water

The city had never seen the likes of it. All those women gathered from around the world, converging on the Chinese capital in September, 1995, for the United Nations Conference on Women. It was a turning point for many individuals and gave inspiration to hundreds of small groups who found kindred spirits around the globe in their determination to give voice to concerns of women of the world.

A number of my Pakistani friends were with their country's delegation. I took them to the Confucius Temple, part of the former Imperial College, that keeps the atmosphere of traditional Beijing.

We stood around the ancient well in the courtyard surrounded by the shadows of looming cypress trees. Claimed to have magical waters, this well supposedly had the ability to help the brush make fine calligraphy and create better essays. As this was the site for the triennial state examinations, students, young and old from all over the country, must have crowded around the well during those times.

This well was so famous that even Emperor Qianlong used its water on his ink slab for writing poetry. In gratitude, he named the well, Lake of Ink Slab Water. On the grounds of the temple, almost 200 stone tablets stand engraved with the names of top-ranked scholars of the exams since 1306. All of those successful candidates probably took a bit of well water to write their essays.

Both Emperor Qianlong and even Confucius never imagined such a spectacle as was happening around the well that autumn day. The shimmer of *saris* and *shalwar/kameez* with flowing scarves made colorful movement as the group peered down into the dark recesses from the raised well stone. Unfortunately, no ladle was available for them to try the waters' powers.

As we walked on, only the playing of an earthen whistle in the main hall broke the solitude of the temple. It was ironic for these delegates to the Conference on Women, that we should be paying homage to the Sage who put women in a lower place for centuries. Just as there was no female name among those on the carved stones, the emancipation of women in every culture is taking a long time. And that is exactly what this historic conference was addressing.

# Stories Heard Round the Well in the Valley of Gujishan

Although Guji Mountain is only a one-hour drive westward from central Beijing, it feels incredibly remote. Surrounded by mountains on all four sides, it takes about another hour on foot to traverse a long gully to reach the secluded mountain valley of ancient monasteries. Vestiges of its history can be seen among its scattered remains.

Stonecutters and wood gatherers are a feature of the roadside landscape along with a few shepherds guiding their flocks to graze on the sparse hillside vegetation. Near the remnants of the first temple complex an elderly couple stood beside a stone well sorting baskets of freshly picked persimmons.

Ms. Feng, 71, and her husband Liu, 77, serve as caretakers of what is left of this centuries-old temple complex. They live at Lingjiuchansi (Temple of the Sacred Vulture) whose stone structures date from 600 years ago, but now stands completely empty.

The monastery complex continues up the mountain where there is a hexagonal stone hall. Above that, three pagodas perch on three small hills. The entire setting was planned as an architectural whole with a balance of temples on the west *Yang* (Sun) side, while the east *Yin* (Shadow) side was devoted to nunneries and graves. Temple compounds were built at different heights up the valley, but were united in balance with layers of history blended together. Ming halls, for example, were perfectly aligned to the remaining Liao pagoda at the top of the central hill. Artisans respectfully incorporated the past into their new design.

A barely legible stone tablet dated 1078 says that Buddhist monks from central China came here in the mid-9th century to escape the Tang authority's religious persecution. Another inscription inside one of the pagodas reads, "A monk named Huike was responsible for bringing Buddhist holy relics here in a crystal bottle from the Great Goose Pagoda in Xi'an. The Ming emperor ordered the pagoda built to protect the relics." Today visitors can crawl beneath the pagoda but the crystal bottle has long gone and only drawings are left etched on stone. The inscription also proclaims that the

Ming emperor vowed to "cover the upkeep expenses forever."

Ms. Feng didn't know anything about the emperor's promise. She was just intent on drawing water from the stone well. It took a long time for her to winch the bucket of water using a green rope with a rusted pulley. Finally the aluminum bucket emerged. It was only half full. Feng explained that she and her husband don't use much water. That is just as well, because drawing water from the deep well is apparently quite a chore. Again she dropped the bucket in the well. Feng's worn hands unreeled the rope slowly. "The well is at least 30 meters down," she said, resigned to the time it takes to get just one bucketful. "This water is really fresh, but there isn't a lot of it." That wasn't always so. Her husband, Liu, told the story. "During the war, Japanese soldiers dumped rocks into the well to prevent the Chinese Eighth Route Army soldiers from getting water. It blocked up part of the natural water flow."

Another local, Ms. Yang, 68, was tending to persimmon trees planted by her father more than 100 years ago. They had grown tall and she was using an extended pole to snatch persimmons way up at the top. Ms. Yang was born here in the valley and knows much of its history.

She began with one story of monks who had forgotten their vows, stealing young girls from neighboring valleys through an underground tunnel. She then talked about more recent history. She said her family was very scared when Japanese soldiers arrived in Gujishan Valley, so they climbed over the mountain crest and hid in another valley for a year. "We lived in a stone cave and foraged for food at night," Yang said adding, "It's hard to imagine some of the sad stories that happened in this beautiful place."

Her real bitterness, though, was directed at the Cultural Revolution. "Many of the small pagodas were demolished at that time. The stone Buddhas in all those halls were smashed. It was awful," Yang said angrily. "In this quiet valley with our good air, how could soldiers and Red Guards dare to come here?" She then turned her attention back to picking persimmons. These stories are reminders of how the nation's history has affected even this remote valley.

# Refreshing Ancient Springs

## Elusive Jade Spring and the Eight Water Courtyards

Safeguarding the best springs of Beijing has had a long history. In many cases, temples and imperial villas were built to control their usage, and their relics today serve as markers of ancient water sources. A number of these springs were extolled for their particularly fine water and wonderful settings and recognized as an auspicious group of Eight Water Courtyards of the Western Hills.

This term was coined under the reign of the Jin emperor Zhangzong at the end of the 12th century when the Jin imperial retinue enjoyed hunting the valleys and camping at the springs of temple compounds built at these sites. With strong nomadic roots from the cooler northwest, their restless spirit propelled them out of the stuffy capital and into the hills. The emperor either restored earlier temples or built new ones so that the monks could serve as caretakers and control the spring water.

The fact that the sites were nicknamed as "water courtyards" shows that the spring was the crucial factor in the setting. In all of these places stone aqueducts led the water in and around the temple and imperial villa grounds. In several cases the choice water was even channeled into the capital city.

Which of the famous springs are included in the set of eight is still debated by historians, but the Jade Spring, was certainly in the group as it was considered the city's premier spring. However, its restricted access today means that the site has eluded me and I've only been able to enjoy it through journals of the past or by

appreciating it from afar. In fact, a Qing Dynasty painting of the imperial gardens of the western suburbs puts the Jade Spring Hill right in the middle. The hill is beautiful as the backdrop to Kunming Lake. Where the prominent pagoda stands on the hill is the former location of the Hall of Hibiscus, the Jin emperor's hunting lodge.

In honor of the rainbows that often appeared where the spring flowed, the site was also one of the Jin emperor's Eight Vistas of Yanjing, "Cascading Rainbow at Jade Spring Hill," resurrected in the Ming from the Jin emperor's poems. Later in the Qing Dynasty, these vista sites were given special consideration by Emperor Qianlong who inscribed the ancient poems for the eight vistas on giant stele erected at each place. The Jade Spring, thus, became the supreme symbol of suburban Beijing. Not only was it one of the Eight Water Courtyards, one of the Eight Vistas of Yanjing, but it also was declared by the Emperor Qianlong to be the Finest Spring Under Heaven. That gave it a stature hard to beat. Its setting was inclusive of all the elements of natural and man-made beauty that could not be surpassed.

The hill was also incorporated into the Qing Garden of Tranquility. Buddhist temple halls and pagodas were built and carvings of Lama Buddhist figures were engraved on rocks. An early 1920s detailed map of the place by the Belgian engineer Bouillard shows there were ten temples, four pagodas and a number of pavilions like the Lake View Pavilion, where guests gathered to

tween two hills, probably the best place for viewing the lake and writing poetry.

There is a rumor that the famed springs are now dry. Yet I like to think of the image created by the spring's nickname, "spring of snow flakes", such was the delicacy of shimmering water droplets that whirled like snow from the spray created by the spring's fountain. I can only sip its elegant illusion.

write poetry. There were in fact two springs. The map makes it clear how the water flowed from the Jade Spring into a small lake and then down the hill via the Golden River. And from there it passed along aqueducts and canals all the way to the Forbidden City.

The best vantage point to look closely at Jade Spring Hill is to stand by the canal right outside the walls guarding the tight security enclosure. There, fishermen gather on the banks by two ornate marble gates. With the recent opening of the Fifth Ring Road, it is possible to have an even closer look at the scenery and the four pagodas. One structure fits snugly in the dip be-

## A Tea Stall Revived

Shijingshan District has a large garbage landfill for Beijing waste disposal. The road there is covered in multi-colored plastic bags, a virtual installation art created by the wind and man's excess. Every tree branch and every bush is colorfully decorated with bags flapping in the breeze, nicknamed the "flowers of winter." The streams around here have dried up, and many springs have gone dry as well. In the midst of this grim landscape, though, is Shuangquansi (Temple of the Twin Springs).

The temple, dating from the late 12<sup>th</sup> century, is only a skeleton of its former self, but several trees and a pair of stone tablets still keep an aura of the past. Once it was known as a designated "Water Courtyard" with facilities for imperial visits. There were in fact two springs, one on each side of the temple.

Ms. Si Li, whose family has had a special relationship with the little temple for many generations, lives next door. She came out of her house to find me peering down the white marble opening for one of the famed springs. She pointed over to a junk filled ravine, "There's the original dragon spout sticking out of the slope." After cleaning it up a bit, I could see a pair of carved marble horns, and she added, "that is where the water used to come out, but it got clogged so we now get water from the new opening."

A couple of boys passed by, struggling with a wheelbarrow lugging a red plastic 20-liter water container. "They're selling it down by the road!" Si said. "Some outsiders paid the local government for the right to sell our water. But we don't complain, because there seems to be enough water. Even when

it is dry in Beijing and all around, the water flow here doesn't change."

Si, 52, was born in a side hall of the temple. Her father's family had been in charge of a tea hostel run by the temple, which was especially crowded at traditional festival times. A pilgrim path leading from one set of mountain temples to another passed right by their front gate. This was a convenient place for travelers to rest.

"We even have a green glazed water basin with the words 'Tea Stall of the Temple of the Twin Springs' inscribed on it," she stated proudly. "My cousin next door keeps it." There in the shed of rusting tools and useless television sets, was a green-glazed basin. Its faded inscription confirmed its authenticity.

We sat together by their front door on small wooden stools and discussed the selling of spring water by outsiders. Our talk turned to the bad smell of the huge garbage dump just up the road and chaotic ugliness of those flying plastic bags. I inquired about the pagodas that used to be in the vicinity. According to Si, they were all destroyed in the 1960s. The cousin then pointed at the dark gray bricks making up part of the shed wall and said, "Those old bricks are from the pagodas. No reason to let them go to waste!"

The cousin's wife then brought out some spring water. It was refreshing. As we gathered in a semi-circle, perched on the stools, the old time tea stall seemed to have been revived. All they had to do was get out that green-glazed water basin and the time slip would seem complete.

# Water Flows at Temple of the Dragon Spring

Water flows again along the stone aqueducts of Longquansi (Temple of the Dragon Spring) when they want it to. The local officials can now turn on the water or divert it to a nearby fish-pond and a restaurant as needed. The spring source is protected at the back by a locked cover. That way the flow can be monitored. But to see the water flow through the relics of the temple grounds is like having the place come alive again. The water spouts forth out of a marble dragon mouth and bubbles along the stone trenches directing its path through the temple yard.

Local legend recounts that the first monk,

Jisheng, often spotted a red-scaled golden dragon as he practiced *Qigong* in the vicinity of the spring. So he named it Dragon Spring. Others have noticed that when the sunlight hits the water as it passes along its winding course, the steam that rises up gives the impression that the water has just come out from the warm body of a dragon.

A monk in residence from southern China claimed that he found the temple by just looking at a map. I thought that was a splendid way of choosing a spot to live, just find a name and try it out. Any place that mentions a spring may provide fine lodging.

Stone steps lead to a platform where the main hall had once stood facing east toward the rising sun. This place harks back to the 10th century Qidan rulers of the Liao Dynasty. An aged ginkgo tree of great girth seemed refreshed to have the water flowing once again, gliding by its roots. Its fallen gold and green leaves floated along with the rippling water.

## Swapping Spring Stories in the Cherry Vale

In the ponds behind the Temple of the Sleeping Buddha lily pads were a clean dark green in the aftermath of yesterday's heavy rain. Yellow acacia petals floated in clumps on the surface of the water giving flower arrangements in motion as they moved with the light

breeze. The narrow valley Yingtaogou in the hills behind the temple, known as the Cherry Vale, is a favorite hiking spot for the citizens of Beijing. The reason is that in summer the thick forest gives a dense shade and water flows again in the usually dried up streambeds. And they also love to taste the spring water.

I met a retired doctor, Wang Yongzheng, 70, standing by the spring. In his plain white shirt, black pants and cap, I had watched him approach, walking at a clipping pace up the stony trail. Once at the spring he got right down to the small crevice where the water drips, collected some in a cup, took a sip and smacked his lips. "I've been to all the springs of Beijing," he boasted. "It is over 3,000 steps to Yuhuangding spring, yet only 2,700 steps to the Cherry Vale." He continued. "In the old days the stream continued on and was directed into

Kunming Lake." On the way up I had come across the willow tree-lined route of narrow stone aqueducts cutting through the Botanical Gardens, so I knew what he was talking about.

Squatting on the rocks by the spring's shallow pool, the little community of visitors swapped spring stories. Wang was obviously the expert and opinionated. He proclaimed that the best tasting water in Beijing is the spring at Cibeiyu Village in Changping. However, he noted, it wasn't easy to get to, so he comes to the Cherry Vale instead. Dr. Wang took his leave and walked briskly down the other side of the streambed, mumbling as he went along. He must have been recounting the steps.

## Mystifying Temple of the Iron Tiles and Its Spring

There were a lot of unanswered questions after I came across an unusual temple located in Hebeizhen Township of western Beijing. It stands between a river and the curvature of a hill behind it. Dominating the grounds is a great ginkgo tree over 35

meters in height. Originally known as the Convent of the Wonderful Spring, it had a name change during one restoration, to Iron Tiles Temple. Both the spring and the unusual tiles still exist, making it an interesting place to visit.

The spring maintains a forceful flow where it spews forth from a spout into a pond just below the temple, now the local government offices. Many people gathered by the pond to collect clear water and wash dishes and clothes. But the origin of the spring is not here; it comes from further up the craggy mountain in back. There I found a small locked cave. Peering in between the cracks I could barely see a marble pool where water was once collected for temple use. This, though, was not the source, said the caretaker, it is deeper in the mountains, but he didn't know exactly where.

Inside the temple compound is a round hall with a hexagonal roof in the shape of a six-petaled lotus with a lotus flower-like ball at the center. The roof is covered with rust-colored iron tiles. It is certainly a rare building in Beijing. Now known as the Iron Tiled Hall, it had an earlier curious name, The Pavilion to Remember One's Child.

The iron tiles each weighing four kilos give some clues. Printed on the surface are dates, referring to the years 1505 and 1515. In addition, some are stamped with Wutaishan, Pusading, Tiewasi (Iron Tile Temple) or Wutaishan, Wanshousi, Tiedian (Iron Hall), both temples on Wutai Mountain in Shanxi Province. The tiles

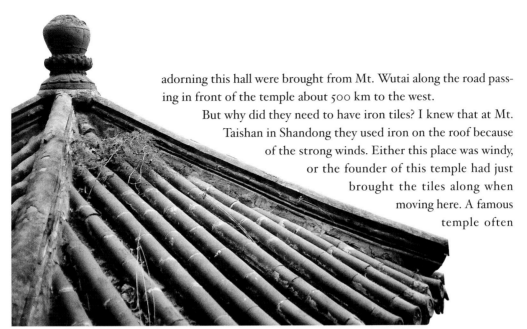

adorning this hall were brought from Mt. Wutai along the road passing in front of the temple about 500 km to the west.

But why did they need to have iron tiles? I knew that at Mt. Taishan in Shandong they used iron on the roof because of the strong winds. Either this place was windy, or the founder of this temple had just brought the tiles along when moving here. A famous temple often

had branch locations, so it is likely that this was considered a subordinate temple to one of those mentioned on the tiles.

Why was the hall round? This feature may be connected to the fact that this was originally a nunnery and that such a round pavilion has a feminine quality. A stele on the grounds writes about a lady who became a nun here because she was saddened by the loss of her husband. Was it she that gave the name Pavilion to Remember One's Child? Was she a member of the imperial family? These are questions that yet to be answered.

The stele was written in the year 1682 when the hall was repaired after an earthquake and laments that there isn't much known about the founding of the temple. It talks about the spring saying it tasted like "fragrant dew" and mentions how it passes under the temple with a strong, clear flow. The inscription also pointed out that local people were free to use the water as they pleased. The spring today is called Sacred Spring, and even though there is an official new sign telling people not to wash their clothes there, it seems the tradition of free use has predated the sign for so long that it is joyously ignored.

I carried the investigation of this temple to the holy Wutai Mountain. The Pusading mentioned on the tiles is no other than the temple on Lingjiu Peak in the center of Wutai community. I climbed the 108 steps, but found no iron tiles nor round pavilion. I had better luck at the Central Summit. Snow still hugged the ground and a strong wind swept across this barren landscape. At the pinnacle of the summit the temple roof was secured with iron tiles. I finally confirmed their necessity.

I also found the ruins of Iron Tile Temple down in a valley, southwest of central Wutai, well protected from any wind. No iron tiles around, but the earth was rust-colored. If this was the parent temple of the one in Beijing, did tiles fired here have iron ore?

I am still intrigued by the origin of Beijing's Iron Tile Hall. And after more than eight years since I first went there, people are still using the water as they please and I am continuing to look for more clues to its history.

## Spring of Longevity

On a rural road in far eastern Beijing, my eye caught a crude sign: "Dragon Spring Valley Health Scenery Spot." A whim of the moment made me turn and enter through a narrow pass in between two giant boulders. It immediately felt like a special place. "If you walk through the Longquan Valley, You can live to be Ninety-Nine," read a signpost.

At the Spring of Sacred Water, located not far from the road, a couplet described the feeling there. "The spring flies forth like a drooping rainbow. It cries out with a deep gurgling." Locals call it The Spring of the Goddess Guanyin that Helps Bring Children. And there are many

stories of successful families resulting from drinking at the spring.

The water gleamed as it rolled out of a mossy aperture in the hillside and down into a small clean pond below it. One Japanese lady had brought a set of utensils for the tea ceremony. Spontaneously, inspired by the lush green setting and pure water, we quietly had tea there. We gazed upon the clear spring trickling along the rocks and listened to its rumble from deep in the earth.

Further along the chasm was the Strange Spring. The Qing Dynasty emperor Qianlong is supposed to have written the following couplet about this site: "The magnificent rocks can prolong life and the aromatic waters keep the doctor away." Beside it was a research center for the study of Tibetan Medicinal Herbs, situated quite appropriately where the old shrine to the God of Medicine once stood. On the mountain above

is the Old Hermit's Cave where, according to local lore, the monk Sheng Ming lived to a ripe age in the 15th century.

Longevity in the village of Great Dragon Gate is well known. The secret must be the aromatic waters. Thus, I assumed that tea drunk in this valley, as advertised, would be effective in keeping the doctor away. The irony was that my companions that day were doctors.

## Spring of the Cheating Eunuch

In the 14th century Yuan Dynasty monk Huang Long built a temple named the Temple of Clear Water, in honor of the spring nearby. Located in the western suburbs at the base of Nine Dragon Hill, it is still a popular place. The spring comes out by the side of the temple ruins and, as usual, a crowd has gathered. There is even a better flow high up the hill, but it is easier to get the water here near the road. Water used to be even more plentiful, they asserted, however mining in the neighborhood affected the underground water level.

Well-wrought stone aqueducts indicate that the water once flowed through the temple before running into the stream below. It was interesting to see how the thin slabs of slate lining the bottom of the troughs neatly overlapped one another. Further up the compound a small bridge spanning over the water conduit has the

ruins of a pagoda on top. Its stone animal reliefs now lay scattered about. These and the intricate carvings on remaining stupas tell of a temple that was once very well off.

But the wealth of the temple came by an unscrupulous man. A stone inscription on the mountainside relates the background story. In the 15th century Ming times, the land around the temple was the property of Yao San, a shepherd and farmer. However, the powerful court eunuch Wu Liang tried to get the land so that he could use this as his retirement monastery and tomb. But Yao San refused the request. Determined, Wu Liang approached Emperor Xuande and the eunuch received the temple as his own.

When Yao San continued to graze his sheep on the grassy hills around the temple, or used the spring, this further upset Wu Liang. Again he used his imperial connections. In 1480 the emperor commanded: no tilling, no cutting of trees, no grazing or other disturbances of the peace of the temple, any offenses would be punished. And the name was changed to Chonghuasi (Temple of Lofty Transformation).

The cheating eunuch got his wishes, but over time his legacy and temple have gone to shambles; the view to the south is an ugly coal heap, sheep are grazing on the hills and people take the water away in large plastic containers any time they wish. And there is no one to pray for the soul of Wu Liang, his grave now gone with the winds of time.

# The Quest for Water Is a Rite of Beijing's Springs

Legend has it that the Dragon King and his consort stole all the sweet-tasting water in Beijing. They are supposed to have carted up all the water into nearby hills for the private use of the Dragon King's family. A young warrior, Gao Liang, gave chase, but succeeded only in breaking a barrel of bitter-tasting water that flowed back into the city in a great torrent drowning him and his horse. That is why, it is said, the capital's wells and natural springs taste bitter and one has to climb up into nearby hills to drink sweeter mellow-tasting water.

At the crack of dawn on any day, hikers converge at some of Beijing's best-known springs in hills west of the city. People of all ages and backgrounds trudge up well-worn stone paths in search of good drinking water. Their rucksacks are jammed with empty plastic 1-liter bottles, ready to be filled. Often these springs are barely more than a trickle of water, so water gatherers must arrive early to get in line.

"I take the 4 a.m. bus to the zoo, then transfer for the ride to Xiangshan, the Fragrant Hills," remarked an elderly gentleman known to all "Old Liu." The 72-year-old waited for the slow flow of the spring to fill up his bottle. "I come three or four times a week. It's a good hike in the fresh air. I like to get here before others," and then he ducked down behind the stone boulder and used his homemade ladle, a coat hanger wrapped around a plastic cup, to scoop up fresh spring water. "Only a tiny bit of water here these days," he mumbled, pouring the water carefully into an empty Coke bottle.

By 6:30 a.m. Liu had bottled 20 liters of water. Others waited patiently and even helped him arrange the filled bottles in his sack. A long line had formed, not just elderly people, but young

couples as well. There is a courtesy and decorum among the water gatherers: friendly chatter, sharing water stories. The atmosphere is low key. "Won't you take a sip from my bottle as you're waiting," Liu offered, even though it had been a painstaking job gathering the water. "Don't mind, I'm not afraid of your germs," he said laughingly. He then turned down the stone path, looking for all the world like a Santa Claus with a loaded sack slung over his shoulder going on his rounds.

At another spring in the hills, site of an ancient temple, a similar water gatherer, Wang Qingshan, 66, knows all about good water. He worked for 34 years as a geologist in the deserts of western China and relied on spring water for survival. "Where there's water, there's people; no water, no people" was his short assessment of life in that harsh environment.

After he retired Wang returned to his home village north of Beijing to live with his son's family. But he missed the sweet taste of pure spring water. So he now walks about 45 minutes one way several times a week to the spring of Jinshansi (Temple of Golden Mountain). "It's the stones that make the water," he spoke confidently. "It's good water here, you know. Yes, there are other good springs in the neighborhood, but this is just as good as the others, and it's free," he bantered on.

Wang lined up his empty bottles by the "Spring of Golden Mountain" to make his place before others come along. The spring here flows out of a pipe because it has been diverted from its original channel. "One doesn't really need very much for a decent life," Wang reflected, weighing simplicity over the growing consumerism of today's urban life.

Wang had adjusted his pack, loaded with 17 liters of painstakingly accumulated water just as some motorists arrived with large empty drum cans to fill up for sale. Wang, though, just takes enough for his family. He'll be back in a couple of days. One can move on to the next valley and the next to search out the springs. And there usually is a line of water gatherers with their plastic bottles defying the old Dragon King!

# Wandering along Historic Canals

## "Shadow on the Grand Canal"

The late afternoon sun glanced off the Grand Canal. Bright green fields of winter wheat crowded its banks. Soon deep shadows began to appear. That was exactly what I was waiting for. Where the Tonghui canal cuts due east from Beijing and intersects with the Grand Canal at Tongzhou, stands a famous

pagoda that has stood at this spot for 1,000 years. Its shadow is also famous. It is mentioned in a Ming Dynasty poem that reads, "On a clear day the shadow of the Randeng Pagoda falls five *li* and crosses the Baihe River."

That sounded like something to investigate. November 12, 1996, was a very crisp day and the late afternoon shadows were clear. Finding the pagoda at the west bank of the canal was one thing, finding the right shadow was another. I photographed a lot of false shadows. Gradually I moved down the row of silhouettes and finally recognized the pagoda's true shadow. It did peak above the rest.

At 4:40 p.m. the shadow stretched a long way. First it cut across the houses lining the road, then across vegetable plots in the process of harvesting Chinese cabbage, then crossed the Grand Canal, and its outline was clear against the newly planted fields of winter wheat, like a black paper cut-out on a giant green carpet, and, at last, the end of the shadow curled up at a row of trees planted in the distance, on the banks of the Baihe (or Chaobai) River. The old saying was right! In just a few minutes the shadows reached their maximum length, then slowly their muted shapes evaporated into the darkness as the sun disappeared beyond the mountains of the west. At 4:46 p.m. the shadow was gone. People thought I was mad to chase down a dark

reflection, and even more so by attempting to photograph its blank form. But this is what made my excitement grow, I could feel the Ming poem, and authenticate its image.

With the last glow of light, pigeons glided in formation around the old pagoda's pinnacle, the setting sun shimmering off their wings. I recalled another important fact: the pagoda was also a kind of flood warning service for the city of Beijing. When water passed the tip of the pagoda, only then would the higher land of the capital be in danger.

This pagoda is dedicated to the Buddha of the Past, Randengfo, who was not only the teacher of Sakyamuni but also known as the Buddha of Eternal Light. So it was fitting that the pagoda served as a lighthouse for the barges and boats plying the two canals.

A small skiff appeared with fishing nets piled at the bow. The fisherman rocked the long rudder back and forth with a grace learned from many centuries of such rhythmic handling. It made a short curve and turned into the smaller canal heading westward toward Beijing. Just then Randengta sparkled with electric lights, illuminating the way in the growing darkness.

The soft jingling of myriads of bells hanging from its thirteen story octagonal eaves made this a very soothing place to be. In the old days, light burning from the pagoda's lamps would greet passing travelers; moreover, the ringing bells would make a chorus of welcome as well. And the pagoda's shadow impressed all who were lucky enough to catch it at its maximum length.

## Community Commemorates Ancient Setting

South of the CCTV television tower on the third ring road inside a large residential complex, there is a historical site that one has to be pretty determined to find: an imperial sponsored temple, Puhuisi (Temple of Universal Kindness), that once stood there.

There isn't much left, only two lofty ginkgo trees and one stone pillar all dating from about 800 years ago. In the 1990s there was a community effort to help locals remember the roots

of their neighborhood. A new stone monument was erected with a sketch of what the temple used to look like in Ming times. In the sketch, the ginkgo trees and pillar have their place in the ancient setting. It is possible to visualize how the temple looked when it hosted the imperial retinue stopping here to admire the scenery.

Why had the emperors chosen this location? Looking carefully I realized that this was positioned on a slope. It was actually once a high hillock. A monk in the Liao period built a temple here facing east. Later, a Ming eunuch rebuilt the complex with an enclosing wall of more than 300 meters in circumference. With many trees and gardens it became a very popular temple.

What was their view? The site overlooked the Jinkouhe canal dug in 12th century Jin times which passed just below it. Imperial excursions lingered here so that the emperor could enjoy the engineering accomplishment that once brought the forceful water of the Yongding River into the capital. Water still flows along the canal bed coming from the Summer Palace into Yuyuan Lake.

Dwarfed by high-rise apartments, the ginkgo leaves turned to gold as residents lingered in the small park that now keeps the memory of this particular spot.

## On the Tracks of an Old Waterway

Empress Dowager Xiao, the Queen Mother Chengtian was a powerful woman of the 11th century Liao Dynasty. Claims of her campsites and legends of activities are found in many places in rural Beijing. There are several sites with flat-topped hills that are referred to as her "cosmetic table."

When she reigned as regent for about 30 years on behalf of her young son, she ordered the building of a canal from lakes by the capital city, extending it some 50 km to the southeast, to link up with the Grand Canal. It still exists, bearing her name 1,000 years later, cutting through

rural landscapes now poised for urban development. It has survived because of its sturdy banks of hard-packed yellow earth.

Even with a map in hand it was difficult to find the exact waterway, but most locals knew this ditch by its proper name, even though they might not know much about the empress herself. A bus route follows part of its meandering path. But it was easy to get confused since numerous small canals and ditches run on an east/west axis weaving their way across the same farmland.

At Majiawan Village, the canal is quite wide, suggesting that this spot was probably a port. Then it narrows again looking almost like a small creek, slithering under the modern Jingshen Expressway. After that it became enlarged again to the size of a small lake where fishermen dipped their nets from one-man flatboats.

The canal port of Zhangjiawan was once a crucial rice storage zone. Even today, a restored granary sits by the banks. The Liao period wooden bridge was rebuilt in stone during the Ming reign and it continues to provide passage over the canal at the same site. Locals refer to it as Stone Lion Bridge. On the map it is Tongyun Bridge.

Crossing the bridge I noticed deep ruts dug in the pavement, groves made by cart tracks loaded with grain. But this is no longer a busy thoroughfare. There was only an occasional tractor, a few motorbikes and group of children returning from school crossing over it.

In the failing light I joined sheep and dogs wandering below the bridge. There I could clearly see its three arches formed out of large stone blocks. Water was only passing through the central arch as the other two were clogged with silt and dirt. A dragon head scowled out from under the main arch. It is a fine looking bridge standing with the dignity deserved of this site: a crucial juncture, where the importance of the canal for grain transport and development of commerce was so evident.

From there the Xiaotaihou (Dowager Xiao) Canal joins with the Liangshui River and as a wide expansive waterway it spills into the Grand Canal by the Yulinzhuang locks. There are neither barges nor boats. It was such a peaceful scene.

But in the past the place must have been full of boats with throngs of people milling about.

One village south of Zhangjiawan named Maying refers to the horse pasture of the Liao soldiers. There used to be a hill where Empress Dowager Xiao camped with her men. She was famous for standing at the front of her troops when going into battle. Her valor and support for the people by ensuring grain was transported to the region, by developing agriculture and by not over-taxing the peasants, made her one of the most respected women of Chinese history. No wonder that Empress Dowager Xiao's canal has kept its original name and that stories of her exploits still linger as local lore around Beijing even today.

# The Lady of Fragrant River

The Chaobai River is the major river system of eastern Beijing. At one point it forms part of the border between Tongzhou District and the province of Hebei. Where it turns to flow eastward toward the sea, there is a rough and tumbled town named Xianghe, Fragrant River, that is a fast developing "border town", laying just outside the Beijing Municipal District. It is where workers and goods congregate for permission to enter the city.

My purpose for going there on a cold blustery day was to check out a story I'd heard of a saintly woman who miraculously became a natural mummy in 1992. The lady, Zhou Fengchen, was a pious rural lay Buddhist and a healer. Because she was such a holy woman, it was said, she was able to control her body even after death so that it did not decay. Pamphlets about this phenomenon were being handed out at temples.

Without really knowing what to expect or even the real address of her home, I set out on an early winter November day in 1996 to look for her village outside of Xianghe town. Icicles were dangling from bushes in the countryside and there was such a strong wind that people on bicycles had trouble going against it. Thus, there weren't many people standing around on the rural roads. I got directions from a local shopkeeper. "Oh, you want to go that way," he chuckled, "I went to see the old lady, too." But the directions weren't easy and I had to keep asking the whereabouts of the "Old Lady." But as I got closer, all I had to say was "Where is that?" and they pointed me onward replying, "That is over there." Finally I stopped at the front door of an unassuming local farmhouse, the home of the Lady of Xianghe.

The eldest son, Mr. Yang, let me in, although he admonished, "You should have let us know you were coming." He led me past the German Shepherd on guard, an unusually friendly dog, almost a blessed being himself. Then we entered the reception room. It was full of posters and pictures of old lady Zhou's life with explanations of this miraculous occurrence.

"She was always different from us," her son explained. "She could tell when things would happen like her granddaughters' auto accident. Or she could go to a new place and know her way around." He continued, "She was a kind mother and never struck us or used harsh words.

She read the Buddhist sutras and prayed daily."

Mr. Yang pointed to some of her pictures, saying, "We knew she had a special ability to diagnose and treat diseases. But near her death she seemed to be preparing for something unusual, by getting rid of all waste and fasting. Then one evening she said that she would now fall asleep and that was how she died."

The son then showed the way to the "Old Lady's" room. Above the window an awning was unfurled as a protection from the glare of the winter sun. He then slowly raised the yellow silk curtain on the outside. I walked close to the window and peaked in to her bedchamber. There was a glass casket on a carved wooden base. This, in turn, was resting on the earthen bed on which she had died. Lady Zhou's face shone like polished leather and her gray hair still curled over her ear and on to the blue pillow. A bright yellow silk cloth covered the rest of her body.

Her son continued, "Because she seemed to be sleeping so peacefully, we decided not to cremate or bury her. We didn't really feel she was dead." Over the past four years her body has naturally dried, but it has been kept in a normal environment all the time.

Other family members gathered around us and spoke proudly of the "sleeping" lady's spirit. "When we realized that this was an unusual phenomenon, we contacted the authorities," related the daughter-in-law. "Buddhist leaders and scientists have visited our home regularly since then."

As the news of the Lady Mummy spread, the small village has attracted believers in miracles and the curious as well. Zhou Fengchen's body is now under the care of the Academy of Social Sciences and her worthy life is being used as a model for piousness and self-discipline. Even though I was a total stranger, the family saw me off at the gate and the sweet German Shepherd wagged its tail.

# Water Traces of Imperial Capitals

## Imagining a Former Water Gate and High Walls

It was 1990 and another construction project was under way on the northern banks of the Liangsui River just south of You'an Gate. As they dug deep into the earth, large slabs of marble and a long culvert of more than 21 meters were uncovered. What in the world was this? The archaeologists agreed that this must have been part of the Jin Dynasty's Zhongdu Capital Walls and because the stones were low and ran toward the river, once functioning as the Jin outer moat, this was indeed one of the early capital's water gates from over 840 years ago.

Rather than apartment blocks, a museum was constructed on top of the excavated water gate. I visited the museum soon after it opened in 1996. One of the resident scholars, Zhang Yan, in her late thirties, took me to the basement to see the ruins. Four ends of the culvert bend outward where it once collected water from the city drainage system and then released it into the moat. Large stone slabs sit over a wooden frame. Ingot-shaped iron, wood and stone pins, similar to butterfly clasps, joined the stones together. We could only imagine the shape of the high wall of firmly packed earth and its arched opening built above it.

A vivacious and dedicated researcher, Zhang Yan insisted that there is a lot of history to be found in the area. "I'll take you to see the walls," Zhang offered. "It's

almost impossible to find them yourself." They can only be reached through a maze of unpaved roads.

Among the sprawl of brick shanty dwellings in the southern part of the city is an area called Wanquansi Village. There within the grounds of an air conditioner factory, a locked gate surrounded one of the remaining sections of Jin wall relics. The lady in charge let us in. Standing in modern platform shoes she wielded a pair of pliers to unravel the thick twisted wire. Looking at her struggling with that cumbersome lock, I gathered that there weren't too many visitors.

The Jin walls, though, were not too impressive to look at, just a pile of rammed yellow earth, overgrown by bushes and grass, and now protected at the base by a new stone wall. "This is near the corner of the southern walls, the moat was on this side," Zhang Yan explained. We then went around to the other side to find the extension of the wall. Actually it was inside a house built right up against it. The owner didn't mind us barging into his patio. "Just go right to the back," he motioned.

A few old discarded doors leaned up against it. Zhang Yan pointed out, "This wall was once 22 meters wide and 20 meters high." She patted the packed dirt, now only about three meters wide. A songbird was chirping from a cage dangling near the top, some three meters up. It took a lot of imagination to visualize the historical significance of the place. In truth, the Jin Water Gate without its walls had been far more

impressive.

Yet these two remnants were what sparked my passion in the history of the Jin Dynasty's sojourn in Beijing. Seeing those plain unadorned dirt walls and the raw remains of the water culvert was the beginning of my fascination with anything from those times. And more often than not, it has meant imagining the past with just a single stone, tree or wall to go on.

## Navigating the Vanished Imperial River

It is surprising that so little of the Imperial River's route has altered since Mongol times. The only problem is that over the past 50 years it has been covered over, its bridges flattened, its locks removed. I set out one day to know its path better. It was dry sailing, but by following its gentle curves and straight stretches, there was a semblance of a river voyage.

From the late 13th century, this river, known as the Yuhe (Imperial River), was developed into an important canal linking the inner city lake port with the canal going east. It was on these waterways that barges brought foodstuffs into the capital. Even though in Ming times the water dwindled and could not support shipping and the commercial sectors moved further south, the river continued to flow for more than 650 years, until it gradually was transformed into an un-

derground drainage ditch.

Starting at Shichahai's Front Sea Lake, the path of the Imperial River meanders east by southeast through old *hutong*s until it hits the eastern Imperial City Wall, at which point it turns due south and continues all the way to where it hits the moat outside the Ming City Wall. Once known as the

Jade River, then the Imperial River, it is still remembered in the names of *hutong*s that keep references to water and old bridges. Fortunately, it is also remembered by the long-term residents along the former banks.

The river begins at Wanning (or, Houmen) Bridge. Recently restored, I went down to greet the marble sculptured dragons standing on both sides of the old locks that used to control the water level between the river and the lakes. Some of the original weathered bridge stones can be seen on either side of the road. Next door, the Temple of the Fire God, the oldest shrine in the district, is also being repaired.

Freshly dredged, the canal goes eastward for almost 60 meters, and then it begins its underground passage. I cruised on top. This was Dongbuya Bridge *Hutong*, formerly known as Horsetail Slanting Street, because it followed the whims of the river. Standing at the juncture with Bent Stick Alley, Mr. Wang, 71, knows a lot about the river as he grew up here. Nostalgically he pointed out the bends and wriggles of the road and talked as if he was looking at the water he had splashed in when he was a small boy.

The voyage on the Imperial River continued. At one turn was an old nunnery. According to a

man selling tobacco and sundry goods from his store attached to the abandoned hall, one 80-year-old nun is still living in the neighborhood. He also noted that this had been the site of a flat bridge over the river.

The road angled on to East Di'an Gate Street where the Dongbuya Bridge once spanned the river. "Dongbuya" means that it doesn't press against the wall. When widening the road in 1998, many grand stones of the original bridge were brought back to light. Moving south, this sense of being adrift on a road gave a different way of looking at things.

At Beihe Alley, for example, I told residents that I was following the old Imperial River and since this section was the last part that flowed above ground, didn't they remember it? A lady in her mid-60s answered directly, "My house is on it. Where your car stands was the bank of that ditch. Can't you see the slope on the other side is higher?"

I drifted east until hitting the newly created Imperial City Wall Park. In the old days the Imperial River ran along inside the wall with both arched and flat bridges passing over it. They have all disappeared, but the names of streets and *hutong*s hint at the earlier scenario. The road that runs south carries the name, Beiheyan and Nanheyan, meaning North River Bank and South River Bank. One cross street is Silver Locks Alley. My journey's sails were set for due south on Nanheyan.

Arriving at the intersection with Chang'anjie

(Avenue of Eternal Peace), my imaginary boat had to pause at the place where the bridge was flattened in the 1930s. It was an auspicious juncture where the Changpu River formerly brought the waters from springs of the Western Hills to join the Imperial River.

In the fall of 2002, the Changpu's banks were made into a very tastefully done park and its water glides under the Cowherd Bridge of Nanchizi street as far as the Heavenly Maiden locks at Nanheyan where the water used to connect with the Imperial River. I was glad to know that this stream links the Heavenly Maiden and Cowherd, representing the Milky Way of folklore.

Navigating across the wide avenue, the Imperial River entered the area known as the Old Legation Quarters. In the 1920s the river was covered and it used to flow under today's green park on the median of Zhengyilu (Government Road).

At the end of the street I docked for a bit to question a gray-haired bicycle repairman. I inquired if he remembered the Sanguanmiao (Shrine of the Three Officials) that once spiritually oversaw the deliveries of goods coming up the canal. He looked me straight in the eye and pointed to his feet. "This is it! They built the post office on it in 1985." This reference helped me get my bearings. The Sanguanmiao was indicated on a 1920s map. This was the terminus of the Imperial River where it passed through a water gate into the outer moat.

# Forbidden City's Bath House

There is still debate about the origins of the bathhouse behind the Wuyingdian (Hall of Military Prowess) inside the southwest corner of the Forbidden City. This complex has had an interesting history, but few people know about its ancient bath. Was this built, as was believed for many years, for the favorite of Emperor Qianlong, the Fragrant Concubine, or was this originally a bathhouse for the earlier Mongol emperors?

The shape is certainly unique. The inside is like a yurt lined in smooth bricks fired with a white glaze. The corners are cut before being fired so that they fit perfectly in with the curvature of the round gradually regressing ceiling. A round glass transom protrudes out from the top affording a skylight. Water once poured out from holes in the wall.

Entering the building was also strange, like sneaking in through a secret passage, with a couple sharp turns before getting to the door to the bath itself. Perhaps this corridor keeps

moisture and heat in the bath area, or else to ensure privacy. I wondered if they showered or was this place a kind of steam bath? Interesting that on this hot summer day, the brick "House of Bathing Virtue" was comfortably cool.

Outside there is a well protected under a special pavilion ten steps high. From there the water runs along raised stone aqueducts held up by narrow marble pillars with a curvature similar to a Roman vase. Along the way, the water passes through a stove where it is warmed before release into the bathhouse through several apertures.

The custom in imperial China was that the court ladies generally stayed in the Inner Sanctum. The Empress Dowager Cixi, for example, never even walked into the complex, much less the bath. This Hall of Military Prowess area was where the officers of China's army had their waiting rooms, and some of the other rooms functioned as an important printing press and publishing house. It also has good *fengshui* because the auspicious Jinshuihe (Golden River) passes in front of the hall, going under the marble Broken Rainbow Bridge as it winds its way eastward into the main courtyard of the palace.

Was a bath at this important location created just to please the Fragrant Concubine from Kashgar? The emperor did have a mosque and the "Home Looking Pavilion" built to help her overcome homesickness. Whatever the real case, the people of Beijing have kept alive a story

that associates the bath with this lady who was finally laid in peace back in her family mosque in Western Xinjiang.

The Fragrant Concubine, it is said, was escorted from the Inner Sanctum to the bath every day. Despite her royal retinue, she was supposedly bothered by a pesky monkey who peaked in the top windows while she was bathing. She finally threw a jade ladle, a gift to her from the emperor, at the unwanted Peeping Tom. But the monkey hid it in the clutches of one of the stone lions on the Broken Rainbow Bridge. From that day on whenever the emperor passed, so the legend goes, a cloth was always put over the lion. That way he never found out about the incident.

Checking out the locale of the legend, I felt that the Fragrant Concubine must have had a very strong arm to pitch the ladle way up to the skylight of the bathhouse with enough force to break the glass. Furthermore, it appears that one of the stone lions on the Broken Rainbow Bridge now actually looks like the pesky monkey. One thing is certain; whoever regularly used this bath did indeed have a special position, because it must have been the height of luxury.

*Unforgettable People*

## Coming across Mao's Shoemaker

South of Tian'anmen Square is the bustling shopping street of Qianmen Dajie. It was the central axis passing through the southern walled city. To the east and west of this main thoroughfare were numerous alleyways filled with the common residents of the city. Most maps show several narrow ditches east of the main axis winding their way diagonally to the southwest. One of these ditches began at the "Grass Market" (Cao Shi) and curved along the alleyways to the famed Gold Fish Ponds north of the Temple of Heaven. A larger ditch, the infamously fetid Longxugou (Dragon Beard Ditch) also began here and finally emptied into the southern moat.

Today Qianmen Street is lined with modernized shops. But just behind these new storefronts are narrow alleyways, with their small shops and cluttered courtyard homes. No stinky channel anymore, yet where the ditch once started was an alley formerly named Tail of the Ditch. I wandered to the back of one of the overcrowded courtyard houses, where about six families shared a communal tap. The following encounter made this corner of Beijing an absorbing documentary of life.

A 81-year-old cobbler lives there with his son's family, all in one room. Next door is his home shoe factory, where he carries on the traditional craft of fashioning cotton and leather shoes. Mr. Peng Jizeng proclaimed, "No one makes them like mine anymore, mine are all hand stitched," he bragged as he turned in his chair to grab a piece of leather. He was surrounded by piles of paper designs, wooden molds, leather sheets ready to cut into shoe patterns, and stacks of boxes with completed shoes. His old foot-pedaled stitching machine stands next to his chair. Peng then took out his light hammer and began hitting small tacks on the leather sheet as he worked it around a wooden mold.

"I began this trade when I was eleven, my parents were poor farmers," he recalled. "First I was making riding boots, but after Liberation, I returned to Beijing and worked at a famous shoe store off Qianmen Street." He retired after working there for 23 years and has been making shoes at home ever since. He lamented the fact that very few people make shoes by hand any more. "It is the mass production, not the individual fit that now seems more important," he said.

Peng then reached high up on a shelf and pulled down a pair of wooden shoe molds. "These were for Mao Zedong's shoes," he boasted. "He ordered just one pair of cotton shoes (*buxie*) a year." Going over the mold with his hand, Peng explained that the opening at the top is called the mouth or *kou* and that Mao preferred the *dayuankou* or big opening. He held up the mold sideways to show the length, "Mao's shoe size was 41.5," Peng said. Then he chuckled, "Well, I never met him though." He went on to explain how one of the assistants came with the foot pattern and, "I just made the mold from the pattern!" After that he made a new pair of shoes for Chairman Mao each year.

Premier Zhou Enlai also liked the cotton *buxie*. "He asked for the medium opening on the top, *zhongyuankou*," recalled Peng. "This was an old design, so most shoemakers didn't know how to do it anymore, and the Premier had a hard time finding them in Beijing, until he found out that I could make them."

The cobbler then moved over to his stitching machine and began to make a cotton inner sole by sewing together several layers of thick cotton already cut into a shoe size. Cloth slippers at 180 *yuan* are a good buy because the soles are leather. Peng used to make five pairs a day, but now he has slowed down to only one pair.

On another table he was in the process of making another pair of shoes. But these were tiny, just 12 centimeters in length and suitable for a small child. He pulled out the mold, "Oh, this one's for the 'Golden Lily', the bound feet of aged ladies." Peng explained that a 91-year-old lady in his neighborhood still requires these small shoes. "I must make special molds for each foot because they are twisted so differently. She's a tall lady, and has to stand on those small feet. My shoes help her walk," said Peng proudly. He carefully hammered the soft leather around the mold; his hands seemed to move on their own. Peng was immersed in his next creation.

# Precious Water Resources

## Residents of Thirsty Village Persevere

I first met Ms. Liu feeding cornstalks to her two donkeys as a light snow fell on the western face of the Cuiwei Hills. "There are only about 100 families left here in Chenjiagoucun (Gully of the Chen Family Village)," she told me. "There is no water, the wells are barren."

When I inquired what was the most common family name, she quickly retorted, "Chen, of course. My husband is Chen." And sure enough, her 80-year-old neighbor was also a Chen. "I was born and raised right here in this village. So were my father and grandfather," boasted Chen Wanzhi as his wife and daughter looked on. They had seen me photographing their rustic stone house and Chen yelled at me to come inside. Chen is a straightforward talker, a man with a lot of true grit. I felt an immediate familiarity with this swarthy-faced and hardy elder sitting on the *kang* bed of his living room.

Their *kang* is well designed. The flue also has an outlet for cooking, and three small earthen pots, buried where the flue goes under the *kang*, have water continually warmed by the embers. "We wash our face with the warm water in the morning, and have warm water at night to bathe

our feet. Very convenient," declared Chen. It certainly is a humble amount of water. "The wells are deep, but they are as dry as a bone now." Yet those villagers, who have remained, endure their plight.

The main well dried up two years ago. Even before that, dry spells caused much of their valley to become a thirsty land. Those that have no water supply like this village are supported by the district government and get water delivery from the city once every ten to twelve days. It is not door-to-door service; rather it must be fetched from a truck parked on the road below. People who live here have resigned themselves to being under a water ration. It is all they have for washing, cooking, drinking, nourishing animals, and for watering their gardens and vegetables. Chen talked about his family of three

sons and one daughter, who now all live in the towns below, and only visit the ageing parents on the weekend. "There's a project to bring running water here," he added, "but for now my children bring us what we need."

Winding through the village is a well-trodden stone path. Mr. Chen remarked that when he was young, this route was very crowded at festival times. Pilgrims went back and forth over the hills to pay their respects at the many temples in these connecting valleys. This austere village is now hushed. It is this peacefulness that keeps Chen and his wife in such a parched place.

Today's snow was bringing much needed precipitation. It will help their carefully rationed water go a bit further. All the Chen families here know the value of every drop.

## Lotus Pond Gets a Facelift

Just below the West Station is one of Beijing's oldest water sources with a deep underground reserve. This is Lianhuachi (Lotus Pond). The capitals of the Liao and Jin Dynasties from the 10<sup>th</sup> to 12<sup>th</sup> centuries depended on the water from Lianhuachi, known then as Xihu (West Lake). Their palaces were located to the southwest of the lake, then much larger than its present size. The 12<sup>th</sup> century scholar Zhao Bingwen described its scenery in a

poem (translated by Yu Danqing) as follows:

*"Reflections of flowers and branches*
*shimmer in the clear water*
*As some people amble along the bank of the pond.*
*But there aren't many visitors this year.*
*It is not only the easterly wind that draws us here,*
*it is also our feelings."*

In the 1990s the pond was an ugly wasteland. Some of the dirt hills where the poets of the past had climbed for a good view remained, but they were overgrown with weeds. Squatters' brick homes closed in around the banks. And the sorry looking mud flats looked unlikely to be rejuvenated with water. It didn't seem possible that even the open space would survive. However, when the modern railroad station was constructed, Beijing University's Prof. Hou Renzhi argued successfully for the preservation of the ancient water source. It was designated as a park and the ensuing massive landscape project brought the natural lake back to life.

Reincarnated from the mud, lotus blooms and water lilies rise up once again around the edges of the pond. There is an unobstructed wide expanse of sky. Summertime magnificence can be enjoyed just as in ancient times. Once again "reflections of flowers and branches shimmer in the clear water."

# Hamlet of Peace and Tranquility

Bright yellow wild flowers covered the small opening in the stone wall of Taipingzhuang Village, just down the road from Beijing's oldest temple, Tanzhesi (Temple of the Pool and Mulberry). Most of the doorways stood open. Every wall of every home is also the neighbors' wall.

Residents told me the origin of the village name. From way back this place was just called Lower Apple Orchard. But one day the great Emperor Qianlong rested here on his way to the temple. To acknowledge the fine character of its people he renamed it Village of Peace and

Tranquility.

Village elder, Mr. Chen, 80, said that they always had a spirit of helping others. "In the past we always cooperated to build each others' homes and repair the road. This village was serene as the name indicates. Even in the Cultural Revolution, things didn't get as bad as at other places, but that frame of mind is now weakening."

Chen had worked at Tanzhesi for 16 years, so he knows a lot about local history. "There's an ancient cave where the first priest of Tanzhesi, Hua Yan, lived while he was building the temple. We villagers actually hid out there when the Japanese first came into our valley."

We were standing by the bridge over a dry riverbed. I asked where the water had gone. The village, he said, originally had a lot of water that ran from the temple's Dragon Spring. It was very clear water that flowed in abundance. The rich bamboo groves of the temple were naturally seeped in water. "Our river bed was always full!" he exclaimed. Tanzhesi was actually first named after its spring at least as early as the 8<sup>th</sup> century.

"Along the road leading up to the temple were several tea stalls," remarked Chen. They all used the fine spring water to welcome pilgrims. One stall by the village was huge. He remembered Japanese soldiers holding a big festival celebration there. "The other tea stalls disappeared when they widened the road," he added.

In 1967 all water stopped flowing. They are not sure why, but they heard it was because of some coal mine drilling on the other side of the

mountain that caused the water's flow to change direction. Now they have to be given water. In fact the village gets it water by pipes from a well that was dug at the temple.

Chen is trying to keep the continuity of their community spirit. He preserves stories and oral history, as well as stressing the tradition of cooperation. "We must live with the Taipingzhuang philosophy of peace and tranquility, it is the true spirit of our village."

## Porridge, a Bonding Ritual along the Great Wall

The isolated Xianggoucun (Village of the Fragrant Gully) nestles deep in a valley with remnants of the Great Wall running along a ridge high above it. One of the wall's ramparts offers a stunning view of the wall extending on and on to the eastern horizon, snaking along the crest of the mountains. The wind howls through this section of the mountain pass. From that vantage point it is easy to see the village down below. It is one of a few inhabited spots in this tough terrain.

It is there that the family of Wang Junfeng, 64, lives. While they are used to the rugged life, they worry about an exodus of neighbors. More and more people are moving away from the mountain region. Many of the villages in this area are becoming deserted, veritable "ghost towns." "It's the drought," said Wang. "Fortunately, we have a spring only 500 meters away. Fifteen years ago or so, we put in pipes to bring the spring water to the homes of our village. So we have water. But the village down the way has none because the river dried up. They come to our village everyday for water." The villages seem devoid of life because all the young people have gone to Beijing or neighboring towns for work.

The villages in this region are historically intertwined with the Great Wall. In olden times, soldiers camped at small forts every 100 to 200 meters and stood guard from the towers. The local villages were important suppliers of food, water, laborers and wood for smoke signal communications. Upkeep was expensive and the necessity of spreading out military forces so thinly was an additional burden. Thus, the Great Wall's strategic importance diminished and the nearby villages lost their livelihood. Residents then turned to wood gathering and planting fruit orchards.

Wang's entire family — his four sons and their families — all gathered in the main room of their house on the coldest day of the year, the winter solstice. According to the Chinese Lunar calendar, it was also the 8th of the twelfth month or *Laba*, the day to eat *Labazhou* porridge. The thick gruel is made of whole grains, dried fruit, nuts and whatever else is in the family traditional recipe. *Laba* gruel is always eaten on this day and is an important rite of family bonding. Great pots used to be prepared for neighbors to share as well and the porridge gift to neighbors had to

arrive before noon on that day.

The Wangs did not know the origins of the dish. Some say it came from the time when a big monastery in Shanxi Province ran out of food and locals gave whatever they could spare to feed the hundreds of monks living there. Others have a more bland explanation: a meal concocted by a housewife at her wits end, who just threw everything in the pot. The creation was a hodge-podge of whatever was in the cupboard.

Wang's wife, Wang Xiuying, 57, was stirring the *Laba* porridge over an open fire. This nutritiously rich dish appeared to be a specialty. Her recipe included red beans, corn, gaoliang meal, millet, chestnuts, jujubes, almonds, crushed walnuts, glutinous rice and kidney beans. When it was ready, she and her daughter-in-law, Sun Xiumin, rushed in with steaming bowls and called out, *"Labazhou, Labazhou!"* Everybody spooned on a little sugar for extra taste.

The electricity winked on and off, "It's the wind," Mr. Wang proclaimed as he brought out candles. Even when the single light bulb in the room came back on, it only offered 25 watts of power, creating a comfortable darkness. Another *Laba* tradition is the steeping of garlic cloves in vinegar for *Laba suan* and a bowlful was eventually put on the table to accompany cold side dishes of mountain vegetables. There was also a dish of wild plants with a strange name of *heigoujianr*, Black Dog Sinews. "Good for your health," Wang proclaimed as he downed Chinese liquor straight.

Being senior, Wang sat at the warmest part of the *kang*. First son Wang Shaoli sat next to his father with his two children. The three other brothers and their families also gathered around. As the biting wind tore through the passes of the Great Wall, the Wang family bonded with the slurping of hot porridge.

*"We have to leave something, both cultural relics and good water, for the following generations"...*
(Professor Hou Renzhi)

# Epilogue

These related encounters are my way of presenting various threads of Beijing history from the angle of its natural setting. I hope these stories give yet another dimension from which to appreciate the city's great heritage. It was my own mixed background and environment that probably led me to look at Beijing in this peculiar way.

Originally an American, I focused on East Asian history and geography in university and graduate studies. Later, I received a grant to study Chinese language in Taiwan. It was there that I met my future husband, a young Japanese diplomat. In 1970, we married and went to live in Japan. In fact, I moved in with my mother-in-law, who later became a Buddhist nun. At the beginning I spoke no Japanese, so she and I communicated in written Chinese. Our meals often had a mix of Western, Japanese and Chinese food.

Growing up by the Mississippi River near the marshes and bayous of southern Louisiana, I was used to seeing water everywhere. When it rained too much, we just got out our pirogues (canoes) and paddled down the street. The damp climate in Tokyo was thus easy for me to get used to. I love the Japanese rainy season. But when we lived in Beijing, I found the arid and dusty North China plain was something else. Water is not taken for granted. So I naturally took notice of springs and gradually saw through local eyes the importance of the lakes, rivers and reservoirs.

Maybe one reason I am fascinated with hills and stoney mountains of Beijing is because my hometown of New Orleans had only one man-made hillock called Monkey Hill where children could climb and run down on weekends. It is only half the height of Beijing's Coal Hill, but for me growing up, that was the extent of my mountain climbing. While in Beijing, the mountains are like the Sirens of Ulysses always beckoning me out. I can always tell the finest weather by how clear Miaofengshan or Yinshan peaks appear on any day.

New Orleans is known for its giant Live Oak trees with huge branches, able to seat six people, bending to the ground. Japan's old trees are considered sacred and special belts of entwined rope are wrapped around their middles. Shrines were usually built to honor them. Trees at sacred sites in China were mostly planted after the original temple was established or tomb constructed, their longevity ensured by the sanctity of the compound. I was impressed that Beijing's old trees have endured long droughts as well as the traumas of history.

Japan and China have much common culture and history including the Buddhist tradition. But I knew only one Buddha as a child. This was the Buddha seated in a garden in Avery Island, home of the famous Tabasco hot sauce. It turns out to be from a lama temple in the Beijing area, sold to antique dealers in the 1920s and ended up in the Louisiana swamp. But for me, that was "the Orient", never realizing that I would one day swap domiciles with this Buddha.

I also felt at ease in Beijing because so many of the homes in my native New Orleans have a layout with a garden or patio in the middle of the house, quite like those of the *siheyuan* (courtyard houses). In my youth I used to walk the alleys of the old French Quarter. In many ways they are similar to Beijing's *hutong*s. Likewise, whenever we lived in Japan, I would often organize field trips with my students to the old parts of downtown Tokyo to find footprints of the past. This rambling around to discover history is what I did and continue to do, during our three postings in Beijing.

My first visit to Beijing actually was in 1976 during the last months of the Cultural Revolution. A pivotal year with many important events, it was easy to remember that our trip was after Zhou Enlai's death but before the Tangshan earthquake and Chairman Mao's passing away. While we stayed at the Beijing Hotel, photos of Mao and patriotic slogans were the only advertisements. What struck me the most about that time was the general lack of energy among the people.

We were told that as foreigners we were allowed to visit only six tourist spots in all of Beijing. Every other place outside of a radius of 15 km from Tian'anmen Square had restricted access, with signs saying "No foreigners beyond this point." With small children, of course we took in the Beijing Zoo.

Behind the Great Panda pavilion near the area of the bears is a small lake and pavilion, left from the time when this site was a Ming imperial villa. It was later part of the Garden of Ten Thousand Beasts made for Empress Dowager Cixi. We rested there on rocks and posed for a photograph.

It turned out to be a very important photograph for us. From then on, we took pictures at the very same site in early summer whenever our family was together in Beijing. It always entails searching for the exact stones and willow tree and replicating the same angle with the lake and pavilion as a backdrop. But the

pictures can never be exactly duplicated, of course, as over the 28 odd years, only the rocks and pavilion stayed the same.

When we moved to Beijing to live in 1983, I looked forward to the gradual access to new areas that foreigners could visit. There were only vague maps of famous tourist sites available, so I compiled an extensive collection of old maps and atlases that helped me pinpoint those places off the beaten path. I also traveled across the country and by 1986, had managed to go to all the provinces, usually traveling by train with my husband and two children, son Yusuke and daughter Mika. As a social studies teacher, I thought it was important for my children to learn by seeing the country they were living in, my "walking and talking" method. And I am glad that as a result they are comfortable in their three cultural homes.

When my husband was named as minister in the embassy in 1995, then as the Japanese ambassador to China in 2001, I was overjoyed. I could come back to live in my "third country." I expanded my adventures all over Greater Beijing, and my dog, Nike, on her two postings here, has also gone with me on many adventures hiking the hills, continuing these ramblings in the changing Beijing. I also had changed. Previously, I used to shrink away from the cold, but Beijing winter days had found a way into my heart. From these experiences I found that explorations were best on clear cold days. It was also easier to photograph as there are many days with deep blue skies and the old pagodas, trees and temple roofs showed up so much better in this bare season.

Although many old sites have since been beautifully restored, I still much prefer the places that remain as time has let them age. In my view, protecting history is more important than rebuilding it. Furthermore, even one stone left, one tree standing or a bucket of spring water can in themselves present a strong image of the past, enriching our view of Beijing's soul.

Virginia Stibbs Anami
Feburary, 2004

# Chronology of Beijing History

**Paleolithic** (旧石器时代), **Neolithic** (新石器时代), **Shang** (商) **c.600,000-1027 B.C.**
Peking Man (北京猿人), Upper Cave Man (山顶洞人), Donghulin sites (东胡林遗址)

**Zhou** (周) **1027-221 B.C.**
State of Ji (蓟国) c.1000 B.C.
Ji capital of State of Yan (燕国蓟城) c.475-221 B.C.

**Qin** (秦) **221-206 B.C.**
City of Ji (蓟城)

**Han** (汉) **206 B.C.-220 A.D.**
City of Ji, Princedom of Yan (燕国蓟城)

**Three Kingdoms** (三国) **220-265**
City of Ji, Guangyang Prefecture (广阳郡蓟城)

**Jin** (晋) **265-420**
Capital city Ji, State of Former Yan, Youzhou region (前燕幽州蓟城) 337-570

**Northern and Southern Dynasties** (南北朝) **317-589**
City of Ji, Yan prefecture, Youzhou region (燕幽州蓟城)

**Sui** (隋) **581-618**
City of Ji (Yan), Youzhou region, later as Zhuo prefecture (幽州蓟城)

**Tang** (唐) **618-907**
City of Ji, also known as Youzhou city, State of Yan, Youzhou region (蓟城，幽州)
Youzhou, State of Yan (幽州) 911

**Liao (Qidan)** (辽) **916-1125**
Yanjing or Liao Nanjing (Southern Capital) (燕京，辽南京) 938

**Jin (Kin, Jurchen)** (金) **1115-1234**
Jin Zhongdu (Central Capital) (金中都) 1153

**Yuan (Mongol)** (元) **1271-1368**
Yuan Dadu (Large Capital) (元大都) 1272

**Ming** (明) **1368-1644**
Beiping (the North Pacified) (北平) 1368
Beijing (Northern Capital) or Jingshi (the Capital) (北京，京师) 1421

**Qing (Manchu)** (清) **1644-1911**
Beijing (Jingshi, the Capital) (北京，京师) 1644

**Republic of China** (中华民国) **1911-1949**
Beijing, Beiping (北京，北平)

**People's Republic of China** (中华人民共和国) **1949-**
Beijing (北京)

# Index of Place Names